7

AND THE ~~MEDIA~~

**FROM THE IRAN
HOSTAGE CRISIS TO
THE WORLD TRADE
CENTER BOMBING**

TERRORISM
AND THE MEDIA

FROM THE IRAN HOSTAGE
CRISIS TO THE WORLD TRADE
CENTER BOMBING

Brigitte L. Nacos

Columbia University Press
New York

Columbia University Press
New York   Chichester, West Sussex
Copyright © 1994 Columbia University Press
All rights reserved

Library of Congress Cataloging-in-Publication Data

Nacos, Brigitte Lebens.
    Terrorism and the media : from the Iran hostage crisis to the
World Trade Center bombing / Brigitte L. Nacos.
        p.   cm.
    Includes bibliographical references and index.
    ISBN 0–231–10014–0
    ISBN 0–231–10015–9 (pbk.)
    1. Terrorism in mass media—United States.   I. Title.
P96.T472U66   1994
303.6'25—dc20   94–4602
                                                              CIP

Casebound editions of Columbia University Press books are
printed on permanent and durable acid-free paper.

Printed in the United States of America
c 10 9 8 7 6 5 4 3 2
p 10 9 8 7 6 5 4 3 2 1

For Jimmy

CONTENTS

PREFACE TO THE
PAPERBACK EDITION

THE OKLAHOMA CITY BOMBING
AND THE UNABOMBER CASE

In the fall of 1994, when the hardcover edition of *Terrorism and the Media* was published, American terrorism experts as well as the public at large associated this sort of violence against Americans and America primarily, if not exclusively, with *international* perpetrators and their causes. Since the late 1970s major acts of terrorism had occurred either abroad or, as the World Trade Center bombing demonstrated, in a major American city with well-known symbols of U.S. influence and power. Foreigners, not Americans, were the culprits. All of this changed in the wake of the Oklahoma City bombing on April 19, 1995, when the Alfred P. Murrah Federal Building was gutted within seconds by a car bomb that killed at least 168 men, women, and children and injured many more.

"This happens in Beirut or Jerusalem or New York," people in the stricken city and state said again and again as they tried to deal with the deadliest case of domestic terrorism in America's modern history, "something like this does not happen here!" But it had hit the American heartland. As horrifying pictures of the destroyed Federal Building were projected onto television screens, anchors, reporters, and radio talk show hosts compared the wreckage with strikingly similar images of bombings that had hit U.S. embassies in Beirut and elsewhere a decade or so earlier. There were also references to the 1993 World Trade Center (WTC) bombing in New York and the four men, all Moslems, already sentenced to lifelong prison terms for the most devastating act of international terrorism that had so far happened on American soil. Moreover, when the bombing in Oklahoma City occurred, the trial of Egyptian Sheik Omar Abdel Rahman and nine of his followers was taking place in a Federal Court building in downtown Manhattan. The fiery Islamic fundamentalist preacher and his codefendants were charged with a conspiracy to bomb major buildings and transportation links in New York a few months after the WTC bombing.

Perhaps not surprisingly, most Americans concluded almost instantly that international terrorists had struck again within their borders and that Islamic fundamentalists were the logical suspects. More surprisingly, almost all terrorism experts consulted by the media pointed in the same direction. But as soon as Timothy McVeigh was identified as the primary suspect, the assumed foreign and Islamic connection fell by the wayside; suddenly, there was no doubt at all that home-grown terrorism, not the foreign variety, was responsible for the Oklahoma City carnage.

Probably miffed by the tremendous attention the mass media paid to the Oklahoma City bombers, the mysterious Unabomber, who had already killed two of his victims and injured close to two dozen over a span of seventeen years, put another of his homemade explosives in the mail.[1] The intended victim, the director of the California Forestry Association, Gilbert Murray, was killed instantly when he unwrapped the package in his office. Judging from the unknown sender's choice of targets over the years, the agents of the FBI's special Unabom task force had earlier suspected that the mailbomber blamed advanced technology for most of modern humanity's problems.[2] This was confirmed and detailed in a letter the Unabomber mailed to the *New York Times* while the Oklahoma City bombing was still dominating the news. Claiming that the bombs of the terrorist group FC were designed to promote social instability in industrial society, propagate anti-industrial ideas, and give encouragement to those who hate the industrial system, the bomber proposed a deal: If the *Times* or another widely read, nationally distributed publication would publish a lengthy manifesto explaining his group's grievances and ideas, he would stop his terrorist activities. Otherwise, he threatened, his deadly campaign would continue.

When a 35,000-word manuscript arrived at the offices of the *New York Times*, the *Washington Post*, and *Penthouse* magazine at the end of June, the media organizations were in a bind: In order to save the lives of innocent targets, should they give in to the demand and publish the long tract within the three-month time limit given by the Unabomber? Or should they resist striking a deal even if that meant additional killings? To demonstrate once more that he meant business, the Unabomber orchestrated a bomb scare at the Los Angeles Airport over the July Fourth weekend that turned out to be a costly and most inconvenient hoax. The *Washington Post* published the full manifesto on September 19, 1995—five days before the deadline expired. It was revealed that the decision had been made jointly by the two news organizations on the recommendation of the Justice Department and the FBI. The *Post* and the *Times* shared the printing costs.

Although my book deals primarily with international terrorism and how this kind of political violence exploits the linkages between the mass media, public opinion, and governmental decision makers, it does contrast the news coverage of anti-American terrorist events outside and inside the United States (see especially chapter 2). My research concerning major terrorist acts abroad and the World Trade Center bombing established that the latter case was covered by and large like any other domestic disaster, home-grown terrorism included, and strikingly different from major incidents committed against Americans abroad. From my data, I concluded that international terrorists are quite able to exploit the U.S. media for their purposes, when they strike Americans and America abroad, but are not very successful in this respect, when they hit inside American borders.

The developments since the fall of 1994 underline this point with respect to the World Trade Center bombing and the plot to commit subsequent bombings. Because television cameras were not allowed inside the courtroom, the trial against Sheik Rahman and his followers did not become the major news event one might have expected. To be sure, the murder trial against former football great O.J. Simpson in Los Angeles overshadowed other important events as well, but even without the live television coverage of the sensational O.J. case, the nontelevised terrorism trial in New York lacked steady media and public attention. As a result, Sheik Rahman and his codefendants did not have much of an audience in front of which to articulate their grievances. The Sheik and his trial were also upstaged by the dramatic capture of two primary suspects in the World Trade Center bombing: the alleged mastermind of the plot, Ramzi Ahmed Yousef, and his longtime friend, Eyad Ismoil. In both instances, American law enforcement pinpointed the whereabouts of the two men who had fled the United States after the WTC bombing, but it was the cooperative stance of foreign governments (in these cases Pakistan and Jordan followed the earlier example of Egypt) that allowed FBI agents to bring the suspects to the United States and to justice. All of these developments strengthen my earlier conclusion (see chapter 7): when international terrorists strike on their enemies' turf, they lose the battle for publicity and are likely to be caught.

What about domestic terrorism and the media? Several terrorism experts who studied the news coverage of domestic terrorism in various countries determined that law enforcement and other government officials are far more likely to dominate and influence the press coverage of such events than are homegrown terrorists and their sympathizers. In this respect, the coverage pattern of domestic terrorist acts and international terrorism committed within the borders of a target country resemble each other a great deal.

I have summarized some of my findings here, because the preface to the paperback edition offers a welcome opportunity to discuss the media perspective of two recent cases of domestic terrorism, mainly the Oklahoma City bombing and to a lesser extent the Unabomber's brazen challenge of the press. While these cases introduce the reader to the major themes of the book, another and perhaps better way to appreciate the differences and similarities between various types of terrorism with respect to publicity, public opinion, and public policy would be to read or reread the remainder of this preface after absorbing chapters 1 through 7.

The Oklahoma City Bombing

As one would expect, once the catastrophic extent of the Oklahoma City bombing was evident, both the local and the national media paid a great deal of attention to the incident. In the hours after the blast, first television and radio stations in and around the city and soon thereafter the large broadcast and cable networks as well reported nonstop or extensively about the disaster and its victims, the dramatic rescue efforts, and other aspects of what soon was understood as an act of terrorism. The tremendous volume and the nature of the news coverage was similar to the reporting mode Americans have come to expect in the event of devastating hurricanes, floods, earthquakes, fires, urban riots, or major acts of anti-American terrorism such as the WTC bombing or the Iran hostage crisis.

Television, radio, and the print press were superb in discharging their function of apprising the public of the facts as quickly as they could gather information. Just as important, the local broadcast and cable stations functioned as conduits of communication between public officials and citizens in the affected city and region. For example, by disseminating officials' appeals to

xiii

the citizenry to donate blood for injured victims, not to enter the disaster area, or to contribute warm clothing for rescue workers, the media provided an excellent public service. Since many officials, who were involved in managing the crisis, followed the news about the disaster, the stations facilitated also the difficult task of coordinating emergency services that involved a great number of organizations and individuals.

Relying heavily on reporters' on-the-scene descriptions of the bombing and its aftermath, the media recorded also the utterings of survivors, rescue workers, eyewitnesses, families and friends of victims, and other ordinary residents of the shell-shocked city. Otherwise, political leaders (i.e., the U.S. president, the governor of Oklahoma, the mayor of Oklahoma City, members of Congress), law enforcement officials (from the FBI, Bureau of Alcohol, Tobacco and Firearms, local and state police, etc.), rescue coordinators (from the Oklahoma City Fire Department, the area's medical facilities, etc.), and other public figures were the dominant news sources. Analysis and commentary were provided by the media themselves (anchors, reporters, editorial writers, columnists) and by experts in terrorism, trauma, and other fields dealing with the consequences of disasters.

In all of these respects, the media coverage fit the usual pattern of domestic terrorism or other domestic calamities. After all, when terrorists commit violence in the territory of a government that is the source of their grievances, they cannot actively pursue their publicity goals. While domestic terrorists, too, use the media to communicate with the public and with government officials in their own land, they lack the safety of their international brethren who strike in the territories of governments that support or condone their violent activities. The captors of the American hostages in Tehran during the 444 days of the Iran hostage crisis (1979–1981) and in Beirut during most of the 1980s, for example, were personally involved in exploiting the news for their purposes by providing the press with communiques, videotapes, and interviews and staging news conferences. Trying to escape the arm of the law, those responsible for the Oklahoma City bombing did not attempt to manage the news. They didn't need to, because they left a powerful clue as to their motives. By igniting their devastating bomb on the second anniversary of the FBI's ill-fated raid on the Branch Davidian compound in Waco, Texas, during which cult leader David Koresh and at least eighty of his followers died, the bombers assured that the mass media would explore their causes and grievances.

Still, before they struck in Oklahoma City the terrorists could not have dreamed of a more perfect publicity bonanza for the grievances and emotions that motivated them. Perhaps their sole purpose was to avenge the men, women, and children who perished in Waco. But without the certainty that a major bombing would result in a great deal of news coverage and send strong messages to their soul mates in the right-wing milieu, the American public, and the federal government and its agents, the perpetrators probably would not have acted. Perhaps they planned to communicate their motives at a later date. Either way, the fact that the media once again accommodated the classical terrorist desire for publicity in terms of the sheer volume of news coverage didn't come as a surprise. But the extent to which television, radio, and print press explored the "Waco factor" and other grievances of people in, close to, or influenced by the radical right was far greater than one could have anticipated.

The "Old Media"

Even in the first hours and days following the disaster, when the news coverage in the mainstream media (print press, radio and television news programs) was dominated by sources and reports espousing a Middle East connection, the traditional media, or "old media," did not ignore the possible link between the deed in Oklahoma City and the inferno in Waco completely. For example, two stories on the front page of the *New York Times'* first edition after the Oklahoma City bombing contained references to a possible Waco connection. And once Timothy McVeigh and some of his former army buddies were identified as suspects, the mainstream media reported very extensively about the radical right movement, how it related to the suspects, and how deadly encounters between federal agents and defiant individuals and groups such as David Koresh and his Branch Davidians had fueled its extreme hatred for the federal government. A lengthy report appearing in the *Times* four days after the bombing under the headline "Radical Right's Fury Boiling Over" was typical for this reporting angle. The article quoted the leader of the White Aryan Resistance, Tom Metzger, who said,

> I have told people for years, at least since 1984, when the Order [another tight extremist group] declared war on the central Government of the United States that the Government of this country—what we call the criminals—had better start listening to the dispossessed white people, the dispossessed majority.
>
> Evidently these people [the bombers of Oklahoma City], who I don't know personally, saw the Federal building as a strategic military target, and these are the things that happen at war.[3]

Three days later, a *Times* article linked Waco and Oklahoma City by reporting that suspect Timothy McVeigh had visited the site of the Branch Davidians' compound and, according to his acquaintances, expressed "outrage at the deaths of sect members."[4] This article referred also to a 1992 bloody clash at Ruby Ridge, Idaho, between federal agents and Randy Weaver, a white supremacist, in which Weaver's wife and young son and a deputy U.S. marshall were killed. The incident was described because it fueled, just as Waco did, the militant right's extreme antigovernment stance.

While these kinds of stories were factual, informative, and balanced, others were outright critical of federal decision makers and law enforcement agents. A *Newsweek* article, for example, stated that

> two separate federal investigations have not persuaded even mainstream critics that those responsible for the debacle are telling all they know. Now Waco is becoming a politi-

cal wrangle. Last week, Republicans in the House and Senate announced hearings on the conduct of the FBI and the Bureau of Alcohol, Tobacco, and Firearms, and on the Clinton administration's handling of the incident.

The established facts are damning enough [emphasis added].[5]

"There can be no justification for the terrorist attack last month in Oklahoma City," wrote the author of an op-ed piece in the *Wall Street Journal*, "but likewise there is no justification for delaying asking serious questions about government misconduct."[6] He called the U.S. Senate's decision to postpone hearings on the federal government's action in Waco and in Ruby Ridge "a grave error."

The "New Media"

In the hours, days, and weeks after the Oklahoma City blast, talk radio and cyberspace (the "new media") were dominated by programs and communications that speculated about the likely causes and grievances behind the bombing. Even when the mainstream media and their experts looked foremost in the direction of fundamentalist Moslems, talk radio hosts and their callers discussed primarily the likelihood of paramilitary groups or some of their members commemorating the second anniversary of Waco by lashing out at federal personnel and property. Whether in agreement with the extremists or not, callers seemed well aware of these circles, their mind-set, and their tremendous hate for the federal government.

According to one talk radio expert,

"The mainstream press is out of touch—that's why . . . it did not see the Waco connection right away. It has never acknowledged that a large segment of the population feels that the Branch Davidians were victims. Talk radio audiences have known that all along, and the callers immediately suspected that the bombing was done by paranoid paramilitary individuals who fear the United States government is eroding our civil liberties.[7]

No doubt, this role of the interactive radio talk show format was a novel factor with respect to terrorism's media perspective. Surely, earlier terrorist events had been discussed in radio call-in programs. But the spectacular growth, popularity, and influence of these, mostly conservative, programs in the last several years expanded the reach and importance of talk radio tremendously. Following the Oklahoma City incident, zealots among right-wing talk show hosts and leaders in the paramilitary scene used their radio programs to publicize their extreme positions. One compared the Oklahoma City bombing to a work of art; another encouraged his listeners to defend their homes and aim their guns at federal agents; many claimed that the federal agents had ignited the bomb in Oklahoma City in order to further the police state agenda of federal officials.

Moreover, while Timothy McVeigh and other suspects remained silent, techno-savvy right-wing leaders and followers utilized cyberspace and its bulletin boards to publicize and discuss their views on the Oklahoma bombing, the federal government's role in it, and the Waco connection. Mark Koernke, for example, a leader in the militia movement, got his messages into cyberspace by distributing the transcripts of his shortwave radio show over the global computer network. In one of the transcripts that went on-line he called U.S. Attorney General Janet Reno "the Butcher of Waco" and accused federal officials of having "butchered our cities" and "killed whole population groups."[8]

The Bomb and the Message

If we assume that the men accused of the Oklahoma City bombing shared the views that were so forcefully expressed by radical right-wingers, their message came across clearly and loudly to the American public and to government officials. While the old media reported extensively on the radical right's grievances and causes, the new media devoted far more air time to discussing these issues and was far more sympathetic to them than the established press. Finally, leaders in the right-wing milieu went on-line to spread their provoking gospel, rally their supporters, and try to recruit new ones.

The public was overwhelmingly satisfied with the way the news media covered the bombing incident. A majority rejected the suggestion that radio talk show hosts had encouraged the bombing, but a substantial minority either felt precisely this way or was not sure.[9] Nevertheless, according to a CBS News poll, a slim majority (53%) agreed with President Clinton that "loud and angry voices" in America have encouraged hatred and violence like the bombing in Oklahoma City.

Public Opinion and Oklahoma City

Considering that most Americans depended on the media for information about the Oklahoma City case and considering furthermore that research has demonstrated a relationship between media content and public opinion (see chapter 3), one wonders about the American public's reaction to the blast and the questions it raised.

To begin with, the incident alerted Americans to the dangers of domestic terrorism and caused a solid majority to anticipate similar acts within the near future.[10] Although acknowledging the difficulty of preventing terrorism, shortly after the bombing only about one in ten Americans had no confidence at all in the U.S. government's ability to prevent this sort of violence on American soil; most Americans had a "fair amount" (51 percent), a "good amount" (24 percent), or even a "great deal" (12 percent) of trust that the government could prevent terrorism.[11]

As had happened in the aftermath of most major acts of anti-American terrorism abroad, the Oklahoma City bombing boosted the president's public approval ratings, which are based on responses to the standard question pollsters ask regularly: Do you approve or disapprove of the way [name of current president—in this case Bill Clinton] is handling his job as President? Although survey organizations reported varying degrees of

changes between their last prebombing and their first postinci-
dent polls (Gallup, for example, measured merely a 5 percent
increase, and an ABC News/*Washington Post* poll a 10 percent
jump), a rally effect in favor of Clinton was undeniable. When
asked specifically to rate President Clinton's handling of the
Oklahoma City bombing, 80 percent or more of the respondents
expressed their approval. On the other hand, nearly one-third of
the public believed that the president tried to use the tragedy
"for his own political advantage."[12]

While giving President Clinton very high grades for handling
the bombing, far more Americans believed that Republicans
would generally do a better job than Democrats in dealing with
terrorism.[13] This was probably caused by the still widely held
belief that President Carter did not provide strong leadership
during the Iran hostage crisis, although none of the U.S. hostages
in Tehran was killed during the ordeal. Republican president
Ronald Reagan, on the other hand, is widely appreciated as a
leader who took a tough stand via-à-vis terrorism (i.e., he ordered the bombing of Libya) although hundreds of Americans
lost their lives as the result of terrorist acts (i.e., the truck bomb
attack on U.S. Marine barracks in Lebanon in 1983, the downing
of Pan Am Flight 103 in 1988) during his eight years in the
White House.

Waco, the Public, and Decision Makers

By devoting a great deal of air time and space to Waco and its
connection to the Oklahoma City terrorism and government-
hating right-wing radicals, both the old and the new media, albeit in different ways, reminded the public of an incident most
Americans had probably forgotten. As a result of this news
angle, the raid on the Branch Davidians was placed high on the
public agenda. Shortly after the Oklahoma City bombing, about
three in four Americans believed that the actions of federal
agents had been justified. A Gallup poll of April 23–24, 1995,
found that 73 percent of the respondents approved and 21 per-

cent disapproved of the raid of the Branch Davidian compound. This was in the approval range measured shortly after the 1993 incident. As the mass-mediated Waco debate intensified in the following weeks and months and critical sources in the radical fringes as well as mainstream critics got ample opportunity to voice their opinion, an attitudinal shift occurred: support for the FBI's handling of Waco declined while disapproval escalated. In early May, a CBS News survey found that support had dwindled to 45 percent and opposition swelled to 43 percent. In the second half of July a *Time*/CNN/Yankelovich Partners poll showed even more disapproval (50 percent) than approval (45 percent) for the Waco raid. According to polls, a considerable minority (14 percent according to an April 27 survey by Yankelovich Partners) believed outright that federal agents had deliberately set fire to the Branch Davidian compound, 20 percent of the populace deemed it possible.

Although the Congress had conducted Waco hearings in 1993, when the Democrats controlled the U.S. House of Representatives and the U.S. Senate, critics pressed for a new round of hearings in both congressional chambers following the Oklahoma City bombing—this time around with Republicans in the driver's seat in both chambers. Given the media's extensive coverage of this issue, American attitudes with respect to congressional hearings changed dramatically: in early May, a slight majority of the public (51 percent) was against, a substantial minority (43 percent) for, hearings. By mid-May, half the populace (50 percent) supported Waco hearings and 47 percent believed them unnecessary; five weeks later 60 percent were for and only 31 percent against congressional action in this matter.[14]

Decision Makers and the Waco Controversy After the Bombing

Although in vastly different ways, both the old and the new media were instrumental in moving the Waco controversy onto the public agenda and affecting Americans' attitudes about the bombing and related issues. Not the media, however, but political actors were instrumental in helping those responsible for the Oklahoma City tragedy and their sympathizers to realize their objectives, namely to win headlines for Waco and fuel a renewed public debate about the controversy. Surely, at the time of the Oklahoma City incident strong and legitimate questions about Waco remained unanswered. Well before the incident in Oklahoma City, members of the Clinton Administration and Congress were well aware of radical "Remember Waco" activists and mainstream critics who demanded additional investigations and hearings. None were scheduled before the Oklahoma City blast.

The terrorists achieved what peaceful petitions and protests did not accomplish: their deed, the mass-mediated debate about their likely motives, and the public's reaction persuaded enough influential politicians, presidential contenders among them, to take another look at the Waco case. Senator Orrin Hatch, the chairman of the Judiciary Committee, refused to schedule a hearing on Waco before the Oklahoma City terrorists were brought to justice. He did not prevail. Before the summer was over, Congress held several hearings on Waco and another one on the Ruby Ridge case.

By revisiting Waco as an obvious response to and so soon after the Oklahoma City tragedy, the Congress played into the hands of the bombers and took the risk of encouraging other alienated circles to resort to terrorism. It might well be that law enforcement agencies and their agents needed better guidelines and more scrutiny in the disputed area. Indeed, the agencies under fire did introduce new rules of deployment and engagement as a result of these hearings. But when decision makers in Washington acted so swiftly on what was widely believed to be the paramount grievance of the Oklahoma City bombers, the message they sent was as obvious as troublesome: If you fail by peaceful means in the legitimate political process, you can succeed with violence.

An illustration in *Time* magazine captured this perfectly: depicting a prisoner in his cell and in front of a television screen displaying U.S. Attorney General Janet Reno's features, the picture's caption read, "If he had a TV, accused Oklahoma City bomber Timothy McVeigh might enjoy watching federal officials squirm at the Waco hearings."[15]

The Media and the Unabomber

In the summer of 1995, the publishers and editors at the *New York Times* and the *Washington Post* agonized over the question of whether to devote seven full pages to the Unabomber's manifesto "Industrial Society and Its Future," agree to his request for three annual updates, and possibly encourage other discontents to demand the publication of their tracts under the threat of violence. The news organizations' dilemma was widely debated in the national media. This public discourse was a publicity feast in itself for the mysterious bomber and his deadly crusade against the ills of modernity and technology. Moreover, well before the bomber's deadline ran out, both the *Times* and the *Post* printed substantial excerpts from the treatise that captured the essence of his ideas.

Actually, giving in to terrorists' demands to either publish their writings or shoulder the responsibility for the violent death of innocent victims was not a new quandary for the leading print press. In 1976, at the request of the FBI and the FAA, four newspapers in the United States, the *Times* and *Post* among them, published the statements of Croatian nationals during a lengthy hijacking. While their appeals to the American people on behalf of national independence for Croatia comprised only 3,500 words, the terrorists' goal at the time was the same as the Unabomber's objective: publicity in the national press. The following chapters of this book contain many examples of the print and electronic media publicizing terrorists' communiques, videotapes, or statements made in interviews or news conferences.

Nevertheless, the length of the Unabomber's tracted, the demand for several follow-ups, and the author's past record of terrorist killings constituted a new quandary for the targeted media organizations. For a few observers, columnist John Leo among them, the only sensitive response was to "stop all the agonizing and just print it." Pointing out that the newspapers had already published excerpts without being criticized by the journalistic establishment, Leo wondered "why it would be dangerous and ethically wrong to print the whole manuscript." For Leo the bottom line was simply, "If the newspapers say no, real people die. If they say yes, the only victims are the extra Canadian trees that will have to be put to sleep so the *Times* and the *Post* can publish the bomber's rant."[16] Others, like the *Boston Globe*'s columnist David Nyhan, recommended a tough stand against the Unabomber's demands. "Cover the news, yes; publish under gunpoint, no," was Nyhan's verdict.[17] Still others rejected both extremes and suggested that, as media critic Jonathan Alter put it, "the press should keep the lines of communication open, even publish something, but avoid being completely co-opted by a killer."[18]

There was, as the mass-mediated debate reflected, no easy way out of the Unabomber's heretofore unusual demand for media access—except for Bob Guccione, the publisher of *Penthouse*. Offering to print the Unabomber's treatise "fully and without censorship," Guccione pleaded in a full-page open letter with the Unabomber to accept his magazine as a respectable and widely read publication, explaining,

> The demographic mix of our audience is virtually the same as that of the *New York Times* and the *Washington Post*, but our total readership is many millions more than the total readership of the Times and Post *combined*. *Penthouse* is one of the biggest and most quoted magazines in the history of our industry. For 25 years it was and continues to be the single, biggest selling magazine in the Pentagon. If it's attention you want, you'd be hard pressed to do better.[19]

Suggesting that in the Unabomber's case "killing was merely a means to the end" and characterizing the mystery killer's objectives as "much bolder and infinitely more elaborate," the *Penthouse* publisher sweetened his bid to publish the terrorist's manifesto with the following proposition, should the publication of the treatise fall to him,

> I propose to offer you one or more unedited pages in *Penthouse* every single month for an indefinite period of time. Consider it a regular column in which you may continue to proffer your revolutionary philosophy, answer critics and generally interact with the public. Surely this would be preferable to the three annual updates you are requesting from the *New York Times*, et al.[20]

Simply by offering the Unabomber far more than he had demanded in return for ending his terrorist activities, Guccione ("I'm still the only friend you have in the media") opened a new chapter in the annals of terrorism and the media and possibly a can of worms as well. If printing the manifesto and a few follow-up articles would not entice other malcontents to follow in the Unabomber's footsteps, would the prospect of a regular column prove an irresistible temptation? Alluding to the fact that many professional journalists never realize the dream of becoming a widely read columnist, a *Chicago Tribune* cartoon alluded to the troubling questions raised by Guccione's offer. Depicting an editor in his office and a "Unabomb copycat" ready to ignite an explosive device, the fictitious editor keeps on working while he tells the would-be bomber, obviously a member of his staff, "I don't care, Simpkins, you still can't have your own column."[21]

In the real world, the problems surrounding the Unabomber's demands were far more complex. Ronald E. Graham and Arthur Sulzberger Jr., the publishers of the *Post* and the *Times*, left no doubt that the decision to publish the lengthy tract in a special section of the Washington-based newspaper was a painful one. "Whether you like it or not," Sulzberger explained, "we're turning our pages over to a man who has murdered people. But I'm convinced we're making the right choice between bad options."[22] Concern for public safety had led the U.S. attorney general and the director of the FBI earlier to recommend that the manuscript be published.

Nevertheless, even if the choice was appropriate and saved lives, the Unabomber scored another victory for terrorism.

Brigitte L. Nacos
Manhasset, New York
September 1995

PREFACE AND
ACKNOWLEDGMENTS

This book explores how the mass media, the public, and decision makers in the United States responded to major acts of anti-American terrorism during the last fifteen years. My central argument is that terrorists try to exploit the linkages between the news media, public opinion, and presidential decision making and that they are successful, when they stage violent spectaculars.

The focus is on events that occurred abroad (e.g., the Iranian hostage crisis of 1979–1981, the TWA hostage incident and Achille Lauro case in 1985, the long ordeal of several American hostages in Lebanon in the 1980s and early 1990s, the downing of Pan Am Flight 103 in 1988, and American responses such as the failed Iranian rescue mission in 1980 and the bombing of Libya in 1986). But I also deal with the 1993 bombing of the World Trade Center in New York whenever the dramatic event illustrates the similarities and differences of terrorism inside and outside a target society's own country.

There are different types of terrorism—namely, domestic and international—and different perpetrators—namely, states and groups (autonomous or state-sponsored). Some experts in the field criticize that governmental decision makers, journalists, and scholars are preoccupied with what they see as a relatively minor problem of international terrorism against the United States and its citizens and ignore the much greater problem of state terrorism committed by governments supported by Washington. Without doubt anti-American terrorist "spectaculars" have been very troublesome for the American public and for decision makers during the last decades and need to be understood and explained. The book concentrates on terrorism against innocent Americans who were not in positions to influence directly the actions and policies of their government. With the exception of terrorists and their supporters hardly anyone condones attacks on unarmed civilians. To oppose this sort of violence against innocents does not necessarily deny the grievances of the perpetrators against the United States but rejects their means. Counterterrorist actions that harm innocent citizens of other countries are questionable as well.

Americans have seen, heard, and read a great deal about dramatic terrorist incidents. Therefore, this book is intended not only for politicians, who have to deal with terrorism, for journalists who report these incidents, and for teachers and students who explore terrorism, communication, journalism, public opinion, presidential decision making, and foreign affairs, but also for a broad audience of general readers.

While I researched and wrote this book I relied heavily on family, friends, and colleagues. The project began on a long, hot Memorial Day weekend when David Fan, John Young, and I worked on a comparison of text analyses conducted by human coders and by a computer program developed by Fan. Because I was eager to test the thesis that terrorists seek attention, recognition, and respectability through news coverage, David and John agreed to get involved in my "little extra project." Thus we analyzed how leading U.S. newspapers reported the hijacking of TWA Flight 847 in 1985 using Fan's computer program and its method of successive text filtrations. The results encouraged me to continue and broaden my research in this area. I am thankful to both colleagues.

I learned a great deal about the mass media, public opinion and public policy and their linkages from a leading scholar in the field and a valued colleague, Robert Shapiro. To him, more than anyone else, I am forever grateful for the best advice one could hope for, for tough and constructive criticism, and for always finding the time to discuss one or the other aspect of this project and to read and critique all manuscript drafts.

Many of my students in the courses on American responses to international terrorism that I taught at Columbia University offered stimulating responses to my ideas.

I am thankful to Sara Offenhartz, James E. Nacos, and John C. Nacos for their skillful research assistance and to Joan Gozaloff for patiently and competently assisting in the preparation of the manuscript.

Kate Wittenberg, editor-in-chief of Columbia University Press, showed interest in my project from the outset. I thank her for that and for selecting the two anonymous readers who offered excellent suggestions for the improvement of my manuscript and whose thorough examination and critique of my work I appreciate greatly. It was my good fortune to work again with manuscript editor Leslie Bialler who shepherded my work with great competence and understanding through the various stages of the electronic editing process.

Finally and mostly, I thank my husband Jimmy for his eternal support, encouragement, and patience.

Brigitte L. Nacos
Manhasset, New York
February 1994

CHAPTER ONE

INTRODUCTION:
THE CALCULUS OF VIOLENCE

Terrorists try to exercise influence over targeted officials or nations through intimidation of the public and arousal of sympathy for the social and political causes they espouse. Without widespread publicity, terrorist acts can achieve neither of these effects.

—ALBERT BANDURA

In Wall Street circles "Black Mondays," "Black Fridays," or other "Black" weekdays refer to stock market crashes and damage to their and other people's portfolios. February 26, 1993, however, was a different kind of "Black Friday" for the financial center in downtown New York and for America: the explosion that shook the World Trade Center and its more than fifty thousand workers and visitors with the might of an earthquake was the most destructive act of terrorism on American soil ever, killing six persons, injuring more than a thousand, and causing extensive damage to the world's second tallest skyscraper and the hundreds of businesses it houses. But perhaps more costly than the immediate consequences of the car bomb attack on a preeminent symbol of U.S. economic might was the effect on America's psyche. The

1

explosion in the bowels of the World Trade Center's twin towers dispelled forever the myth that terrorists are simply not able to stage their violent spectaculars inside the United States.

Foreign terrorists tried repeatedly to strike inside American borders before the World Trade Center blast, but alert law enforcement officers and pure luck prevented what could have been previews to the terror of "Black Friday" 1993. One of the more ambitious of these terror plans was foiled in April 1988, when a state trooper checked the driver's license of a Japanese "tourist" at a rest area along the New Jersey Turnpike and discovered three bombs on the car's back seat. Yu Kikumura, a Japanese Red Army member with ties to Middle Eastern terrorist groups, was on his way to New York—presumably on a mission for Libya's Muammar Qaddafi to avenge the U.S. air attack on Libya two years earlier. Among Kikumura's possessions the police found a map of Manhattan on which three targets were marked: the United Nations complex, the garment district, and a Navy recruitment center.

Pointing to these kinds of incidents, some terrorism experts warned years before the World Trade Center bombing that the nation was "on the verge of suffering the first major terrorist attack on American soil."[1] But in the 1980s the American people and decision makers at the highest level of government were preoccupied with anti-American terrorism abroad.

The decade began with the Iranian hostage crisis and ended with an ongoing hostage dilemma in Lebanon with terrorist groups holding several American civilians captive. The period in between witnessed a multitude of ever more shocking terrorist strikes against America. In 1983, for example, explosive-laden trucks blew up the American Embassy and U.S. Marine barracks in Beirut, killing a total of 258 Americans. In 1985 Navy diver Robert Stethem was murdered during the hijacking of TWA flight 847 in the early stages of a seventeen-day hostage ordeal. A few months later terrorists hijacked the Italian cruise ship *Achille Lauro* and killed a wheelchair-bound New Yorker, Leon Klinghoffer. Toward the end of the decade, a terrorist bomb caused the mid-air explosion of Pan Am flight 103 and the death of 270 persons aboard and on the ground in Lockerbie, Scotland.

Whether by bombings, hijackings, or kidnappings, Americans were the primary targets of international terrorist activities. And yet, if one adds up the number of victims and the cost of damages, the results seem to support those who consider international terrorism merely a nuisance.[2] In 1983, by far the worst year in terms of casualties, 387 Americans were killed in terrorist incidents. And in 1988, the second worst year in the record book, 192 U.S. citizens died as victims of terrorist violence. But during each of those years many tens of thousands of Americans were murdered in Washington, D.C., New York, Los Angeles, Chicago, and other places in the United States. During one eight-day period in the summer of 1989, four small children were killed by stray bullets in New York, whereas only sixteen Americans died in terrorist incidents during that entire year.

Do these numbers and comparisons prove that terrorism is not a major problem but merely an irritant? Yes—if simply measuring the consequences of violence for political ends in terms of people harmed and property destroyed, the magnitude of terrorism pales in comparison to domestic problems. The Los Angeles riots in the spring of 1992 caused more human casualties (58 persons killed, hundreds injured) and property damage than all the anti-American terrorism in the three years preceding the riots. The great Mississippi River flood of 1993 was far more costly in human and economic terms than was the World Trade Center blast a few months earlier.

Yet even a casual observer of the American scene has an inkling that the "significance of international terrorism does not lie in the number of lives taken or in the amount of destruction inflicted; it lies in the number of lives threatened and in the amount of fear and terror generated."[3]

Long before the first, spectacular terrorist act took place on American soil, the impact of international terrorism on America's mindset was exemplified by the establishment of concrete barriers around the White House, State Department, and other

3

government buildings in late 1983 and the deployment of counterterrorist forces at events such as the 1984 Olympic Games in Los Angeles, the 1986 Statue of Liberty rededication in New York, and several presidential inaugurations. Even before the fortification of the nation's capital, a former State Department official summarized the effects of terrorism on the lives of Americans:

> We now accept routinely the searches we undergo in boarding aircraft. Our embassies and consulates abroad are heavily fortified. . . . Our ambassadors must now travel in bullet-resistant cars. These measures have been developed to protect the public and American employees, but they represent significant restrictions on our freedom and on the traditional openness of our society and of its representatives abroad.[4]

Anti-American terrorism has had far greater effects on the public and decision makers, on the policies and politics in America, than statistics would suggest. Assessing the influence of terrorism on public opinion and decision making during the Reagan years, one observer concluded, "It is hard to find something that had a more profound impact on the United States in the 1980s than terrorism."[5]

The presidencies of Jimmy Carter and Ronald Reagan were overshadowed by terrorist crises and controversial measures to resolve hostage situations. George Bush, too, had to deal with several serious terrorist actions and threats. And Bill Clinton had barely settled into his presidency when the World Trade Center explosion shocked the nation. In all these instances, the mass media and public opinion figured prominently in the official government responses.

When the Iranian hostage crisis began in November 1979, President Carter's public approval ratings had hit a low point. But neither his major rival for the Democratic nomination, Massachusetts Senator Edward Kennedy, nor Republican hopeful Ronald Reagan were especially popular. Perhaps the decisive factor for Carter's failure to win reelection in 1980 was the long hostage ordeal. On the eve of the 1980 election the mass media focused on the first anniversary of the Iran situation. Carter's White House chief of staff, Hamilton Jordan, observed that "all three networks took their viewers on an emotionally wrenching review of the past year. Rather than drawing the contrasts between the two men who wanted to be President, the news was a strong reminder of our inability after a long year to win an honorable release of the hostages or to avenge the wrong done us by the Iranians."[6] The following day, Ronald Reagan was elected president of the United States.

Reagan was the beneficiary of his predecessor's failure to win sustained public support for the manner in which he handled the Iran crisis. But President Reagan would later face foreign policy dilemmas caused by several terrorist "spectaculars" against Americans or American interests. Eventually, Reagan's own presidency was thrown into turmoil when it was revealed that he had secretly engaged in an arms-for-hostages deal with Iran and violated his official foreign policy precepts. The President blamed the news media for his plunge in the approval polls.

The first foreign policy crisis of the Bush presidency occurred when the killers of hostage Lieut. Colonel William Higgins in Lebanon released a gruesome videotape of his hanging, and threatened to execute captive Joseph Cicippio next. During the early months of the Persian Gulf conflict in 1990, a new dimension of international terrorism threatened the United States and other countries, as Palestinian and Shiite groups warned of terrorism in the event of military actions against Iraq. Also, Saddam Hussein's decision to hold thousands of foreigners, especially U.S. citizens, hostage in his country and to use these "guests" as human shields in military installations, created a potentially unprecedented situation. Focusing on the impending military confrontation between Iraq and the American-led alliance for the liberation of Kuwait, the news media and the public treated the hostages as a secondary problem within the greater conflict and thereby allowed President Bush to pursue his Persian Gulf policy regardless of the hostages.

Following the World Trade Center bombing President Clinton

assured the nation that the government was doing everything in its power to keep Americans safe at home. But in spite of the President's and other officials' seemingly calm demeanor, the White House was reportedly "jittery" and "far more shaken than it has publicly let on."[7] A few months later, an inside informer helped law enforcement agencies to foil a terrorist plot to simultaneously bomb the Holland and Lincoln tunnels, the United Nations headquarters, and the FBI office in New York City in an apocalyptic fireworks display during the July Fourth holiday weekend. On the day of the plotters' arrest, the President okayed a cruise missile attack on Baghdad to retaliate for an attempt on George Bush's life, allegedly masterminded by Iraq's intelligence service, during the former president's visit to Kuwait. But coming in the wake of the New York terror plot and the World Trade Center bombing, the missile attack was also meant as a demonstration of Clinton's tough position toward all kinds of anti-American terrorism. Thus, in his address to the nation following the attack on Baghdad the President warned, "There should be no mistake about the message we intend these actions to convey to Saddam Hussein, to the rest of the Iraqi leadership, and to any nation, group of persons who would harm our leaders or our citizens. We will combat terrorism. We will deter aggression. We will protect our people."[8]

It may well be, as some experts argue, that "most of the damage to U.S. interest done by terrorism has been self-inflicted,"[9] but this is precisely the result of the terrorists' calculus of violence and their intention to manipulate the mass media, the public, and decision makers.

This book is primarily about the effects of and responses to major international terrorist acts—terrorist spectaculars—committed overseas against U.S. citizens. With the exception of the 1993 World Trade Center bombing the most dramatic, brutal, and shocking incidents were staged outside the United States by Mid-Eastern groups with or without the support of governments in the region. The focus of the study is especially but not exclusively on

incidents that involved hostage taking, the quintessential terrorist deed.

Above all, international terrorists want to influence various
targets in specific target countries. How the media, the public,
and decision makers react to violence for political purposes—and
how the three groups interact—determines the official responses
and the extent to which terrorists can advance their objectives.
This book argues that the strategy of terror is most effective when
international terrorists stage violent spectaculars outside their
specific target countries. This is quite different in cases of domestic terrorist events and international terrorist violence committed on the territory of a targeted government and public. In these
instances government officials have considerable advantages in
the battle for media attention, public opinion, and dominance in
the policy debate.

Although this book deals with the effects of terrorism on the
mass media, the public, and the politics of policy making, it is
necessary to sketch the goals and targets of international terrorism before dealing with its impact on various actors in the policy
process.

As Martha Crenshaw has observed, the effects of terrorism are
complex and multifaceted.[10] The same applies to goals, targets,
and methods, which differ from group to group and from incident
to incident. Still, it is possible to construct a typology of terrorist
goals and targets, especially if one views terrorism as the result of
rational political strategies and not as the consequence of psychological forces that compel certain people to commit violent
acts.[11]

International terrorists have three types of goals: tactical or
short-term, strategic or long-term, and universal or overlapping.
Tactical or short-term goals are incident-specific, strategic ends
are peculiar to certain types of groups, and universal objectives
attempt to advance both tactical and strategic designs. For example, a group that stages a hijacking and demands the exchange of
its hostages for imprisoned comrades is pursuing a short-term or

tactical goal that might be obtained by one single action. It is conceivable that the same group has strategic or long-term objectives such as winning national independence for a people it claims to represent—surely an end that will not be achieved by one hijacking or bombing. Regardless of whether a group manages to realize or further its tactical or strategic goals as the result of major acts of terrorism, it will get the attention of its target audience, spread fear and anxiety among citizens, and demonstrate the inability of a targeted government to protect its citizens. The leader of the Popular Front for the Liberation of Palestine, George Habash, recognized early in his terrorist career that by committing violence "we force people to ask what is going on."[12]

Getting the attention of the mass media, the public, and decision makers is the raison d'etre behind modern terrorism's increasingly shocking violence. By resorting to ever more spectacular and brutal deeds and thereby heightening the threshold of violence, terrorists are assured of substantial press coverage and public attention—otherwise, as one terrorist put it, "we would throw roses if it would work."[13]

Terrorists achieve their goals by winning the attention of—and manipulating—their various targets. Figure 1.1 identifies the most important target types that enter into the terrorists' objectives. Domestic terrorist groups such as the Irish Republican Army, Germany's Red Army Faction, and Italy's Red Brigades have traditionally chosen high-level political, diplomatic, military, or corporate leaders as immediate victims of their political violence. International terrorist spectaculars directed against the United States have mostly affected random victims who happened to be in the wrong place at the wrong time. While the perpetrators of such violence are indifferent to whom they harm, "victims of terrorism are not selected purely at random."[14] In most instances the immediate victims' identities do not matter, but their nationality, their presence in certain locations, or their professions place them automatically into an identifiable "enemy" category.

8

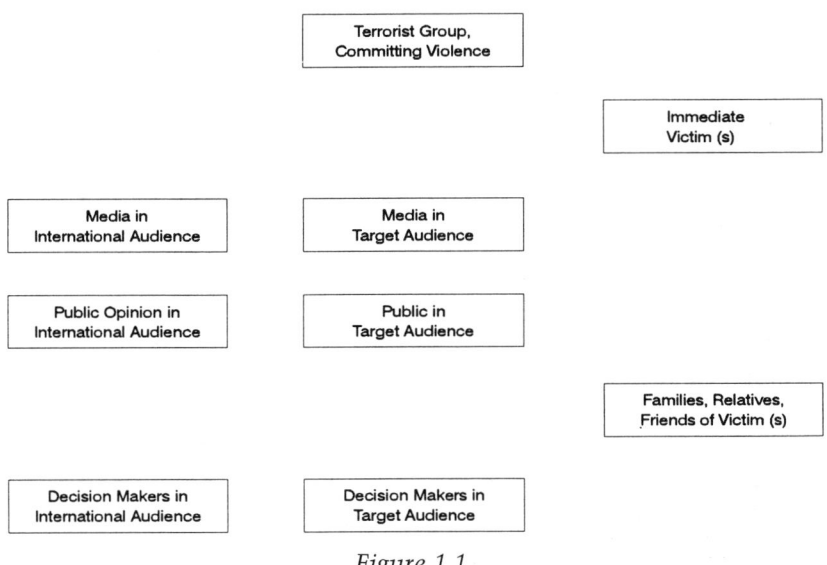

Figure 1.1
The Calculus of Violence

For many years American GIs were targeted by the German Red Army Faction or the Italian Red Brigades because they were members of the U.S. armed forces. Tourists in Israel who have been harmed during terrorist attacks by Palestinian groups were not innocent victims in the eyes of their attackers but guilty simply because of their presence in enemy territory. After the massacre at Lod airport in 1972, during which terrorists killed a number of tourists who had flown to Israel, the leader of a terrorist group argued, "There are no innocent tourists in Israel."[15] The rationale is that if you are not for us, you are against us, or, "If you are not part of the solution, you are part of the problem."[16]

In a letter to the *New York Times*, the group responsible for the World Trade Center bombing revealed that it acted in response to American political, economic, and military support to Israel, "the state of terrorism," and to "the rest of the dictator countries in the region." Implying that in their eyes none of their victims was innocent, the group members warned, "The American people are responsible for the actions of their government and they must question all of the crimes that their government is committing against other people. Or they—Americans—will be the targets of our operations that could diminish them."[17]

By targeting the citizens of a particular country, terrorists calculate that these immediate victims, dead or alive, are sure means to get the attention of the mass media, the public, and policy makers in their target country. Contemporary terrorists are sophisticated enough to understand that decision makers in liberal democracies cannot and do not ignore press coverage and public opinion. It is for this reason that they "try to exercise influence over targeted officials or nations through intimidation."[18]

Further, terrorists need not convince their targets that their cause is morally right. Targeted societies and governments do not lose their usefulness in the terrorist scheme, even when violent incidents result in negative media coverage and public outcries against terrorist brutality. A nation enraged over terrorism may in fact either encourage or inhibit governmental responses in ways that play into the hands of terrorists.

Through the mass media international terrorists gain access to the public at large and to decision makers in their target society. Because the free press is the "primary conduit connecting terrorists, the public, and governments,"[19] violent incidents can advance the terrorists' goals only if these kinds of incidents are widely reported. For this reason the press is frequently accused of providing terrorists their "lifeblood" or "oxygen" in the form of publicity. Some observers argue that if the media were to deny such coverage "terrorism as such would cease to exist."[20]

Even though international terrorist acts are often specifically designed to exploit the interconnections between the various targets in one particular country, they also affect international publics and decision makers in other countries by gaining coverage in the international mass media. Whether intended or not, this dimension of the calculus of terror can obstruct a target government's efforts to find international support for its counterterrorist measures.

President Carter during the Iranian hostage crisis and President Reagan in the wake of several terrorist acts during 1985 and 1986 tried to enlist support for collective responses to terrorism. In both instances the friends and allies of the United States were slow to support even modest proposals for concerted actions. Another example of international terrorists' ability to promote disunity among friendly nations was the investigation following the bombing of Pan Am Flight 103 in late 1988: German security officials dragged their feet when asked to cooperate with American and British investigators, perhaps to cover up mistakes in their own antiterrorist efforts and their lax attitude toward international terrorist groups operating in the Federal Republic of Germany with whom they had an understanding that Germans would not be targeted.[21]

We know more about the roots and forms of terrorism than about its effects on target societies and more about terrorists' goals than about their successes and failures to realize their objectives. According to Irving Louis Horowitz, "Social scientists and historians have made exhaustive analyses of everything from the causes of terrorism, to the nature of the terrorist, to the relationship of terrorism to ideology. But what are the consequences of terrorism—unanticipated and otherwise?"[22] Experts on terrorism deal frequently with the impact of political violence on the mass media and on public opinion. But in most instances, these discussions fall into the anecdotal, legal, or psychological genres.[23]

Several comprehensive studies have examined the most important features of the mass media's terrorism coverage. But even the best of these works do not make clear distinctions between domestic and international terrorism news: they deal mostly with domestic terrorism (political violence involving the citizens and the territory of one country) and only peripherally with international terrorism (involving the citizens or territory of more than one country), even though there are significant differences in the way the media report the two kinds of political violence.[24] Researchers who specifically analyzed the news presentations of international terrorist incidents made interesting findings about the volume of coverage and the media's preferred sources, formats, themes, and topics.[25]

Public opinion researchers have studied the effects of terrorist violence and of governmental responses by examining public attitudes toward terrorism and counterterrorist measures.[26] A few have attempted to estimate terrorism's impact on target audiences in order to establish whether the calculus of terror works. Through innovative experiments Shanto Iyengar and Donald Kinder have demonstrated that television coverage of terrorism affects "the standards by which governments, presidents, policies, and candidates for public office are judged."[27] Viewers "primed" with television reports about the Iranian hostage crisis were thus more inclined to evaluate Jimmy Carter's overall performance as president in light of his foreign policy than people who had not watched the reports.[28] Another of Iyengar's studies traced the connection between viewers' exposure to episodic and thematic television coverage of terrorist events and their preferences for various government policy responses to terrorism.[29]

Gabriel Weimann conducted experiments to study the impact of terrorism news coverage on public opinion and found agenda setting and "status-conferral" functions. Weimann's research established that both print and television coverage of terrorist incidents raise the salience of terrorists' objectives by conferring "status on the problem, the participants and the coverage itself."[30]

While focusing on the American public's attitudes toward terrorism and government policy, Ronald Hinckley has made a strong case for policymakers to be especially sensitive and responsive to public opinion in the area of mass-mediated terrorism.[31]

If one recognizes violence for political ends as one of the most difficult American problems of the recent past and presumably of the foreseeable future, it is important to find out to what extent terrorist groups and their state sponsors have managed to win access to the free press, public opinion, and policymakers, and thereby to the American foreign policy process.

In most areas of foreign policy, debates aired through the mass media are dominated by administration sources; other voices are likely to be heard through press coverage only, if they belong to what the media consider to be authoritative and legitimate sources, especially from the standpoint of Washingtonian political elites. As for peripheral actors opposed to administration policies, their participation in policy debates typically occurs after opposition establishment sources—such as members of Congress, foreign policy experts, and perhaps dissenting administration insiders—have gained access to the media. However, when international terrorists carry out a shocking spectacular against Americans abroad, they are assured instant media access for themselves or for their allies and, just as important, for their victims and their victims' families and friends. Through such actions they are able to derail the symbiotic relationship between journalists and administration officials. As the news coverage of the World Trade Center bombing and its aftermath showed, the symbiosis remains intact when terrorists strike within the United States. Chapter 2 describes the exceptional features of those foreign policy debates in the mass media that are triggered by these sorts of terrorist spectaculars.

It has been suggested that terrorists commit violence in quest of three universal goals—to get attention, recognition, and even a degree of respectability and legitimacy. Critics complain frequently that the American media accommodate these objectives generously. The evidence presented in chapter 3 demonstrates that those who have committed anti-American terrorist spectaculars abroad have been stunningly successful in provoking and manipulating press reporting to further two of their universal goals. The chapter also presents evidence of strong relationships (1) between terrorism coverage and the American public's agenda and (2) between news reporting and the public's collective attitudes toward terrorism.

Public opinion on foreign policy issues has been characterized as volatile and irrational and consequently not worthy of consideration by government decision makers. While public opinion polls reveal frequent opinion changes with respect to American anti- and counterterrorist policies, the central argument of chapter 4 is nevertheless that apparent fluctuations and reversals in Americans' collective opinions are rational responses to changing developments and information.

When international terrorists commit a spectacular act of violence against Americans, the public tends to rally around the president, who is in charge of managing the crisis. But, as chapter 5 demonstrates, the strength and duration of such support depend on the participation of political elites in the debate and on their evaluations of the president's performance as reported in the media. This chapter makes the case for examining the incident-specific presidential approval ratings as well as the president's general approval ratings, which studies of "rallying" tend to analyze exclusively. The book's case studies suggest that approval of a president's handling of specific events is more helpful in understanding such rallies in general, not just in the case of terrorist crises.

Terrorist incidents, especially those involving hostages, are nightmares for presidents, who are often forced to choose between protecting Americans' lives (i.e., giving in to terrorists' demands in order to win the release of captive Americans) or acting in the overall national interest by not dealing with terrorists, so as not to encourage further hostage takings. The president's political self-interest enters into these considerations as well. Chapter 6 shows that media coverage of hostage situations tends to favor sources closely associated with the hostages and their loved ones. The chapter demonstrates that policies formulated with the national interest in mind are the first casualties when decision makers are forced to make hard choices.

The last chapter considers the implications of the book's findings, acknowledging that international terrorists are successful in furthering or achieving at least some of their goals. If the calculus of violence has worked quite well against the United States, as the evidence strongly suggests, what can and should be done about it? Whereas several other liberal democratic countries have enacted laws restricting various aspects of terrorism coverage, such restrictions are unlikely in the United States, as are other methods that curb the press elsewhere. In spite of suggestions that media organizations should exercise self-restraint and critique one other as to the volume and quality of terrorism reporting, there is no realistic prospect for disrupting terrorism's exploitation of the media. Yet terrorists should not be allowed to succeed when they target innocent victims. Rather, as the concluding chapter proposes, presidents and other officials must themselves learn and educate the public about the intricacies of terrorists' schemes and the dilemma the calculus of violence poses for the public and for political leaders. Otherwise terrorism will continue to succeed.

CHAPTER TWO

TERRORISM, THE MEDIA, AND FOREIGN POLICY

Power, said Karl Marx over a century ago, is control over the means of production; that phrase, said Arthur Schlesinger, Jr., recently, should be changed—power in America today is control of the media of communication.
—THEODORE H. WHITE

Friends and foes of the mass media agree that the press has political power. In his in-depth analysis of the American foreign and defense policy making process Roger Hilsman observed, "No one doubts that whoever controls the press wields power."[1] We can better understand the complex question of media power by first recognizing that "one dimension of power can be construed as the ability to have one's account become the perceived reality of others."[2] Those actors who manage to get their views and positions most often and most prominently covered by the mass media have the best chance to influence the perceptions of others—the general public, the attentive public, and elites alike—and thereby gain an advantage in efforts to affect foreign policy processes and outcomes. The evidence presented in this chapter shows that terrorists, their supporters, and their victims, unlike

16

other non-establishment individuals and groups, have no trouble whatsoever in winning access to and even dominating mass-mediated foreign policy debates.

Many past and present government decision makers, scholars, and even media insiders share the view that recent technological advances and the advent of worldwide communications networks have fundamentally changed the processes by which foreign policy is formulated, debated, and decided. In the global village, a powerful international communications network is considered to be "capable of circumventing the control of any national government"—including the American government.[3]

In the mainstream view, the communications revolution and what Senator Richard Lugar calls a new "medialism" have altered the foreign policy process in fundamental ways, diminishing the dominance of the president, White House advisers, and other decision makers. By instantly and indiscriminately providing information from all over the world and from all kinds of actors, the news media, especially television, are believed to have opened up the foreign policy process to a diversity of views and influences more typical of domestic policy making. Foreign policy makers in Washington pay increasing attention to the media; they believe in the growing influence of the global media network on public attitudes toward foreign policy.[4] Inside and outside of government the perception grows that the once-sharp distinctions between the domestic and the foreign policy making processes have faded. No wonder, then, that one study of the media's influence on federal policies—both domestic and foreign—revealed a growing belief among administration officials that press coverage is "so much part of policy-making as to be indistinguishable from it."[5]

However, this understanding of the foreign policy process in which the number and the diversity of participants are said to have "increased dramatically in the past twenty years,"[6] is based mostly, if not exclusively, on the observations, anecdotes, and perceptions of those who emphasize the problems that an emerging global and populist democracy poses for managing foreign policy problems and crises. The normative core here is the enduring Madisonian contempt for the public's tendency to base political judgments and actions on passion rather than reason. In this vein the communications revolution is believed to have magnified the dilemma of decision makers in that, as White House adviser David Gergen has argued, "television can awaken people's interest, but it does not have yet the capacity to educate them."[7]

But whether they like it or not, modern-day decision makers know that they cannot ignore the attitudes of a public whose interest has been stirred by what policy makers perceive as an open mass-mediated foreign policy debate. Like a growing number of former administration insiders, Lloyd Cutler, counselor to Presidents Carter and Clinton, has described the significant effects that television news has on both the timing and the substance of important foreign policy decisions. In Cutler's view, more than the print press, television news "has major consequences for the foreign-policy agenda of any administration. To sustain its foreign and national security policies, an administration must not merely satisfy the minority of print readers who care about issues; it must now satisfy the entire national television audience as well."[8]

Recent systematic research does not support the view that the result of global communications networks is a foreign policy process spun out of decision makers' control and, as David Gergen argues, a wide-open teledemocracy.[9] Questioning the conventional wisdom that government policy makers have lost their dominance to either increased democratic participation or competition among numerous interests, Lance Bennett and others insist that developments in communications and mass media have not fundamentally altered the influence and power of the foreign policy establishment. Rather, they suggest that the most important factor in the production of foreign policy news—i.e., the symbiotic relationship between press and public officials—has not changed much, if at all.[10]

Demonstrating that in the first two months of the Persian Gulf conflict of 1990–91 the three leading Washington news beats (the White House, Department of State, and Department of Defense) dominated the television networks' news about the Gulf conflict, Timothy Cook's work supports Bennett's argument.[11] Television news gave sources in these three locations about the same amount of airtime as all other domestic actors taken together to shape the perceptions of the public and elites. Before the communication revolution, Bernard Cohen had recognized a symbiosis between journalists and public officials that served their respective organizational goals,[12] and this cooperative arrangement still existed in the global village of the 1980s and 1990s. While the free marketplace of ideas remains the ideal of the American media, the press remains dependent on economic markets and the political arena. Moreover, as Robert Entman has persuasively argued,

> the continuing dependence of reporters on self-interested elites helps perpetuate the journalistic status quo. . . .
> Each side peddles something the other needs. The elites have newsworthy political information, the indispensable raw material needed to construct the news. Journalists can provide publicity that can be slanted favorably or unfavorably.[13]

Even journalists themselves are struck by the degree to which "foreign coverage is shaped by Washington, by White House and State Department reporters"[14] and their attitude about the primacy of the executive. In the words of the Washington bureau chief of a major media organization, "It's Reagan who counts"[15]— or, of course, Carter, Bush, Clinton, or any other sitting president.

Bennett has concluded that the enduring symbiosis between reporter and official, the increasing routinization and monopolization of international news production, and ever more sophisticated news management within administrations do not necessarily add up to an expanded range and diversity of information in mass-mediated foreign policy debates. On the contrary, the combination of continuity (in personal relationships between reporter and official) and change (in international news production) may in fact limit the input and influence of many different view-points.[16]

Of course, a model of democracy along the lines of the Jeffersonian ideal depends upon a fully informed citizenry that has access to all kinds of views and opinions. And, as Robert Entman and Benjamin Page remind us, "autonomous reporting at least potentially allows the public to assess policy critically and thereby to participate in genuine policy discourse."[17] Whether or not the news media present readers and audiences with a comprehensive record of a particular policy debate depends in large part on the presence of disagreement among "authoritative" sources inside and outside the administration.[18] It is only when conflict persists among actors whom journalists perceive as "important" or "authoritative" that "the news gates tend to open to grass roots groups, interest groups, opinion polls, and broader social participation in media policy debates."[19]

This pattern of news reporting has existed for decades. My own systematic content analyses and comparisons of news coverage in three leading U.S. newspapers (the *New York Times*, the *Washington Post*, and the *Chicago Tribune*) of two similar foreign policy events in the 1960s and 1980s (the invasion of the Dominican Republic of 1965 and the Grenada invasion of 1983), showed striking similarities—although the communications revolution occurred in the years separating these crises. In both cases administration officials were the most frequently cited and in terms of front page placement the most favorably treated domestic sources. And in both cases the range of diversity of opinions presented in the news pages was by and large determined by the existence of conflicting voices within what one might call the "loyal opposition"—especially in Congress. The press accounts of the two U.S. interventions mostly reflected consensus or disagreement among institutional actors and elites.[20]

Even when the press covers a wide range of views and opinions on a particular foreign policy case, chances are that administration officials led by the president and his supporters receive preferential treatment as their positions have a far better chance of being cited on the front pages or early in individual news stories than other sources.[21]

This lack of consistent autonomy on the part of the news media runs counter to the widely held view that the Vietnam war and the Watergate scandal marked the end of the post World War II policy consensus and the beginning of press hostility and cynicism toward the president and other decision makers. After his four years in the Carter White House, Hamilton Jordan commented on what he perceived as drastic attitude changes in news organizations and individual journalists: "I believe that Watergate and Vietnam pushed the American media from wholesome skepticism and doubt into out-and-out cynicism about the American political process generally and the Presidency specifically."[22]

One could assume that different foreign policy issues, problems, crises, and wars result in different kinds of reporting. But while the open and closed models can easily coexist with ample room for variations in between, research points overwhelmingly towards the dominance of a relatively closed model despite contrary claims that a wide-open "medialism" has significantly changed the foreign policy process.[23] The most persuasive accounts of growing media control and diminished decision makers' control over the foreign policy process come from former and current administration officials who were closely involved in anti- and counterterrorist decisions in the 1980s. In this respect, Democrats, Republicans, and independents describe the press as, in the words of Simon Serfarty, "an independent force" that adversely affects the timing and the range of decision making.

Robert Oakley, director of the State Department's Office for Combating Terrorism during the Reagan presidency, hints at one particular dimension of the media's impact on the foreign policy process. In his view, when the United States is faced with terrorism, these events "tend to be more publicized and emotion-laden, and generate greater political heat, than other developments."[24]

The perception is that a spectacular attack or merely the threat

of violence against innocent Americans by a small group of terrorists, whether supported by state authorities or not, manages to
alter the American foreign policy process. By exploiting the need
of the media—especially commercial television—to compete in
the economic marketplace, terrorists are believed to forge a symbiotic relationship with the press, weakening the entrenched ties
between journalists and officials at the three most important
news beats in Washington. Terrorists are believed to succeed
where other challengers to the administration's dominance
almost always fall short: they get all the media coverage they
want. In addition, these kinds of events seem to open the mass-
mediated foreign policy debate to a diversity of domestic views
and thus do away with the relatively closed process that prevails
in most foreign policy areas.

From Theory to Actual Cases

To explore whether or not international terrorist incidents
indeed alter the traditionally closed foreign policy debate as the-
orized above, I examined several major international terrorist
and counterterrorist incidents. The Iranian hostage crisis
(November 4, 1979–January 20, 1981) and the TWA hijacking
incident (June 14–June 30, 1985) were the most shocking and sensational hostage spectaculars to that time. The ordeal of the
American hostages held in Lebanon for many years during the
1980s and early 1990s was the longest incident of this kind. The
hijacking of the Italian cruise ship *Achille Lauro* in October 1985
involved the taking of hostages and the murder of one American
passenger by Palestinian terrorists, and it was the first case in
which the United States succeeded with a rather difficult counterterrorist operation. The bombing of Libya in April 1986 was a
retaliatory and preventive counterterrorist strike in response to
what the Reagan administration believed to be Libya's long-term
support of and direct involvement in terrorist activities against
the United States. Finally, the bombing of Pan Am flight 103 over
Lockerbie, Scotland, in December 1988 killed all 259 passengers

and eleven people on the ground, by far the most deadly terrorist attack to date.

I analyzed the content of television and print press terrorism coverage during the first five-and-a-half months of the Iranian hostage crisis, during the entire TWA hijacking, and during the days immediately following the *Achille Lauro* hijacking, the American air raids on Libya, and the destruction of Pan Am flight 103. The focus was on the CBS Evening News but in order to examine similarities and differences in television and print press coverage, I also analyzed the *New York Times*.

The Iran Hostage Crisis

When so-called students stormed the U.S. embassy in Teheran and took Americans inside hostage, the media at home reacted as they would to any routine foreign policy event: the first CBS Evening News broadcast after the takeover opened with a summary of the Teheran happenings by anchorman Walter Cronkite. This was followed by correspondent Marvin Kalb at the State Department describing the reaction of administration officials, especially of Secretary of State Cyrus Vance who stated calmly, "I have received assurances that they [the American hostages] will be kept safe and well by the Iranian government, and I expect the Iranian government to carry out those assurances." The lead stories in the following four CBS Evening News broadcasts originated at the State Department—one of Washington's "golden triangle" news beats in foreign affairs. (The two other leading news beats being the White House and the Department of Defense.)[25]

However, as soon as it was deemed likely that the Teheran situation might be more serious than a similar episode at the Embassy several months earlier and as soon as correspondents were in place, CBS and the other TV networks began to pay an extraordinary amount of attention to the actual crisis spot. In fact, the very first CBS report directly from Teheran was the lead story on the November 9 CBS Evening News. Following Arden Ostrander's report, Cronkite described the filmed scenes of anti-

American demonstrations in Teheran, pointing out that "the demonstrators burned an effigy of President Carter, shouting, 'Burn, Carter, burn.' The effigy, with a goat's skull in place of a head, was topped with a hat resembling the American flag."

During November, while the Carter administration tried to pressure the Iranian authorities to end the hostage situation by freezing Iranian assets in American banks, by ordering an oil embargo, and by initiating deportation procedures against Iranians, there was no domestic criticism of Carter's crisis management, and Washington's golden triangle was the leading domestic news beat with 39 reports (19 originating from the White House, 18 from State, and two from the Pentagon). But a total of 48 reports from other domestic beats were aired—among them 12 concerning hostage families or released hostages and three originating from Capitol Hill. In December, February, and March, administration news beats were more frequently covered by the CBS Evening News than all other domestic locations taken together, but in January and April more stories came from other domestic news beats than from the golden triangle. From the start of the crisis to mid-April, when the final decision to launch a rescue attempt was made, about the same number of reports originated at the golden triangle as at other news beats in the United States. (See table 1 in the appendix.)

To take this nearly even split as an indication of a tilt in coverage in favor of the administration's dominance in the foreign policy process would ignore the dual character of the most dramatic news beat—Teheran and the U.S. Embassy itself. Teheran was in a very real sense as much domestic as foreign: much of the reporting from around or inside the U.S. Embassy was based on what the American hostages said in interviews with western reporters and their captors, or what they reportedly mentioned in telephone and personal conversations with their families and with American and foreign officials allowed to visit them. In fact, Washington's golden triangle, other domestic news beats, and the Teheran location were evenly represented on the CBS Evening News, with about 30 percent of all reports originating at each of the three.

Experiments have demonstrated that reports placed at the top of news programs are more likely to affect the public agenda than non-lead stories—in the words of Shanto Iyengar and Donald Kinder, "Stories that appear first tend to matter more."[26] Reports from White House and State Department correspondents accounted for 39 lead stories while reports by other domestic correspondents accounted for 7 lead stories. But 50 lead stories originated in Iran. More important, a significant number of the Teheran reports centered on the American hostages and were thus also domestic in nature. (See table 2 in the appendix.)

While the frequency with which news beats are used and placed at the top of newscasts provide valuable clues about reporting patterns, we need to take a closer look at the opportunities for political actors at the various news beats to participate in the mass-mediated foreign policy debate. Clearly, the most likely administration sources are White House officials, especially the President, and State Department and Pentagon officials. But during the Iran crisis White House and State Department correspondents regularly gave non-administration actors the opportunity to voice their support or opposition to President Carter's handling of the crisis.

During November and December these "outsiders" were overwhelmingly in favor of Carter's handling of the Iran situation. Members of Congress, governors, interest group leaders (e.g., AFL/CIO president George Meany), and foreign policy experts (e.g., Henry Kissinger) expressed support for the official U.S. policy. The families of the Iran hostages were no exception: on November 9, for example, Lesley Stahl reported that President Carter and the families of the hostages had issued a joint statement, after a meeting at the White House, that clearly indicated their agreement.

But even at the golden triangle posts, the consensus did not last very long. During the January 2 broadcast, Roger Mudd observed, "In the name of national unity, the presidential rivals of Jimmy Carter at first refrained from attacking him on the Iranian crisis, an issue that has sent him climbing in the polls. But now, carefully worded dissent is being heard."

This dissent, not always carefully worded, was also reported by correspondents stationed at the White House and occasionally by those at the State Department. The families of the hostages also aired their growing dissatisfaction with the administration's policies. On February 4, for example, Jacqueline Adams reported that First Lady Rosalynn Carter had met with the families of the Iran hostages at the State Department. The meeting did not go well:

> Jacqueline Adams: But after ninety-three days of waiting, the families want more from the State Department than simple reassurances.
> Kenneth Timm [stepfather of a hostage]: It's just totally frustrating to go through ninety-three days and to almost be told we are no closer to any negotiations than we were at day one.
> Allyssa Keough [daughter of a hostage]: They're getting fed up with what's going on which is nothing, basically nothing. They're getting to the point where they're tired of not hearing anything. Many of them feel they're getting the shaft from the State Department, from the whole government as a whole.

Other domestic news beats—especially those covering the campaigns of the Democratic and Republican primary candidates and the families, friends, and supporters of the Iranian hostages across the country—contributed greatly to the range of views and opinions in the crisis discourse.

Television news programs are structured around distinct news beats and their correspondents, whereas the print press tends to cut across many news beats. In the *New York Times*, for example, a typical front page story about the Iran crisis carrying a Washington dateline would often cover developments at several news beats inside and outside the administration and the capital city. Therefore, the fact that the *Times* carried ninety-two first page stories datelined Teheran as against eighty-three datelined Washington during the first five-and-a-half months of the Iran crisis reveals little about the representation of news beats and their primary sources at the time. (See table 3 in the appendix.)

While front page stories are more important to readers than those published on a newspaper's inside pages and are more likely to be read and remembered, Entman and Page also suggest that "a picture may be more noticed and better remembered than many words."[27] In their preliminary analysis of the news media's coverage of the 1990–91 Persian Gulf conflict, they found that even during the most intensive public discourse over the Gulf conflict "the visual rhetoric of the coverage [in leading U.S. newspapers] appears much more under control of the administration than the verbal. . . . Visual portraits of the administration leaders appeared to us very favorable if not heroic in most cases."[28]

President Carter and others in his administration did not enjoy such an advantage during the Iran crisis. In purely quantitative terms, administration leaders fared well in being depicted in photographs on *New York Times* front pages: officials at golden triangle news beats appeared in fourteen front page photographs compared to sixteen photographs for all other domestic actors combined, including the Iranian hostages. (See table 4 in the appendix.) But numbers do not tell the true story of the "visual rhetoric" and its probable impact on public and elite opinion. Even during November and December, when few domestic actors second-guessed Carter's handling of the crisis, the visual images on the front pages were not helpful to the administration. After multicolumn pictures of the captors, their hostages, Teheran demonstrators with anti-Carter and anti-Shah banners, and an Iranian using the American flag to carry garbage, the *Times* finally printed a routine shot of Jimmy Carter signing a presidential order freezing Iranian assets in U.S. banks. A day later, another photograph showed the President and close relatives of the hostages during a prayer service at the National Cathedral in Washington. These first two pictures of Carter foreshadowed the impression of him as a weak and "do-nothing" President, a perception that would soon come to haunt him.

The nine occasions on which the President appeared on the

front page of the *Times* during the first five-and-a-half months of the crisis magnified the contrast between the passive posture of Carter and the high drama and human tragedy expressed in the nine photographs of the captive Americans in Iran and their worried loved ones. The twelve photographs of the anti-American captors in Teheran and their supporters probably contributed even more to the increasingly negative public and elite opinion of Carter's performance.

If still photographs are likely to be more influential in the formation of public opinion than printed words, one would also conclude that visual images on television are far more persuasive than words. Although this study does not attempt a systematic analysis of visual rhetoric in television broadcasts, a close look at the transcripts of CBS News crisis coverage provides some clues about the news presentation as a whole, because the congruence, which has been found in the photographic images and the text of print media coverage, is even more plausible with respect to television.[29] Television images depend, of course, on the choice of film material that is used in newscasts. It is also clear that television pictures are not unrelated to the news sources who are shown speaking or acting directly or are quoted, paraphrased, or otherwise described by reporters and anchors. An analysis of the CBS Evening News reveals that sources who invoked images of an administration and a President unable to solve an increasingly frustrating Iran crisis overshadowed administration sources who made great efforts, as State Department correspondent Marvin Kalb observed in early December, "to counter the impression of inaction in the face of continuing provocation not only from Iran, but from other countries in the area."[30]

During this period there was nearly as much coverage of President Carter's foes in Iran (14 percent of the paragraphs in CBS Evening News transcripts) as of administration sources including the President himself (15 percent). Another 7 percent of the coverage relied on the hostages, their families, and friends as news sources. After an initial reluctance to criticize the President's handling of the crisis, Carter's rivals had begun to attack his fail-

ure to solve the Iran problem: about 3 percent of the Iran reporting covered Democratic and Republican presidential contenders.
Thus, not counting the critical voices among experts, congressional sources, and the public at large, significantly more coverage was based upon sources who either explicitly attacked the
President (the students in Teheran and their supporters led by
Ayatollah Khomeini, the President's election year rivals, and relatives of the hostages) or provided images of an impotent leader
in the White House (especially hostages shown in Teheran) than
upon administration officials. Compared to the CBS Evening
News, the coverage in the *Times* was more favorable to President
Carter and administration officials (with 20 percent of the Iran
news based on these sources) than to foes in Iran (14 percent),
hostages and their families (4 percent), and Carter's rivals for the
White House (1 percent).

Even reporters' descriptions, background information, anchorpersons' comments, and transition texts contributed to the image
of failure during the crisis. Anchorman Walter Cronkite's daily
reminders that it was day forty, sixty, one-hundred-and-twenty,
of the Iran hostages' captivity illustrate this point, as well as
remarks such as:

> Cronkite: The Iran crisis appears to be just about back to
> square one. (March 10, 1980)
> Cronkite: To the Carter Administration, the one-hundred-
> forty-three-day-old Iran crisis is becoming more and more
> like a tunnel with no light at its end. (March 25, 1980)
> Cronkite: The Carter Administration, which has met failure
> in all its efforts to end the one-hundred-forty-five-day-old
> Iran crisis, held out new hope today. But it gave no
> specifics. (March 27, 1980)

The President and administration officials were far from being
the dominant sources in television or newspaper reports. Only 15
percent of the Iran coverage in the CBS Evening News and 20 percent in the *New York Times* was based on Jimmy Carter and others in his administration; far more coverage was devoted to other
domestic actors (68 percent in the CBS Evening News, 54 percent

29

in the *Times*). The leading domestic news sources were reporters, correspondents, editorial writers, columnists, and anchorpersons offering descriptions, background reports, analysis, interpretations, and opinions. (See tables 5 and 6 in the appendix.)

Analysis of the selection and placement of news beats in CBS broadcasts, the imagery in front page pictures in the *Times*, the choice of sources in both media, and the comments and observations by anchors and correspondents, all show that the news concerning the Iran situation deviated from the reporting patterns of other foreign crises. From the early weeks of the hostage ordeal, when domestic opposition was virtually non-existent, the constant attention to the predicament of the hostages and their loved ones as well as to their aggressively anti-American captors dramatically diminished the usually dominant, preferential treatment of administration officials in mass-mediated foreign policy debates.

The TWA Hijacking Crisis

While the Iran coverage distinctly deviated from the media's tendency to favor the president and other administration officials as prominent sources, the news of the TWA hijacking drama five years later was an even more striking example of the ability of terrorists to upset the routine reporting patterns of the American press during such emergencies.

The CBS Evening News of June 14, 1985 opened with the partial replay of a communication between the distraught pilot of TWA flight 847 and air controllers at Beirut airport: "[Voice of pilot] They are beating the passengers. They are threatening to kill them now! They are threatening to kill them now! We want the fuel now!!"

This lead set the stage for the coverage format during the following sixteen days: much of the news relied on the actions, orders, and demands of the hijackers and their Lebanese supporters and the plight of their American hostages.

During the seventeen days of the ordeal, reports about the

TWA situation were the lead story on the CBS Evening News six-teen times. But only one of those lead stories originated at a gold-en triangle location: On the twelfth day of the crisis Bill Plante's White House report was deemed the most newsworthy and placed at the top of the broadcast. All other lead stories came from foreign locations—ten from Beirut, two from the London CBS studio, and one each from Algiers, Israel, and Cyprus. This lopsided selection of lead stories filmed abroad constituted a stunning departure from the usual placement advantage of reports originated at the White House and the Departments of State and Defense during international crises. The poor showing of administration news beats was not merely a remarkable shift of media attention from Washington to foreign locations but also a deviation from the usual placement advantage of golden trian-gle spots over all other domestic news beats.

Algiers, where the TWA airliner landed during the early phase of the hijacking; the CBS studio in London, which moni-tored the developments surrounding the incident; and most of all Beirut, where most of the drama unfolded, were "foreign" news beats in a geographic sense only. Like Teheran during the Iranian hostage situation, all of these beats relied as much—or more—on domestic sources (hostages, freed hostages) as on for-eign ones. The hijackers and their Amal militia friends under-stood the value of American news sources. For the American media and for their own purposes they frequently made the hostages available for television interviews, or provided infor-mation about their captives.

In these kinds of crises neither the distinction between domes-tic and foreign news beats nor placement in television newscasts reveals very much about the relative importance given to various sources by the media. During the TWA hijacking twenty-five sto-ries on the CBS Evening News originated at the golden triangle in Washington, while thirty-five reports came from other domestic locations. But in ten of these, the domestic locations, such as CBS studios in New York, were in fact merely domestic locations of transatlantic interviews with Nabih Berri and other Amal offi-

31

cials in Beirut. On the other hand, as mentioned earlier, a great many foreign news beats relied heavily on Americans abroad as sources, especially hostages or released hostages. (See table 7 in the appendix.)

During the TWA hijacking the President lost control over the golden triangle news beats and the accompanying benefits of the usual cooperative relationship between reporters and officials. Forced to wait and see instead of taking the initiative, officials simply did not have very much to say. The CBS Evening News on June 17, 1985 aired a typical White House report during this crisis: following one sentence statements by President Reagan and State Department spokesman Bernard Kalb, four relatives and one friend of a TWA hostage expressed their growing dissatisfaction with the administration's passivity.

A day later, another White House report opened with a film clip of President Reagan in a phone conversation with Patricia Stethem, the mother of the young Navy diver who had been murdered by the TWA hijackers. Introduced by correspondent Lesley Stahl, who described growing frustration among members of Congress and their constituents, Representative Judd Gregg (R-New Hampshire) demanded, "When an American sailor is singled out and murdered simply because he is an American, the time has come for America to meet force with force." In contrast, House majority leader Jim Wright (D-Texas) called for national unity, saying, "I am not going to criticize the Administration. I think it's time for all of us to join ranks and face this problem together."

Although both reports originated at administration news beats, their dominant messages and visual images conjured impressions of a President unable to deal with a handful of terrorists and their backers and unable to free his citizens from captivity. Sources triggering these kinds of images were by far more often represented in the TWA coverage than were administration officials who tried to transmit assurances that they were handling the crisis effectively. In this respect, the Reagan administration did even worse during the relatively short TWA ordeal

[handwritten margin note: Why is admin. not being heard? are reporters going to them first?]

than President Carter had during the far longer Iran crisis. While the CBS Evening News relied on President Reagan and other administration officials for about 7 percent of its TWA hostage coverage, it used the hostages, their relatives, the terrorists, and their supporters in Lebanon as sources in 21 percent of its crisis reports. (See table 8 in the appendix.)

Based on his content analysis of the complete TWA coverage on ABC, CBS, and NBC News, Tony Atwater found "homogeneity in the topical emphasis of network evening news programs."[31] Furthermore, his research established that reports concerning the hostages, families, and the acts and demands of the hijackers and their supporters accounted for 53 percent of all stories, while 17 percent of the coverage concerned the U.S. government reaction.[32]

In the *New York Times* 17 percent of the crisis news came from the President and other administration sources, and 19 percent from the hostages, their relatives and friends, and the terrorists and their Lebanese supporters. However, the pictures published on the front pages of the *Times* were far more likely to evoke dissatisfaction with an ineffective administration than confidence in the President. For eight days these photographs showed either the terrorists, the hijacked plane, several American hostages or released hostages, and in one case mourners at the funeral of Robert Stethem. On the ninth day of the crisis, the front page carried a portrait of the U.S. Ambassador to Lebanon, Reginald Bartholomew: it was the first page one picture of an administration official involved in the crisis. Four days later, a photograph of President Reagan made the front page along with pictures of the other three key players in alleged secret negotiations to solve the crisis—Nabih Berri, Syria's President Hafez al-Assad, and Israel's Prime Minister Shimon Peres.

Of twenty-three front page pictures depicting a total of twenty-five actors in the TWA drama, twelve showed the terrorists, their sympathizers, or the American hostages, but only three showed administration officials. The visuals on page one were overwhelmingly tilted toward what the captors and the captives in Beirut tried to communicate to America at the expense of administration efforts to convey the impression of strong presidential leadership.

The President and other administration officials—normally dominant in foreign policy debates—figured in only 7 percent of the reports in the CBS Evening News. The *Times*, too, relied far more on domestic sources outside the administration (60 percent) than on the President and other administration officials (17 percent). (See table 9 in the appendix.)

Thus, in both the CBS Evening News and the *Times* the TWA crisis coverage departed drastically from normal reporting patterns: the golden triangle news beats were not the dominant reporting locations and administration officials were not the dominant news sources during this crisis.

The *Achille Lauro* Case

The day after Palestinian terrorists who had seized control of the Italian cruise ship *Achille Lauro*, brutally murdering one of their American hostages, surrendered to Egyptian authorities and left Egypt as free men, the CBS Evening News opened with the jubilant revelation of yet another dramatic twist in the Mediterranean hijacking saga:

> President Reagan: These young Americans sent a message to terrorists everywhere. The message: you can run, but you can't hide.
> Jimmy Dell Palmer [former TWA hostage]: I almost felt like standing up and cheering for President Reagan. He's done something.
> Dan Rather [voiceover]: A plane today on the ground of the NATO base in Italy: symbol, finally, of U.S. can-do, will-do, symbol of poetic justice. Hijackers intercepted by U.S. jets and forced to land here so they will finally face the justice of a jury.
> Good evening. This is the CBS Evening News, Dan Rather reporting.

What a difference a day makes. An amazing, daring U.S. intercept of the plane bearing four men accused of hijacking the *Achille Lauro*. Tonight, instead of safe passage from Egypt and out of range of justice, they are in Italy and charged with murder, hijack, and other charges, courtesy of U.S. Navy jet pilots.

Indeed, what a difference a day had made: twenty-four hours earlier, the CBS Evening News had portrayed a fumbling and stumbling President unable to deal with terrorists, unable to do something, anything. Twenty-four hours earlier Dan Rather had introduced a report by White House correspondent Lesley Stahl with the critical remark, "President Reagan, who has said little during and after the hijack, today stunned even some of his aides with conflicting statements about what should be done with the hijackers and who should do it." In Stahl's report Representative Tommy Robinson (D-Arkansas) blasted the President and his terrorism policy. "It's time to rename your State Department the Capitulation Department. Get off of your stick, Mister President," Robinson said. "The American people are sick and tired of being kicked around."

And on October 8, one day after the hijacking of the cruise ship, CBS had given one American who had been on a shore excursion when the terrorist takeover occurred the forum to castigate the Reagan administration. Obviously referring to Washington's handling of the TWA hijacking a few months earlier, the distraught woman said, "I'm mad at my government for fooling around the last time and not really coming to a decisive impact that this should have happened again [sic]."

Such criticism stopped immediately once Americans learned of the interception of *Achille Lauro* terrorists in the air. Leslie Stahl reported that "official Washington reflected the mood of the country over the success of the operation—outright elation." To underline this point, Representative David Dreier (R-California) was shown saying, "For this morning, the American giant stretched out its little finger and exacted a fitting bid of retribution."

35

CBS newscasters gave their audience a taste of the new sentiment in America by playing excerpts from radio call-in programs:

Woman: I just want to call and tell you that I never felt so good since World War II ended.
Man: My president came through and I'm proud and I show it."
Woman: I thought America did the most wonderful thing they ever did. I'm telling you and it's true.
Male Student: I think it's about time the U.S. stood up and took some type of action.

Correspondent Bob Simon cited the headline in New York's tabloid *Daily News*—We Bag The Bums.

But in spite of the sudden counterterrorist initiative by the Reagan administration, the media's record for the eleven days following the hijacking (four days before the interception, seven days after the interception) did not reflect administration dominance in terms of lead stories, news beat frequency, or source selection. During the first four days of the *Achille Lauro* crisis (October 7 through 10), the CBS Evening News opened twice with the CBS studio as the location and once each with reports from the White House and from Cairo. During the following week, beginning on October 11 when the news of the interception broke, the lead stories came once from the White House, once from cities and towns around the country reacting to the hijacking, and four times from overseas (on one of the seven days the CBS Evening News was preempted by a sports event).

During the first four days of the crisis a total of five reports came from the golden triangle, eight from other domestic locations, and seven from abroad. Actually, the administration fared worse in the days following the interception, when only four stories originated at White House, State Department, or Pentagon, while other domestic locations contributed seven stories, and foreign correspondents fourteen stories. The focus on overseas news beats affected the selection of sources by correspondents and anchors alike. Only 15 percent of the CBS Evening News about the *Achille Lauro* came from administration sources, 62 percent from other domestic sources, and 23 percent from foreign ones. (See table 2.10). The *New York Times* used administration sources more frequently (for 22 percent of its *Achille Lauro* coverage) than the CBS Evening News, but its editors and reporters, too, based more coverage on foreign sources (30 percent) and significantly more on domestic sources outside the administration (48 percent). (See table 11 in the appendix.)

More important, the visual images on the *New York Times* front pages were not at all reflective of the bold and highly successful U.S. counterterrorist measure. Of the seventeen front page crisis-related photographs during the eleven days after the takeover of the cruise ship, none showed President Reagan or other administration officials involved in the decision to intercept the Egyptian plane carrying the *Achille Lauro* terrorists. The Italian cruise ship itself, with and without terrorists, was shown four times; the American hostages, ex-hostages, and their relatives or friends were portrayed in six, foreign officials in four, and the captain of the *Achille Lauro* in two photographs. Perhaps the only picture that conveyed a clearly pro-administration image was the one of the intercepted Egyptian plane on Italian soil.

During the eleven day period, Marilyn Klinghoffer appeared in three front page photographs—at first in a snapshot with her husband and later, surrounded by friends and relatives, as the widow of the one hostage killed by the hijackers. In addition, the *Times* published a picture on page one of Syrian soldiers carrying the coffin of Leon Klinghoffer. While there were two front page pictures of the Italian Prime Minister, Bettino Craxi, who was highly critical of the interception, and the head shots of four terrorists in defiant demeanor, there were no visuals that communicated the enthusiasm with which many Americans reacted to the first American counterterrorist spectacular or the satisfaction of its architects in the White House and the Pentagon. President Reagan's decision to take the initiative and show terrorists that Washington was tired of its usual "wait-and-see" role in these situations did not help his administration to dominate the mass-mediated debate of the incident.

The Bombing of Libya

On April 14, 1986, twelve days after a terrorist bomb exploded aboard TWA flight 840 en route from Rome to Athens and nine days after a second bomb went off in Berlin's La Belle disco, patronized by American GIs, the CBS Evening News conveyed the expectation of an imminent retaliatory strike against Libya by the United States. Leading into a taped report, anchorman Dan Rather explained: "America's allies in Europe today pleased the United States by naming Libya as behind recent anti-U.S. terror bombings, but, as Tom Fenton reports, they refused to approve any economic crackdown against the Libyans." A few minutes later, Jeffrey Fager and Allen Pizzey were on the phone from Tripoli with dramatic news:

> Fager: Dan—Dan, if you can hear that in the background, there's a little bit of—a few blasts going off right now. The attack—the actual attack has been going on for about ten minutes now.
>
> Rather: What kind of attack, Jeffrey?
>
> Fager: We're not—we're not quite sure what hit. There's smoke in the distance, about a mile from where we are in the hotel. The lights have all gone out here.
>
> Rather: Jeffrey, just one second, if you will, because this is coming as new information. We'd heard reports. Is there an attack on the way in Tripoli at the moment and can you hear it out the window? If so, put your microphone out that window and let us hear it.
>
> Fager: Yes, Dan, we can—it's—it's—it pauses every once in a while. We hear some pops. Here you go [artillery fire]. I don't know if you were able to pick that up.

Even before the administration had released any information about the bombing of Libya, CBS reporters in Tripoli were telephoning the news directly into an Evening News broadcast in progress. Correspondent Allen Pizzey offered a first, short summary of his observations:

> Dan, about three o'clock this morning there was a sound of jets going overhead. It sounded like at least two coming in

very low, very fast. There was a series of loud explosions, then anti-aircraft fire opened up and what a—what could have been missiles. There were streaks of light into the sky, certainly a lot of anti-aircraft fire, then a series of explosions. And these jets, and I think there were at least two, possibly more, made several runs very low, quite near the hotel. We could hear explosions, the sound of heavy impacts of bombs hitting the ground, a lot of smoke in the air.

After what Rather characterized as an "excellent on-scene report" by his colleagues in Tripoli, and after the news about American air strikes against targets in Libya had been broken by CBS and other media organizations, presidential spokesman Larry Speakes entered the White House press room to officially inform the American people of "carefully planned air strikes against terrorist-related targets in Libya." The announcement, which blamed Libya for the disco bombing in Berlin and the resulting death of an American soldier, and the following question-and-answer session was carried during the newscast. But the news value of the Speakes statement and of the President's subsequent address to the nation were clearly overshadowed by earlier, live reports from Libya.

This aggressive, counterterrorist American move did not result in a dominant role for the golden triangle news beats in the coverage of the raids. On the contrary, the record of the CBS Evening News shows that news beats within Libya were nearly as frequently represented as the three leading administration beats in the eleven broadcasts following the raids— fourteen stories originated at the golden triangle news beats and eleven at either Tripoli or Benghazi, Libya. Twenty-six stories originated abroad while twenty-two came from domestic news beats. While reports from CBS correspondents at the White House, the State Department, and the Pentagon were chosen four times as lead stories as against two lead stories from Tripoli, foreign news beats were selected on seven days and domestic ones on only four days as lead stories. The typical "domestication" of foreign policy news did not occur in the Libyan case.

On April 15, the day following the U.S. bombing of Libya, maps at the top of the front page of the *New York Times* pinpointed the flight route followed by American bombers from Britain to the Mediterranean Sea and their targets within Libya. In the lower part of the page, the newspaper carried the photograph of a determined looking President Reagan explaining the air attack on Libya. But while this initial visual portrayal was undoubtedly advantageous to the administration, it was quickly weakened by front page images during the following days: prominently placed pictures showed a heavily damaged residential area of Tripoli, the destroyed living quarters of the Qaddafi family, and coffins said to contain the bodies of Libyan civilians killed by American bombs. These visuals underlined charges that instead of surgical strikes against terrorist targets, the U.S. had in fact hit purely residential areas and harmed innocent people.

Even a front page photograph of Pentagon spokesman Robert Sims holding an image of a heavily damaged Libyan airfield suggested the administration's need to prove the success of its action. The same was true of the picture of the U.S. Representative to the United Nations, Vernon Walters, defending the U.S. bombing raids at a session of the UN Security Council.

In addition, front page photographs of Americans hastily evacuating West Beirut in an effort to escape terrorist retaliation for the Libyan bombing, and pictures of slain British journalist Alec Collett, allegedly killed in Beirut in retaliation for Prime Minister Thatcher's support of the U.S. move against Libya, stirred fears of renewed terrorism against Americans.

Finally, by placing a picture of Muammar Qaddafi with a short, factual caption on its front page, the editors of the *Times* granted Qaddafi the same placement privilege that President Reagan had enjoyed a few days earlier. Altogether, the visuals on the front pages of the *Times* were far from dominated by pro-administration images and were compatible with the reservations toward and skepticism about U.S. military actions against Libya that one study found in the coverage of the newspaper before and after the bombing raids.[33]

While significantly more of the Libyan coverage by both the CBS Evening News and the *New York Times* was based on domestic than on foreign sources, the record attests to a by far more open discourse than is the norm in foreign policy debates. CBS—which depended for 17 percent of its coverage on administration officials and for 15 percent on foreign sources—based a great deal less of its reporting on Washington and on foreign sources than did the *Times* where 27 percent of the coverage stemmed from administration officials and slightly more (28 percent) from foreign sources. (See tables 12 and 13 in the appendix.)

The Bombing of Pan Am Flight 103

On December 21, 1988, a grim Dan Rather opened the CBS Evening News with the shocking announcement that a Pan Am airliner en route from London to New York had crashed near Lockerbie in Scotland. Studio reports came from London, New York, and Washington; at the end of the newscast the first reports by people who had witnessed the catastrophe came in from London.

Opening the next day's Evening News, Rather spoke of indications that the crashed plane had been downed by an act of terrorism. The CBS News audience learned that officials in the "administration of President Reagan and President-elect Bush" had decided not to reveal an earlier bomb threat against another Pan Am flight from Frankfurt, Germany, where the flight had originated. Thus, even before the first reports by correspondents David Martin and Wyatt Andrews with official reaction at the Departments of State and Defense were aired, the possibility of a terrible error in judgment by officials had been thrown into the debate.

Even though the downed Boeing 747 belonged to an American airline and most of the victims were U.S. citizens, officials at the White House and elsewhere made no credible effort to take the lead in the widening debate surrounding Pan Am flight 103. The State Department failed to satisfy the relatives of American victims, as they were soon to complain, while the administration and even the "great communicator," President Reagan, seemed strangely quiet in the wake of Lockerbie.

The media reports reflect this subdued response of official Washington in reaction to the most deadly hit-and-run attack in the history of terrorism. In the ten CBS Evening News broadcasts following the Pan Am bombing none of the programs opened with a story from golden triangle news beats. Instead, reports from Lockerbie were placed at the top of the newscasts five times and stories originating at domestic CBS studios twice. On the three other evenings CBS chose lead stories other than the Pan Am catastrophe. From December 21 through December 31 only seven stories on the CBS Evening News were contributed by correspondents at administration news beats (five from the golden triangle and two from the Federal Aviation Administration) while twenty stories originated at other domestic locales and fifteen at foreign news beats.

Given that British investigators needed one week before announcing their finding that a bomb had definitely caused the destruction of Pan Am flight 103, the administration's low profile was unusual. Ten days after the bombing, on December 31, President Reagan finally addressed the Lockerbie disaster in his weekly radio broadcast. That evening Bob Schieffer referred to the President's comments while showing film clips from the crash site in Scotland. The visual images of death and devastation outweighed the spoken words and probably stirred feelings about the government's inability to fight and to defeat terrorism.

The visual images on the front pages of the *New York Times* were even more likely to suggest the government's and especially the President's inability to effectively respond to terrorism. During the eleven days following the downing of the Pan Am jet, the newspaper carried five crash-related photographs on its front pages—three of the crash scene, one showing a boy placing flowers outside the Lockerbie town hall in memory of the victims, and the last one picturing the British Chief Investigator Mick Charles and Chief Constable John Boyd announcing their finding

that a powerful bomb had destroyed the airliner. There w
pictures of a reassuring President or any other administ
official and thus no visuals that might have somewhat weal   _
the images of terrorists' ability to strike against America and its
citizens.

Media Autonomy and Terrorism

If one measures the media's autonomy to shape the mass-mediated foreign policy debate and discourse in terms of journalists',
editors', and producers' dependence on and independence from
administration sources, especially at the golden triangle locations, the cases of terrorist and counterterrorist spectaculars represent clear cut exceptions to the usual administration-centrist
and elite-driven coverage of foreign policy events and crises.
None of the five cases described in this chapter fits the model of
the relatively closed debate that has been found typical for other
kinds of foreign policy issues.

These findings support the new "medialism" school and its
argument that, with global communications, the press can shortcircuit the dominance of the president and a relatively limited
circle of establishment members by opening up the discourse to
a multitude of views, voices, and interests. Whether one likes
wide-open foreign policy debates or not, it must seem ironic to
both advocates and opponents of the perceived global "teledemocracy" that increased press autonomy from government officials
derives from the actions of actors who pursue their political goals
outside the legitimate democratic process.

The enduring symbiotic relationship between journalists and
government officials, which is the key to the dominance of decision making elites in the foreign policy process, crumbles quickly when publicity-conscious and media-savvy terrorists and their
supporters manipulate the news media for their own purposes by
peddling dramatic and touching "human interest" news. In
exceptional cases such as the TWA hostage incident one symbiotic relationship—between the press and administration actors—

is overshadowed by a new one—between the news media and terrorists. While regaining some of their autonomy from administration officials, the media forfeit it to news manipulators among terrorists and their allies. This has been especially pronounced when hostages are involved. In most of these situations the media coverage is dominated not by the terrorists or their supporters but by the hostages they hold and the relatives of their captives. The case studies also demonstrate that even in the aftermath of deadly hit-and-run attacks or counterterrorist measures the news coverage is extraordinary when it comes to the selection and placement of news beats, sources, and visual images.

When covering foreign policy unrelated to terrorism, journalists tend to focus on perceived "authoritative" actors within the political establishment. Voices critical of a president's foreign policy have the best chance to make the news when they are "legitimate" actors such as members of Congress, former administration officials, or leaders of major interest groups. But chances are that these rules of the game are ignored in the event of terrorist spectaculars. Situations which involve hostages create an instant "special interest" outside the foreign policy establishment with high stakes in offering views clearly independent from those of decision makers. Precisely because of their central roles in such human dramas, the captives of terrorists and their loved ones are assured of very generous media access regardless of their stands on official government positions. Contrary to the norm in foreign policy discourse, during major hostage situations like the Iran or TWA crises non-authoritative critical voices are heard loudly and often regardless of the authoritative actors and the foreign policy elite.

Studies have shown that in other foreign and even domestic policy areas there is little chance that policy debates will be sustained from below.[34] But when it comes to hostages held by anti-American terrorists, the policy discourse can be sustained from below even if the president and other decisionmakers attempt to discourage public debate. The best examples of this are the insistent appearances in the press by Peggy Say on behalf of her broth-

er Terry Anderson during his years as a captive of a Shiite terrorist group in Lebanon, as well as similar activities by the relatives
of other hostages who were held in Lebanon. Shortly after her
brother was taken hostage, Mrs. Say had been told by a representative of the Department of State that officials wanted her "to
keep a low profile."[35] But the relatives kept the issue of the
hostages alive.

In cases of terrorism, one finds instances of the media's willingness to remind administration officials and even the president of their failure to make good on stated policies and promises. Immediately after Ronald Reagan's 1981 inauguration, shortly after the 444-day Iranian hostage crisis had ended, he warned,
"Let terrorists beware that when the rules of international
behavior are violated, our policy will be one of swift and effective retribution."[36] More than four years later, however, during
the TWA hijacking in June of 1985, Dan Rather made the following comment during a studio discussion with former administration officials:

> One week into his first term, President Reagan met at the
> White House with what were then the just returned Ameri-
> can hostages from Iran. He vowed then that if terrorists
> struck again against the United States, quote, Our policy
> will be one of swift and effective retribution.
> But now, confronted with the hard reality of terrorism,
> what can and should be done?[37]

It would be a mistake to take this or similar cases as sure signs
of the media's increased insistence on holding decision makers
accountable for their words and deeds in the realm of international terrorism. Policy makers and specially presidents still have
considerable opportunity to get away with inconsistencies and
misrepresentations in this area of foreign policy as in others. For
example, President Bush's acceptance speech at the 1992 Republican convention in Houston contained several references to terrorism that deserved to be challenged. Bush mentioned in a list of
great foreign policy accomplishments during the Reagan and
Bush presidencies that "every hostage held in Lebanon is free"

45

without alluding to the arms-for-hostages scandal of the mid-1980s. He also referred to "American blindfolded hostages" during the Iran crisis as attesting to the foreign policy failures of the Carter administration without admitting that no American hostage was killed by terrorists during the Iran crisis, whereas several U.S. hostages were murdered by terrorists during the Reagan and Bush years. Neither the news media nor Bush's political opponents took issue with his misrepresentation of successes and failures in recent brushes with terrorism.

The evidence presented in this chapter demonstrates that media coverage of anti-American terrorist spectaculars abroad deviated in most respects significantly from the usual foreign policy coverage, a striking exception to the rule. My findings seem irreconcilable with those of several other researchers who concluded that official government sources and the perspectives of target governments are dominant in terrorism coverage. Several studies found that with respect to television's portrayal of terrorism, 'open' programs—those presenting a diversity of perspectives—appear far less frequently than 'closed' ones.[38]

The puzzle of these vastly different findings is quickly resolved if one identifies the types of terrorism and the locations of violent acts that were examined. Researchers who found that target governments and their views had the upper hand in media reports scrutinized and based their findings on the coverage of political violence committed within the borders of target governments and societies—in most instances the deeds of domestic terrorists. Alex Schmid and Janny de Graaf, for example, concluded that target governments and their security forces are "the main sources for the media in regard to insurgent terrorism." But they also touch upon a difference between news coverage of terrorism inside and outside a target country. "Reliance on government sources is strongest," they observed, "when the reported terroristic news is national."[39] My research shows that the U.S. media's reliance on administration sources was weak when terrorists staged highly dramatic events against Americans outside the United States.

46

The coverage of the World Trade Center bombing differed greatly from the way the press reported earlier anti-American terrorist spectaculars committed by similar groups for similar reasons outside the United States. The news media treated what was headlined as "terror in the towers" like any other domestic disaster with primarily local rather than nationwide consequences. Thus, the *New York Times* carried the bulk of the stories surrounding the explosion, apart from what appeared on the front pages, not in the national but in the metropolitan New York sections.

The World Trade Center blast and the subsequent plot to hit New York with simultaneous bombings wore, in one observer's view, "the label of domestic crime."[40] The coverage reflected this label: local, state, and federal officials, and especially law enforcement agencies, were the dominant news sources in what was mostly treated as a domestic event. The same patterns were observed in the wake of earlier terrorism inside the United States (e.g., bombings in New York by the Puerto Rican FALN) as well as within other countries (e.g., violence by the Red Brigades in Italy and the IRA in Great Britain). This led to the conclusion that whenever terrorists strike within the territory of a target society, its "authorities arrive first and are there to provide details, explanations, and their interpretations to the press."[41] Under these circumstances, like in any other domestic crisis, the media and journalists "become teammates of officialdom in attempts to restore public order, safety, and tranquility."[42]

Thus, the difference between news coverage of terrorism inside and outside a target country is striking: when terrorists hit their enemies at home, they can inflict greater damage but they lose in the battle over media access and predominant perspectives. While terrorists manage to shortcircuit the dominance of government officials and other establishment elites as news sources by staging spectaculars outside a target country's borders, this exceptional feature does not reveal to what extent the mass media facilitate terrorists' specific publicity goals. This issue will be explored in the following chapter.

CHAPTER THREE

TERRORISTS AND THEIR GOALS

If the media were not there to report terrorist acts and to explain their political and social significance (the motives inspiring them and so forth), terrorism as such would cease to exist.

—JOHN O'SULLIVAN

Years ago *The Saturday Review* published a cartoon by Robert Mankoff depicting a young son's strangely perceptive inquiry, "Dad, if a tree falls in the forest, and the media are not there to report it, has the tree really fallen?" With respect to terrorism it seems appropriate to ponder: if terrorists kidnap, injure, or kill innocent people and the news media do not report it, have those violent events really happened?

Assume for a moment that no wire service, newspaper, television network, or radio station reports the takeover of a U.S. embassy or some other American facility abroad. Unlikely as this might be, from the perpetrators' point of view the unreported event would have the same effect as if it did not happen at all, because they would have failed to reach their target audiences— U.S. decision makers, the U.S. public, and the international community—with whatever messages and demands they set out to get across. The absence of media coverage would "defeat the whole purpose of the exercise—the deed would pass unheralded or unrecognized."[1]

Some critics of the media's seeming eagerness to cover terrorism go so far as to claim that without press attention "terrorism as such would cease to exist."[2] Media coverage is critically important to modern-day international terrorists, and the unfettered mass media in democratic states, especially in the United States, extensively report incidents of politically motivated violence. Yet there are those who question the crucial role of the press in the calculus of terrorism by pointing out that this type of violence was practiced and feared long before the printing press was invented and long before today's worldwide communications network existed. But most of the earliest perpetrators of political violence were as aware as contemporary terrorists that such actions accomplish little without publicity.

Nearly 2,000 years ago the Jewish Zealots "were inspired by messianic hopes to seek maximum publicity" and thereby generate a mass uprising against Romans rule.[3] According to David Rapoport, the Islamic Assassins (1090–1275) "did not need mass media to reach interested audiences, because their prominent victims were murdered in venerated sites and royal courts, usually on holy days when many witnesses would be present."[4] The Thugs who acted on behalf of the Hindu goddess of terror tried to avoid publicity, and there is a question as to whether they were indeed terrorists.[5]

The communication revolution of the second half of the 20th century, allowing live broadcasts from anywhere on the globe, guarantees international terrorists the widest publicity for their spectacular violent acts. In 1972, an estimated 800 million people worldwide watched live television coverage as the Palestinian group, Black September, attacked and captured members of the Israeli Olympic team in the Olympic village in Munich in an act of violence that ended in a bloody massacre at a Munich airport. While watching the drama, millions of people all over the world learned for the first time about the Palestinian—Israeli conflict, the existence of Black September, and similar terrorist groups.

Just a few months earlier, in May 1972, at the Tel Aviv airport, three members of the Japanese Red Army killed 28 foreign tourists and Israelis and injured many more by throwing hand grenades and firing automatic weapons into the crowd. One of the captured Japanese terrorists stated that they had acted in support of their Palestinian comrades as "a means of propelling ourselves onto the world stage."[6] Considering the world-wide media coverage of the massacre they surely accomplished their goal.

In recent decades, journalists covering terrorist incidents—especially hostage situations—have been struck by the sophistication with which terrorists stagemanage the news for their own purposes. Reporting from Iran in late 1979, CBS correspondent Tom Fenton recognized that the "students" holding more than 50 Americans hostage in the U.S. Embassy in Teheran were very resourceful in their efforts to get their side of the story before the American public. As Fenton pointed out: "It did not take them long to realize that this is a media event. The students have even attempted to buy off television networks by offering an unpublished American embassy secret document in return for five minutes unedited air time."[7]

Correspondents who reported the TWA hijacking in Beirut found that the terrorists and their Amal allies were well aware of the reach of various American media organizations, of press pools, and of the vastly different audience sizes of the electronic and the print media. They staged news conferences, interviews, and briefings with selected hostages, Amal leader Nabih Berri, and other figures in the TWA drama like seasoned American press secretaries or publicity agents. According to one account, graduates of media studies programs at American universities attended meetings in the house of Nabih Berri at which tactics for handling the news media were discussed and worked out.[8]

The media experts working with the Shiite terrorists recommended preferential treatment for American television networks and very limited access for the U.S. print press because they wanted to reach the largest possible audience. NBC News anchorman Tom Brokow, one of those who reported from Beirut and benefited from this media strategy, later observed: "But the fact of the matter is that television had a great deal of access and my friends in print were really standing not just outside, but outside in the street. There was a judgment made by the Amal, especially, that they wanted to deal primarily with television."[9]

Even before the Beirut drama ended, U.S. television networks became the targets of massive criticism for carrying the terrorists' political messages at unprecedented length into American living rooms. One critic characterized the television coverage as "terrorvision" and attacked the "schizophrenic pattern of individual journalistic achievement and collective news mindlessness" of the reporting.[10] Television was simply responding in the way J.B. Bell had described it earlier: "These new transnational gunman are, in fact, constructing a package so spectacular, so violent, so compelling, that the networks, acting as executives, supplying the cameras and the audience, cannot refuse the offer."[11]

It is also no secret that popular support for hostagetakers and other terrorists looks different on the television screen than in reality. Tom Fenton described this scene during the Teheran hostage crisis: "The crowds know it's a media event, too. The other day in the midst of a demonstration, while a huge crowd chanted blood-curdling anti-American threats, one of the demonstrators came up to help us set up our tripod and offered advice on the best camera angles."[12]

Others have also pointed out that media attention to anti-American demonstrators in Iran during the long hostage ordeal and in Beirut during the TWA hijacking gave the wrong impression of the situation in those cities. In Teheran, for example, demonstrators were typically restricted to a few blocks. While most citizens went on with their lives as usual, cameras and microphones recorded only the activities of small protesting groups.

One might wonder why there is so much discussion and concern about press coverage of international terrorism. No one suggests that extensive accounts of brutal attacks on innocent people who happen to be at the wrong place at the wrong time result in sympathy and support for the perpetrators within the target audience. While four members of the "El Ruku" street gang in Chicago were charged in the fall of 1986 with offering their services to Libyan leader Muammar Qaddafi and plotting terrorist acts within the United States on behalf of Libya, their response to anti-American terrorists constitute a rare exception to the general antipathy of Americans toward terrorists and their supporters.

Some have suggested that the media's attention to international terrorism causes copycat violence by encouraging existing groups and the formation of new groups poised to use violence of this kind to publicize their grievances and causes. While some terrorism experts have noted "clusters of occurrences in airline hijackings and embassy sieges" in the past, there is no conclusive evidence for the theory of the media as vector of contagion.[13]

The mass media are also blamed for increased brutality on the part of terrorists seeking publicity. In this view the 1988 downing of Pan Am flight 103, the hanging of U.S. Marine Lt. Col. William Higgins, a member of the United Nations peacekeeping force by his Lebanese kidnappers in 1989, and other terrorist spectaculars in the 1980s were in part responding to the fact that "those who spill the most blood will make the biggest headlines."[14] The argument here is that terrorists heighten the threshold of violence to assure the media coverage they want. Unwittingly, the media's appetite for superlatives, firsts, and records, encourages not necessarily more but increasingly spectacular and brutal incidents. According to Alex Schmid and Janny de Graf,

> ordinary things done by ordinary people are not news. Extraordinary things done by extraordinary people are big news. Due to its moral value indifference, the news value system does not distinguish between the pro- or antisocial content of extraordinary news. And since it is so much easier to produce an extraordinary bad event than an extraordinary good event, the temptation to win access to news-making the easy way is real enough.[15]

This argument is supported by statistical evidence: of the hundreds of international terrorist acts that are committed each year only a few are singled out for extensive press coverage. In 1989, for example, 64 percent of all terrorist attacks against American targets took place in Latin America—mostly bombings of oil pipelines owned or co-owned by U.S. corporations. All these Latin American incidents taken together received far less coverage in the U.S. media than two other terrorist spectaculars that occurred the same year: the murder of Lt. Col. Higgins by Shiite terrorists in Lebanon and the inflight bombing of a French airliner over Africa that killed 171 persons, including seven Americans. Studies comparing terrorism coverage by the three traditional national TV networks, ABC, CBS, and NBC, from 1969 through 1980 found systematic undercoverage of political violence in Latin America and overcoverage of political violence in the Middle East. The reporting records of the three competing networks were very similar and "erratic and misleading" as to the frequency and the nature of terrorism in different regions.[16] But the more spectacular cases of terrorism occurred in the Middle East and not in Latin America during this period. Thus, there is no doubt that the media, especially television, "reward" the most shocking violence by overcovering such incidents and undercovering less spectacular ones.

While international terrorists stage their violence primarily if not exclusively for publicity, media coverage is only the means by which these perpetrators try to promote and realize their various goals. The central issues in the media/terrorism controversy can be summed up in the questions: Does the press unwittingly help terrorists to further their goals? Is news coverage, indeed, as former British Prime Minister Margaret Thatcher once charged, the "oxygen" of terrorism?

News Coverage and the Universal Goals of Terrorists

Chapter 1 discussed the tactical or short term, strategic or long term, and universal or overlapping goals of international terrorists. The hijackers of TWA flight 847, for example, settled on one realistic short-term goal—the release of several hundred Shiites from Israeli prisons. But like other militant groups in Lebanon, the hijackers and their supporters had more fundamental, long-term objectives: to remove the Israeli army from Lebanon if not to remove the state of Israel from the Middle Eastern map altogether; and to eradicate western, especially American, influence in the region. Above all, their universal objectives were to capture the attention of American decision makers and the U.S. public and to publicize their threats, demands, and grievances.

The TWA terrorists achieved their short-term objective but failed to realize their long-term goals, although they managed to create a great deal of tension between the Israeli and American governments. Above all, the hijacking received a great deal of media coverage. As a general rule one can assume that terrorist spectaculars, whether successful or not in terms of short- and long-term goals, are likely to advance one or the other of the perpetrators' universal goals.

What are these universal goals which depend on news coverage? First, international terrorists seek attention by spreading fear and anxiety among their target audiences. Moreover, by staging shocking events terrorists demonstrate the impotence of a targeted government to prevent and protect its citizens from terrorism. Second, these groups and their supporters seek recognition of their demands, their grievances, and their causes. The third universal goal of international terrorist groups is a degree of respectability and legitimacy in their target societies.

If international terrorists indeed strive for one or all of these responses in their target public through media coverage, to what extent does that coverage advance their goals? Without relying on systematic and quantitative studies, several students of terrorism have simply charged that the perpetrators of violence for political purposes are successful in this respect.[17] My comprehensive content analyses of terrorism coverage in television and newspapers substantiate some but not all of their intuitive assumptions.

54

Attention

Those responsible for the World Trade Center bombing in 1993 may not have known that New York's tallest building carries most of the city's broadcast transmitters. After the blast, only WCBS, which maintains a backup system on top of the Empire State Building, was able to transmit over the air, and most of the television coverage was available only over cable channels.

Nevertheless, the explosion at the twin towers was, as the *New York Times* observed, "a thoroughly modern tragedy—one in which the television coverage became a central part of the drama. Throughout the afternoon and evening, New York City newscasters gave out emergency phone numbers, urged calm on those trapped inside and praised the work of the city's emergency crews."[18]

The initial news reports in the immediately affected New York area were in the mold of what Doris Graber once described as functions of the press during domestic crisis. According to Graber, in these situations

> the public becomes almost totally dependent on the media for news that may be vital for survival, and for important messages from public and private authorities. The mass media are the only institutions with the capacity to collect this escalating mass of information and disseminate it quickly. When people become aware of a crisis, they therefore turn on their radios or television sets, often on a round-the-clock basis, to monitor the event.[19]

Local news reporting in the hours, weeks, and months after the blast drew nation- and worldwide attention. In this respect the coverage was typical of major terrorist incidents occurring inside a targeted country. An earlier study of violence committed by the Puerto Rican FALN in the United States, the Red Brigades in Italy, and the IRA in the United Kingdom concluded that "terrorists do receive media attention."[20] But killer hurricanes, major floods, and other domestic disasters draw the same kind of coverage.

When terrorists strike abroad, the U.S. media do not direct the immediate victims and millions of other citizens how to cope with the emergency at hand as New York broadcasters did after the World Trade Center explosion. There is no need for appeals to avoid emergency areas or not to report to work the next morning. Yet, we know that over the years terrorist spectaculars overseas have received a tremendous amount of news coverage at home whenever Americans were among the victims. But even this truism deserves a closer examination. How much broadcast time and news space did the electronic and the print press devote to these incidents? After all, it has been charged time and again that television coverage of terrorism in particular is excessive and that the media blows the importance of these events out of proportion.

The Iranian hostage crisis was a case in point. After militants in Teheran gained control over the U.S. embassy on November 4, 1979, every early evening newscast by the three television networks (ABC, CBS, and NBC) for the rest of November and December included long reports concerning the hostage situation. In November, ABC News devoted 54 percent, CBS News 50 percent, and NBC News 48 percent of their early evening newscasts to the Iran crisis. In December, the hostage story captured 52 percent of ABC, 43 percent of CBS, and 38 percent of NBC evening news. Just as important, during November the three networks chose the Iran crisis to lead their newscasts in each of their evening broadcasts. While not quite as prominent during the following months, the Iranian situation remained the most extensively covered news during the more than fourteen months of the ordeal. This coverage intensified in the days following the hostages' release and homecoming in January 1981.

The TWA hijacking in June 1985, although shorter, received even more generous broadcast coverage. During the entire incident, the three networks opened most of their early evening broadcasts with the hijacking drama: 12 of 14 days on ABC, 16 of 17 on CBS, and 15 of 16 on NBC. The four times the TWA crisis did not lead off the newscasts, other terrorism-related stories took its place: ABC led once with the crash of an Air India airliner into the Atlantic attributed to a terrorist bomb and began another newscast with coverage of a ceremony honoring American victims of terrorism in El Salvador; CBS chose a bloody terrorist attack at the airport in Frankfurt, Germany; and NBC the crash of the Air India airliner. Thus, for the full duration of the TWA hijacking incident every lead story in the evening news concerned international terrorism. The networks devoted an average of nearly two thirds of their entire evening broadcasts to the TWA spectacular with ABC (68 percent) offering the greatest amount of crisis coverage closely followed by NBC (63 percent) and CBS (62 percent).[21]

In a congressional hearing, media expert Ben Bagdikian characterized the TV networks' TWA crisis reporting as "excessive for strictly self-serving, competitive reasons," and pointed out that the newscasts had "in the process obliterated other important news."[22] What one media critic found most troublesome about the way the TV networks reported the TWA incident was not "the quantity of time devoted to the hostages but the fact that the victim of this was all of the other news."[23] ABC anchorman Peter Jennings accepted this criticism, admitting, "During the TWA crisis we ignored the lifting of a 25-year-long moratorium on the testing of chemical weapons. Tax reform went by the boards. Defense spending between the Pentagon and contractors went by the boards." But Jennings took exception to media critics' tendency to single out television, charging that in the case of the *Achille Lauro* incident the *New York Times* and the *Washington Post* "devoted a good deal more attention to this story than we did."[24]

Whether those in charge of TV network news truly "learned that there has to be a cutoff point in our very limited time in the evening so that we can devote ourselves to other news," as Jennings argued, or whether the amount of TV coverage of the *Achille Lauro* crisis was circumscribed by the lack of dramatic film footage of a hostage ordeal aboard a cruise ship is subject to debate. Michael O'Neill, a former newspaper editor, described the circumstances: "the terrorists and the hostages were aboard a ship, cut off from television cameras, with only scratchy radio transmissions intermittently linking reporters to the events at sea."[25]

Jennings had reason to take issue with media critics' preoccupation with television news. During the TWA crisis, for example, one observer spoke for many when he said there were no complaints concerning print coverage of terrorism. Perhaps TV networks have been singled out for criticism because they reach much larger audiences than daily newspapers and news magazines.[26] Still, considering that newspapers in the U.S. have a combined daily circulation of more than 60 million and that the leading newspapers influence the other media, including TV network news, print journalism should not be excluded when excessive media coverage is discussed.

Contrary to the conclusions of media critics, newspapers and news magazines give terrorist spectaculars enormous play. For example, during the first 171 days of the Iran hostage crisis (up to the failed rescue mission in the second half of April 1981) the *New York Times* carried hostage-related articles on all but two days. In the first 58 days of the crisis, from early November through December 31, 1979, the *Times* front page carried stories on the hostages in Iran every day.

A tally of news pages containing only news of the TWA hijacking crisis in three leading U.S. newspapers (the *New York Times*, the *Washington Post*, and the *Los Angeles Times*) from June 15, 1985, when the papers first reported the hijacking, to July 1, 1985, when the hostages were released, led to an interesting result: all three newspapers devoted substantial parts of their national/international sections to the TWA hostage news—an average of 19 percent for the *New York Times*, 18 percent for the *Washington Post*, and 15 percent for the *Los Angeles Times*. When all pages that contained partially crisis-related news were included in the comparison, an average of 31 percent of the national/international news pages in the *Post*, 28 percent in the *New York Times*, and 23 percent in the *Los Angeles Times* pro-

vided news reports, analyses, editorials, or columns ab
drama. Indeed, the volume of coverage in the three pap
strikingly similar.[27]

If, as many critics argue, the extent of television coverage during
the TWA situation and other terrorist crises has been excessive, it
seems that newspapers must share in this criticism. However, one
must also consider that the time constraints on TV newscasts are
far more severe than the space restrictions on newspapers. A former president of CBS News had the transcript of one of his network's evening broadcasts (30 minutes minus seven or eight minutes reserved for commercials) typeset to compare its volume to
that of a leading newspaper. He found that the transcript filled less
than two columns of the *New York Times* front page.[28] Accordingly, comparisons between TV news transcripts and daily newspapers show clearly that the print media devoted far more stories and
paragraphs to any given terrorism incident than did television
news. Because newspapers have by far more news space available
than television networks newscast minutes, the print media is in
a far better position than television to cover other news events
while still reporting extensively about terrorist spectaculars. In
this respect the cable TV news network CNN resembles the print
media since in its case even the most extensive terrorism coverage
does not preempt other important news stories.

Unlike television network newscasts, newspapers are seldom
criticized for overcovering terrorist spectaculars and undercovering
or completely omitting other important news events and development. While most discussions concerning the volume of coverage
and the attention-getting goal of terrorists are triggered by and
restricted to specific spectaculars, terrorism coverage over longer
time periods has been abundant as well. Shanto Iyengar found that
between 1981 and 1986 ABC, CBS, and NBC News aired a total of
more than 2,000 stories on terrorism, an average of eleven stories a
month for each network. According to Iyengar, during this period
"more stories were broadcast on terrorism than on poverty, unemployment, racial inequality, and crime combined."[29]

In the terrorists' quest for attention, it does not matter to them whether news reports are critical, neutral, or sympathetic. As Marc Celmer has pointed out, international terrorists "are not seeking approval or disapproval for their actions but public awareness."[30] The terrorists' goal of gaining attention is furthered by every report of a mother's tearful plight to spare the life of her son or a presidential condemnation of a terrorist act.

This attitude can change once a group has attained recognition of its grievances and enters the legitimate political process. Shortly after the *Achille Lauro* incident a PLO publication warned that terrorist acts "outside the occupied territories harm the cause of the Palestinian people and tarnish their just struggle for freedom."[31] The PLO leadership was obviously troubled about the negative news coverage of the *Achille Lauro* affair and its possible consequences for the role Yassir Arafat and the organization had begun to play. However, it was not the attention goal that the article admonished but rather the usefulness of terrorism against innocent victims outside the disputed territory.

But by and large international terrorists, even more so than their domestic counterparts, depend on and strive for media coverage regardless of its content. Some terrorist acts, for example bloody hit and run bombings, are solely designed to get the attention of target audiences and to tell them that, as one suspected terrorist allegedly put it after the World Trade Center blast, "We can get you anytime!"[32] Another part of the message is, of course, that not even the most powerful government in the world is able to prevent deadly terrorism against its citizens. The bombing of Pan Am flight 103 in late 1988 was such a case. The terrorists and their sponsors did not claim responsibility. But thanks to extensive media coverage they were seemingly content to let their enemies guess as to the perpetrators and their motives, and underscored the impotence of governments vis-a-vis the terrorist challenge.

Recognition

About two weeks into the Iranian hostage crisis, the captors allowed CBS News correspondent Tom Fenton to enter the U.S.

embassy for a short "visit." The following is a passage from Fenton's report:

> Fenton: We hoped to gain a better understanding of who these students were who created a major international crisis. We found that they were mild-mannered young people, polite, terribly convinced of the righteousness of their cause, and like most 20-year-olds, difficult to argue with. They spoke bitterly of corruption and murder under the deposed Shah's regime, America's role in supporting him, their deep resentment when he was allowed to enter the United States, and their fears that the American government is trying to topple the new Iranian government.
>
> Fenton (question): You say you will try the—some of the hostages under Islamic law. Does Islamic law allow you to break into a man's house, to lock up his family, and take his papers, and then use that for a trial?
>
> Voice of Interpreter: This place that we occupied was not an embassy to be considered a home or house. We respect international law. But here was a place of espionage and spying against the beliefs, the hopes, of the people of Iran.

Fenton explained that he had not been allowed to see any of the hostages but had sent them a note asking for messages. One of the three written notes Fenton got back stated, "The fact it's taking this long to negotiate our freedom is unbelievable. Return the Shah. His acts are a matter of record. They say they will give him a fair trial, so let them have it."[33] A day later, in another typical dispatch from the Iranian capital, Fenton reported the captors had responded to his request to prove their accusation that the U.S. embassy was in truth a spy nest; they had given him copies of several documents and promised additional material when asked for more conclusive evidence of spying.[34]

Whether coverage concerned the captors, the captives, the Ayatollah Khomeini, other Iranian authorities, or protesters around the embassy—whenever the media reported the grievances repeated again and again by the Iranians, they unwittingly furthered the hostageholders' desire for recognition.

This commonly occurs during terrorist incidents. Hostages publicize and endorse terrorists' demands and causes—either voluntarily or under duress. In fact, hostages are often the best weapons terrorists can deploy for this purpose. At the height of the TWA hijacking drama, five of the forty captives were made available for a news conference that, as critics later charged, turned into a "media circus." One of the American hostages, Allyn Conwell, said the following in his lengthy opening statement,

> It is also our hope, now that we are pawns in this tense game of nerves, that the governments and peoples involved in the negotiations will allow justice and compassion to guide their way. We understand that Israel is holding as hostage a number of Lebanese people who undoubtedly have as equal a right and as strong a desire to go home as we do.[35]

Nabih Berri, the most interviewed personality on American TV newscasts during the TWA event, was even more blunt about the demands and grievances of the hijackers. During an interview with Dan Rather, the Amal leader insisted that the TWA hostages would be freed only if the hijackers' demands were met. Referring to a Swiss offer to mediate the crisis, Berri told Rather, "If they [the Israelis]—they took the 700—the [Shiites] to a neutral country and—I am ready to send all the Americans here with their plane to the same country to—to make the exchange, yes. I—I accept that."[36]

The Americans and other westerners who were kidnapped in Beirut and held for many years were forced to communicate their captors' threats, grievances, and demands by appearing in videotapes or writing letters. On one occasion his captors ordered hostage David Jacobsen to write a letter attacking the Reagan administration—when they did not like the result, they dictated what they wanted him to write.[37] Terry Anderson, in one of the videotapes released by his captors, said, "Mr. President, we in the United States are not absolutely innocent here. Our hands are not completely clean."[38]

Terrorists themselves publicize their causes through the media. In May 1986, for example, NBC News aired an interview with Abul Abbas of the PLO, who had masterminded the *Achille Lauro* hijacking several months earlier. Around the same time, Abu Nidal made the following statement in a published interview: "If there is anything absolute in this world, it is our enmity against American imperialism. Without American help the Zionist state would not still exist."[39] In their in-depth coverage the leading U.S. newspapers did their share in explaining the causes championed by the TWA terrorists and their allies and the widespread support for both groups in Lebanon. In a *Washington Post* report about Lebanese reactions to the TWA hostagetaking, one young Amal member was quoted: "If people [here] are saying they are sorry, they are lying. . . . They think this is the only way to fight Israel—to get America."[40]

The point is not that the media are soft in their portrayal of terrorists but rather that by reporting terrorist incidents objectively and factually, the news media accommodate the terrorists' desire to publicize their cause. Reporters consider it part of their job to cover terrorism in the larger context and beyond individual violent deeds. During a discussion about the news media's coverage of terrorism, Tom Brokow of NBC argued,

> But terrorism often does have political roots and we have to deal with those political roots. It is not always, although it appears that way, a mindless act of sheer terrorism for the sake of terrorism. There is generally some political context as well and I think we have to work harder at putting it into some kind of political context, however strong or weak that context might be.[41]

Former National Security Adviser Zbigniew Brzezinski criticized television in particular for "permitting them [terrorists] to appeal directly to the American people over the head of the government for the acceptance of the demands [related to their political causes]." He added that television "humanizes the enemy, thereby also making it more difficult for the government to respond firmly."[42]

I identified and tallied those text passages in both television and print coverage that appeared to facilitate the recognition goal.

For example, under the headline "Hijackers Free 64, Set New Deadline," the *Los Angeles Times* reported on its front page on June 16, 1985 that the TWA hijackers "set a new deadline for their principal demand, the release of Arab terrorists [from Israeli prisons]." The story also mentioned that the hijackers had told the Algiers control tower, "We are ready to die if our demands are not met." Readers learned of the terrorists' grievances concerning Shiite prisoners in Israel. Furthermore, readers informed about the terrorists' willingness to die for their cause may have recognized that the hijackers must have serious grievances and convictions. During the TWA hijacking about 10 percent of the coverage in the *Los Angeles Times*, 10 percent in the *Washington Post*, and 9 percent in the *New York Times* fit the recognition category. During the same period, 9 percent of the crisis coverage on the CBS Evening News qualified for the recognition goal. When about one of ten paragraphs published or broadcast about a terrorist incident contain quotes or descriptions that appear to facilitate the recognition objective, the terrorists are rather successful in this respect.

This instance may have been exceptional because of all the coverage was subject to an unprecedented degree of news management by the TWA hijackers and their allies in Beirut. Indeed, the coverage in other terrorist incidents was not quite as favorable toward the recognition objective as in the Beirut hostage case. Still, during similar incidents the terrorists were also "rewarded" with reports that furthered their media recognition goal.In the first phase of the Iran hostage crisis (November 4 through December 31, 1979) about 8 percent of the incident-related paragraphs published in the *New York Times* and about 7 percent of the CBS Evening News coverage fit the recognition category. Even during the four days of the *Achille Lauro* hijacking, some 7 percent of *New York Times* and 5 percent of CBS Evening News reporting furthered the goal of recognition.

Michael Kelly and Thomas Mitchell studied the news coverage of a random sample of 158 terrorist incidents between 1968 and 1974 in the *New York Times* and the *Times of London* and found that less than ten percent dealt with the causes and grievances of those responsible. They concluded that terrorism therefore "is not a very effective way to propagandize if one wants issues and goals to be known or understood."[43] But when close to ten percent of the coverage in some way articulates the causes behind violent acts, terrorists may view this as quite an accomplishment.

Categorizing reports aired by the three TV networks between 1981 and 1986 as predominantly "episodic" (focusing on individual acts of violence and their effects) or "thematic" (framing terrorism as a political problem), Shanto Iyengar found that 74 percent of all terrorist stories were episodic and 26 percent thematic. In contrast, only 11 percent of all domestic crime stories broadcast during the same period were thematic.[44] This finding attests to the ability of terrorists to gain media coverage that articulates the root causes behind their violent acts.

Terrorists operating within the borders of their target country have more difficulty getting their recognition messages across to the public without risking arrest. And the police or the press may not make public phone or mail communications. After the World Trade Center explosion the *New York Times* received a letter from the "Liberation Army Fifth Battalion" that enumerated the group's grievances and its motives for the bombing. In its letter the group stated three demands, which at the same time explained the grievances and causes behind the bombing: termination of all U.S. military, economical, and political aid to Israel; all diplomatic relations with Israel must stop; and a guarantee of U.S. noninterference in the domestic affairs of all Middle Eastern countries.[45] The *Times* turned the letter over to the authorities, only publishing it a month later, after several suspects in the World Trade Center bombing had been arrested.

Respectability and Legitimacy

It has been suggested that the press and especially television unwittingly bestows respectability and perhaps even a hint of legitimacy upon terrorists simply by interviewing them, since "the process of interviewing someone, whether he is a terrorist or a foreign diplomat or a government official, is essentially the same process."[46] It does not make a difference whether an interviewer is tough on the terrorist or his sympathizer. The mere fact that the terrorist is interviewed by respected media representatives and treated "as someone whose contribution to public debate is worthy of attention"[47] elevates the person virtually to the level of a legitimate politician. This is a persuasive argument if one reviews some of the actual interviews with terrorists U.S. television networks presented to their audiences. On September 26, 1990, for example, during the Persian Gulf conflict, Dr. George Habash of the Popular Front for the Liberation of Palestine (PFLP) was interviewed by Ted Koppel on ABC's "Nightline" program. Habash used the opportunity to repeat and expand on his previously reported threats of violence against Americans in case of military actions against Iraq and to present Arab and Palestinian grievances against the United States. The Saudi Arabian ambassador to the United States was also a guest on that program. It is not far-fetched to conclude that the respectability and legitimacy of the PFLP was furthered when the leader of this terrorist group shared the stage with a diplomat who represented his government in Washington.

The same applied to the many press conferences and interviews that Nabih Berri granted during the TWA hijacking crisis. In his messages to the U.S. administration, the Israeli government, and the public, Berri insisted that the demands of the hijackers, for whom he negotiated, had to be met. The Amal chief's polished demeanor served him well in gaining ample opportunities to use American television to communicate the demands of the hijackers. Although Berri was working on behalf of the killers of 23-year-old Navy diver Robert Stethem and was directly involved in hiding several dozen U.S. hostages somewhere in Beirut, American television networks treated him like a political leader, virtually no differently than the President of the United States. This was obvious during an ABC "Good Morning America" broadcast, when anchorman David Hartman ended one more interview with

Berri by asking, "Any final words to President Reagan this morning?" While this particular question triggered an immediate debate about its appropriateness, it was but the most extreme example of the way in which TV anchors and correspondents act when granted access to terrorists or their allies.

Former Secretary of State Alexander Haig subscribes to the thesis that the media unwittingly helped the terrorists and their allies gain respectability or legitimacy during the TWA crisis. According to Haig, "when TV reporters interview kidnappers it . . . risks making international outlaws seem like responsible personalities. Television should avoid being used that way. But there's so much competition involved that it's naive to expect such a thing."[48]

Examining the amount of coverage that might further this goal, I identified those paragraphs in the TWA hijacking coverage in three newspapers and in the full transcripts of the CBS Evening News that directly cited either the hijackers and hostagetakers or their allies (being interviewed, giving a press conference, briefing the media, providing information through spokespersons, etc.) The *New York Times*, the *Washington Post*, and the *Los Angeles Times* devoted about 1 percent of their total crisis coverage to interviews, press conferences, and news briefings by the terrorists and their backers. This would seem to disprove the proposition of an accommodating media in this area. But as was mentioned earlier, the men responsible for the actual hijacking and especially their Amal sympathizers sought access to U.S. television while denying it to the print press; to a large extent the press was left to describe and quote from television interviews with Berri and other figures close to the hijackers. Given this situation, it is not surprising that television devoted far greater news coverage than did newspapers to interviews with pro-terrorism personalities.

About 12 percent of the TWA coverage on the CBS Evening News was exactly of the sort that, as media critics charge, inadvertently confers respectability and even legitimacy on the architects, perpetrators, and supporters of violence for political ends. There is no reason to believe that the hijackers and their allies fared worse in the coverage by CBS's competitors.[49] During the TWA incident the Amal militants and the hijackers themselves gave preferential treatment to ABC News, leading some to make the mocking suggestion that ABC stood for Amal Broadcasting Company.

In the case of the TWA hijacking, the newspaper coverage was typical in the percentage of reporting that presented terrorists as politicians who act within the legitimate process while television deviated in an extreme fashion from the reporting norm for terrorist incidents. In the first two months of the Iran hostage crisis (November 4 through December 31, 1979) only 1 percent of the incident-related coverage in the *New York Times* and about 1 percent on the CBS Evening News fit the respectability/legitimacy criteria. And during the four days of the *Achille Lauro* crisis, 0.3 percent of reporting in the *New York Times* and 1 percent on the CBS Evening News fit this category.

With the exception of television's handling of the TWA hijacking, terrorists simply did not receive media treatment that might have advanced their desire for respectability and legitimacy. Studies that concentrated on randomly selected acts of domestic and international terrorism have also concluded that legitimacy seems "seriously undermined by the kind of coverage the news media provide."[50]

The Media Goals of Terrorists

The evidence presented in this chapter so far demonstrates that terrorists gain attention via the mass media and, to a lesser but still significant extent, they also gain recognition. But this does not mean that the content of the news influences public attitudes in the way terrorists would wish.

Public Awareness and Fear

According to an ABC News poll, four days after Iranian radicals invaded the U.S. embassy in Teheran and took more than fifty

Americans hostage, 93 percent of the American public had heard or read about the incident. A week later, a further ABC poll showed that 97 percent were aware of the situation in Iran. Five weeks into the crisis an ABC/AP poll revealed that 99 out of a hundred Americans had read or heard about the hostage crisis. During the following months, public awareness remained well over 90 percent. Other terrorist actions in the 1980s resulted in similar levels of public awareness. Four days after the start of the TWA hijacking crisis in June 1985, an ABC News poll found that 98 percent of those surveyed knew of the tense drama in Beirut. After the hostages' release, 99 percent of the public had knowledge of the developments. Bloody hit-and-run attacks also came to nearly total public attention. A Gallup poll found that 96 percent of the public heard or read about the terrorist assaults on travelers at the Rome and Vienna airports in December of 1985, in which a total of nineteen people, including five Americans, were killed. When terrorists seized a Pan Am airliner at the airport of Karachi, Pakistan, in September 1986, most Americans learned of the incident in which four American and seventeen other passengers were killed. According to an ABC News/*Washington Post* poll, 92 percent of the U.S. public heard or read of the Karachi incident.

According to opinion polls, the prominently covered terrorist incidents of the 1980s not only gained the attention of the American public; each of these acts also caused public anxiety that in turn allowed terrorists to condition the public to further manipulation by terrorist acts in favor of specific short- or longterm goals.

In January 1986, after a series of anti-American terrorist acts—the TWA and *Achille Lauro* cases, the bombings in Rome and Vienna, and the kidnapping of several Americans in Beirut—57 percent of poll respondents indicated that they would recommend that friends planning to go abroad cancel their trips. After the U.S. bombing of Libya in mid-April 1986, the number of Americans unwilling to travel abroad jumped to 79 percent from an already high 61 percent the month before.[51] From early January to late April 1986, with the media reporting regularly about actual and threatened terrorist violence against Americans, three in four Americans believed that a major terrorist attack within the United States was somewhat or very likely. And in late April, after a rash of violence against U.S. targets in Europe, Africa, and Asia, nine of ten Americans were somewhat or very concerned that international terrorists would strike in the United States.[52]

Terrorism Coverage and the Public Agenda

Questioning the findings of earlier studies that found at best minimal media effects on the attitudes of individuals, communications researchers have more recently demonstrated an "agenda setting" function of the press. These findings have confirmed Bernard Cohen's often cited conclusion that the press "may not be successful much of the time in telling people what to think, but it is stunningly successful in telling its readers [and viewers] what to think about."[53] If the media do, indeed, influence the public agenda, one would be interested in knowing about the relationship between terrorism coverage and the public's perception of how important a problem this threat poses.

Surveys frequently ask: "What do you think is the most important problem facing the country?" The answers reveal which issues rank high on the public agenda and which are lesser problems or are not mentioned at all. Most terrorist incidents are of relatively short duration and fade quickly from the media and public attention. For instance, in a CBS News/*New York Times* survey in January 1985, terrorism was not mentioned at all as a major problem for the United States, but by early July, immediately after the TWA hijacking, terrorism was mentioned by 13 percent of respondents, more frequently than any other national problem. About six weeks later, less than 1 percent mentioned terrorism as a major problem.[54]

The Iranian hostage crisis, however, was a longer incident that provides the opportunity to examine the link between media coverage and the salience of terrorism as a public issue. There was a very strong correlation between the volume of crisis coverage in the television network evening news broadcasts and the results of polls measuring the issues considered most important $(r = .84)$.* The relationship was slightly stronger for lead stories about the Iran situation and the level of public concern over terrorism $(r = .86)$. In an earlier study about television news and agenda setting, other researchers demonstrated significant congruence between the volume of issue coverage and the level of public concern with respect to energy problems $(r = .73)$, unemployment $(r = .37)$, and inflation $(r = .53)$. In the case of the Iran crisis, the strong direct relationship between television coverage and the public's perception of terrorism as the most threatening problem indicates, not surprisingly, that news about terrorist spectaculars can have an especially potent influence on the public agenda in the United States.

Recognition, the Press, and the Public

The absence of frequent surveys exploring public attitudes about terrorists' causes and grievances makes systematic comparisons between media coverage and poll data impossible. But it is noteworthy that during times of extensive coverage of anti-American terrorism, including news about the terrorists' causes and grievances, a significant minority of Americans expressed an understanding of the concerns of "the other side."

For example, five weeks after the seizure of the U.S. Embassy in Iran, a Yankelovich, Skelly, and White survey found that 25 percent of Americans questioned agreed with the statement that "Khomeini and his followers (certainly including the captors of American citizens) have a lot of right on their side when it comes to their accusations against the United States government and its support of the Shah's regime." While the majority disagreed, another 15 percent of respondents were "not sure." One would

* Pearson's r, a measure of association, varies between -1 and +1 with $r = +1$ the strongest possible direct relationship. The resukts cited are from seven surveys conducted from early December 1979 through mid-October 1980 by Yankelovich, Skelly, and White. The question asked was: "What are the main issues or problems facing the country that particularly worry you?"

hardly expect that in the midst of a tense hostage drama, at a time when the lives of more than fifty U.S. citizens were threatened, one of four Americans would express some measure of understanding for the grievances of Iranians who were responsible for the embassy takeover or supported it. At the time the survey was conducted, the press carried frequent and prominent reports about the grievances of the Iranian militants. Whenever the Iranians repeated their top demand—the return of the Shah to Iran—they emphasized the U.S. government's steadfast support of the Shah and his regime. The media coverage apparently affected the public's attitude in this respect. During the TWA hijacking a CBS News survey asked respondents whom they blamed for the terrorist incident: 11 percent placed "a lot of blame," 40 percent "some blame," and 31 percent "not much blame" on United States policy in the Middle East, so that a majority of the American public sympathized to a degree with the terrorists' grievances—an attitude probably not unrelated to the way the U.S. media covered the incident.

Experimental evidence revealed that audiences reacted differently to "episodic" reporting that focused on the circumstances of an individual terrorist act than to "thematic" coverage that emphasized the roots of political violence. Iyengar found "that attributions of responsibility differ substantially depending upon episodic or thematic framing of the issue. When terrorism is depicted as a general outcome, viewers gravitate toward societal attributions. On the other hand, when terrorism is framed as a specific act or event, viewers gravitate toward individualistic and punitive attributions."[56] In Iyengar's study, a substantial part of terrorism coverage (26 percent of which was found to be "thematic") made viewers more inclined to recognize deeper causes and grievances behind terrorist violence. Participants in Iyengar's experiments named, for example, "the actions and policies of the U.S. government (including support for Israel, insufficient economic aid to underprivileged nations, siding with repressive leaders, and realpolitik)"[57] as political or societal causes of terrorist violence.

The media coverage of terrorism has facilitated the recogni-

Could terrorist attacks lose their utility if they are too destructive?

tion goal of terrorists, namely to familiarize the American public with their causes and grievances and to convince Americans that these violent acts are justified responses to the wrongs committed against their people by or with the support of the U.S. government.

The News and Terrorists' Legitimacy

In contrast to the other two goals, respectability and legitimacy in the eyes of the American public is only sporadically achieved by terrorist groups. With the notable exception of the television coverage of the TWA crisis, terrorist spectaculars have not resulted in a great deal of news that has granted terrorists and their supporters the same treatment as legitimate politicians.

Any effort to speculate about the ability of terrorists or their supporters to exploit the press to further their respectability and legitimacy must distinguish between interviews and press conferences broadcast or published during terrorist events and those publicized or broadcast at other times. It has been suggested that incident-related interviews reward terrorists directly for a violent act while media appearances made apart from specific incidents do not bestow similar benefits.[58] Yet Yassir Arafat and other PLO leaders received a great deal of media attention during the 1970s and 1980s—in the form of interviews and coverage of PLO news conferences—that was not tied to specific incidents, and it is likely that such generous access to the media contributed significantly to the PLO's increasing respectability and legitimacy in Washington and other western capitals. Referring to the media's approach to covering terrorism, the influential television news anchor, Peter Jennings remarked that "given the present framework and the present state of mind in which we operate, it seems to me that terrorists, having this lock on public opinion, have become a legitimate part of the news story."[59]

To sum up, the media's reporting of terrorist spectaculars helps to facilitate two of the universal goals of terrorism. Terrorists gain attention when the volume and placement of news

73

coverage affects the public agenda. There is also evidence that thematically framed stories that refer to specific grievances influence public attitudes about the roots of politically motivated violence.

The next chapter explores how Americans collectively respond to anti-American terrorism and under what circumstances public support or opposition to U.S. policies and actions is altered by such acts.

CHAPTER FOUR

THE POLLS AND THE
THEATER OF TERROR

*Terrorism is aimed at the people watching, not the actu-
al victims. Terrorism is theater.*

—BRIAN M. JENKINS

The Founding Fathers feared the "passions" and the "errors and
delusions" of the general public and the danger of demagogues
who might appeal to the "passions," not the reason, of the average citizen. There are plenty of references to the irrational and
gullible masses in accounts of the constitutional convention and
in The Federalist. But when James Madison, Alexander Hamilton, and others worried about demagoguery and its threat to
"public tranquility," they envisioned ambitious individuals and
factions within America who might try to whip up public sentiment and exploit them for their own, selfish purposes.[1] When
international terrorists lift the curtain in the theater of terror and
stage a violent anti-American spectacular, they make the
Framers' worst nightmares come true—albeit acting from the
outside. Theirs is demagoguery by violent deeds and words
designed to appeal to the emotions and prejudices of the masses—
fear, frustration, compassion for the immediate victims, and dis-

75

satisfaction with the responses or non-responses of their own government.

James Ceaser distinguishes between "soft" and "hard" demagogues according to what kinds of passions they appeal to.[2] Soft demagogues emphasize their closeness to the people who know best while hard types try to divide the people; as Jeffrey Tulis points out, "typically, this [hard] sort of appeal employs extremist rhetoric that ministers to fear."[3] Terrorists and their supporters use either soft or hard demagoguery or both types. For example, they often emphasize that they have no problem with the American people but in fact trust the good judgment of their target public to influence its government to do the right thing, i.e. what the terrorists demand. But the practitioners and backers of terrorism also utilize the hard approach. When hostage-holders release women but not men, as they frequently do, they point out that they fight against the oppression by male American power-holders just as female Americans do; they make similar efforts to pit group against group, when they explain why they release African-American but not white male hostages.

The American Founders were neither the first nor the last in a long line of political theorists, politicians, and scholars who have characterized public opinion as utterly passionate, volatile, unintelligible, and incompetent. On the other hand, a revisionist school has found evidence of Americans' collectively holding opinions that are responsible, rational, stable, and responsive "to changing circumstances and to new information."[4]

How does the American audience react to the theater of terror? How do Americans respond to the demagoguery of violence? Is public opinion of terrorism rational or irrational, driven by reason or by passion, intelligible or incoherent?

These are important questions, given the close attention paid by decision makers, especially presidents, to opinion polls and the mounting evidence that public opinion is a significant factor in policy making—not only in domestic but also in foreign affairs. One expert, a longtime Washington insider, concluded, "whether one likes it or not, believes it or not, or thinks it should happen or not, public opinion affects policy decisions."[5]

The fundamental problem with Americans' views on public policy issues is lack of knowledge and information. Moreover, as Robert Weissberg has pointed out, "given people's tendency to pay closer attention to events closer to home, knowledge of many basic facts about foreign affairs is especially poor."[6]

However, when it comes to international terrorist spectaculars against U.S. targets and counterterrorist responses, Americans do pay close attention to the burst of incident-related media coverage (see chapter 3), which provides extraordinary amounts of easily accessible information. Not surprisingly, in the public mind, terrorism was among the most salient issues for much of the period between late 1979 and 1991. As Ronald Hinckley found, "on the average three of four Americans viewed it as an 'extremely' or 'very' serious threat to U.S. national security."[7] But he also found that "the more recent the incident, the higher is the salience; the further off is the episode, the lower is the perceived importance of terrorism."[8]

The difficulties in deciphering and analyzing public attitudes toward terrorism and, more specifically, collective views toward policy options do not stem from lack of relevant surveys. During the last decades terrorist incidents, along with other events perceived as crises, have triggered hundreds of opinion polls by a growing number of polling organizations. But their data are not without problems. For example, with the exception of the Iran hostage situation, the most shocking terrorist incidents were of relatively short duration, and most polls were conducted within limited time periods. Follow-up polls after the situations had been resolved were the exception. More important, neither the surveys of any one polling agency nor of different organizations used identical questions to explore over time the public view of one single policy issue such as the use of military force against countries believed to be sponsoring terrorism.

Referring to polls during the Iraqi occupation of Kuwait and the Gulf war, John Mueller observed:

The data . . . were created prodigiously, but not always very systematically, by the polling agencies, who were chiefly trying, of course, to generate data for short-range journalistic purposes, not longer-range academic ones. Although there are many places where the polls failed to ask what a latter-day analyst might consider to have been the right question at the right time, they did manage to create a considerable amount of semi-redundant data on many aspects of the issue, and . . . if several polls in different ways show the same opinion trend to have taken place, one can begin to believe that something like that probably actually happened.[9]

In the past decade or so, many of the terrorism-related polls were also conducted either by media partnerships such as CBS News/*New York Times*, NBC News/*Wall Street Journal*, ABC News/*Washington Post*, or by polling organizations such as Gallup, Harris, and Roper. All of these surveys were tailored to journalistic needs. The electronic and print media frequently and extensively reported the results of polls of American attitudes toward incident-related issues and problems. A search of the Nexis database covering the first phase of the Iran hostage crisis from November 5, 1979 to April 24, 1980 (when the rescue attempt was launched) produced nearly 500 stories which either exclusively or partially concerned poll results relating to the Teheran hostage situation. This is a rather large number of stories given that the available print press material in Nexis was significantly smaller than in the 1990s.

But an increasing number of polls does not necessarily contribute to a better understanding of their meaning beyond the short-term ups and downs which are of interest to the media. At first sight, a great deal of the poll data on terrorism seems to be unintelligible or, in the jargon of communication research, "noisy" and "raw." Only a closer examination of the survey data reveals a rationale for seemingly volatile opinions representing sudden attitudinal swings: because the public is bombarded by contradictory messages—terrorists' threats, immediate victims' pleas, and their own leaders' reactions—rapid

78

changes in American opinion are often the result of informed responses to developments in the terrorist horror show; they are not the "flabby" or "knee-jerk" views which are generally blamed for erratic attitudes.[10]

Even if public opinion of terrorism were raw and volatile as opposed to deliberate and stable, this would not justify discounting popular opinion and its possible effects on government action at a time when political leaders stand accused of governing by holding up their wet fingers to find out from what direction the wind of public opinion is blowing. To put it differently: Whether public opinion concerning a very salient terrorist spectacular is deliberate or raw is irrelevant: what matters is the influence of this opinion on decision making.

However the argument here is that the American public's collective response to terrorism-related policy issues is overwhelmingly rational. Relevant polls reveal that American attitudes concerning terrorism are relatively stable with respect to some policy issues (i.e., ransom payments to terrorists) and rather volatile concerning others (i.e., whether or not to negotiate with terrorist hostage-holders). Seemingly hectic opinion changes occur mostly in response to information about events and developments transmitted through the mass media.

Unpopular Options: Concessions, Ransom

Pluralities and majorities of the American public have repeatedly supported the "no concessions, no ransom" principle which has been the official policy of Republican and Democratic administrations for more than two decades. But during prolonged or very tense incidents, a minority tends to change its mind and show a willingness to compromise for the purpose of freeing fellow Americans held hostage.

Thus during the Teheran hostage ordeal the public was steadfast in its rejection of the demand that the United States hand over the ailing Shah to Iranian authorities. From mid-November through mid-March a clear majority did not want the Carter administration to give in to this condition for the hostages' release—regardless of the ups and down in the negotiations for a peaceful end to the crisis. But while well over half of all Americans backed the President on this issue during this period, the polls disclosed a notable shift in opinion over time: in late November 1979, 68 percent of the public refused to give in to the Iranian demand while 23 percent were willing to make this concession, but by mid-March, rejection of the Iranian demand had declined by 11 percent to 57 percent and acceptance had increased by 11 percent to 34 percent.[11]

Most Americans knew the issues, the arguments, and the options; those who changed their position concerning the Iranian demand were not necessarily giving in to a knee-jerk view—after all, expectations for a speedy release of the hostages, which had been quite high during November, declined rapidly during the following weeks and months. In addition, part of the opinion change may have been in response to the hard demagoguery on the part of the Iranian captors and their supporters and the failure of the Carter administration to show progress in its effort to free the hostages.

Soon after the TWA hijacking in June 1985 the hijackers and their Amal backers made clear that the fate of the American hostages depended on whether or not Israel released more than 700 Shiite prisoners. Israeli officials refused to consider releasing the Shiites unless Washington issued an official request. A majority of the public backed President Reagan's explicit refusal to ask Israel to give in to terrorists' demands. Four days after the hijacking, when the situation in Beirut seemed very dangerous, 51 percent of the public backed the president on this issue, and 35 percent took a contrary stand. But eight days later, when fear for the lives of the hostages had subsided and Israel released 31 Shiites, Americans backed Reagan's position 61 percent to 27 percent.[12] This was a case of Americans collectively reacting to information about new developments concerning the most salient problem at the time.

While a majority of Americans did not want the Reagan

administration to directly ask the Israeli government to do what the hijackers demanded, more than 60 percent of the public expressed the desire that Israel comply without involving Washington. This position was not a thoughtless departure from the American "no concession" position, but probably a response to media reports about White House officials' "hints" that they wanted the Israeli government to help end the hostage crisis.[13]

In late July 1989, Israeli commandos abducted Sheik Abdul Karim Obeid, a Moslem cleric and leader of the Lebanese Hizbollah or Party of God, which at the time held several Americans hostage. Several days after the abduction, another terrorist group released a videotape of the body of U.S. Lieut. Col. William Higgins, who had been kidnapped in Southern Lebanon. The videotape warned that more American hostages would be killed, with Joseph Cicippio next on the list, if Sheik Obeid was not freed by Israel. Faced with this situation, ABC News/*Washington Post* polls found that the proportion of Americans who wanted Israel to release the Sheik topped those opposed by 48 percent to 35 percent in early August, and by 52 percent to 42 percent a few weeks later. In this instance, the public departed again from the "no concession" position in response to both the demands and threats of Lebanese terrorists and the lead of U.S. administration officials who criticized Israel for kidnapping Sheik Obeid, regardless of his role in the Hizbollah organization.[14]

While, as described above, significantly more Americans opposed rather than supported U.S. government pressure on Israel during the TWA hijacking incident, the public was of a different mind some five years later: obviously weary of the long ordeal suffered by American hostages in Lebanon, 48 percent of the American public embraced and 43 percent rejected the suggestion that the Bush administration should pressure Israel into releasing Shiite prisoners in a possible exchange for U.S. hostages in Lebanon.[15]

Americans have consistently opposed the ransoming of hostages. Even after years of feeling helpless and frustrated about the long-lasting captivity of American hostages in Lebanon, the American public was still not willing to support ransom payments. In September 1989, 85 percent of Americans polled opposed paying ransom while 10 percent of the public supported it. In an earlier poll conducted a few days after the announcement that William Higgins had been killed by his captors, 19 percent of the American public had been willing to ransom the remaining hostages while 76 percent had opposed this solution.[16] When Americans feared that the lives of the hostages were threatened, ransoming the hostages seemed more attractive than six weeks later, after the hostage-holders had ceased their threats to kill other hostages in retaliation for Sheik Obeid's abduction.

In October, November, and early December 1980, when no one in the United States could foresee when and how the Iranian hostage crisis would end, pollsters explored public attitudes toward the ransom option: 51 percent of the respondents rejected, while 36 percent approved of, sending Iran military spare parts in exchange for the American captives. This clear stand against ransom was in response to a straightforward question: "Would you favor or oppose President Carter's providing Iran with spare parts for their military equipment in exchange for American hostages?". In two other polls respondents were asked their opinion of "unfreezing the more than $8 billion of Iranian assets in the U.S., including orders for military spare parts." In this context, 48 percent were opposed, while 43 percent in one poll and 45 percent in the other supported the proposition.[17] The wording of the question made clear that the military parts at issue had been bought and paid for by Iran well before the Teheran crisis began. The significant difference in the results indicated that the public understood the fine but not unimportant differences in the presentation of the question.

Once the Iran-Contra arms-for-hostages deals of President Reagan's second term were revealed, generally 80 percent of Americans polled disapproved of the secret transactions.[18] This reaction should not have surprised the Reagan administration: during the Iran hostage crisis and thereafter, a majority had rejected the sale of weaponry in a straight exchange for hostages. Moreover, during the mid-1980s, when the public became increasingly frustrated about anti-American terrorism and especially the ordeal of American hostages in Lebanon, the alternative of selling military equipment to state sponsors of terrorism in order to free American hostages was the least popular alternative among several policy options (favored by only 8 percent of those questioned).[19]

One analysis of American attitudes toward the Iranian arms scandal observed that "it was probably the type of concessions that were made—arms transfers—that bothered people."[20] A large majority of Americans disagreed with the Reagan administration's secret Iran initiatives precisely because it involved the sale of arms to Iran.

Mixed Feelings About Negotiations

When Americans have reason to believe that the lives of American hostages are in immediate danger, a majority want the government to negotiate for their release. During the early stage of the Teheran hostage crisis and in the aftermath of the failed rescue attempt several months later, polls revealed strong support for a negotiated settlement. Both before and after the rescue attempt, efforts to find a diplomatic solution were the cornerstone of the Carter administration's approach to a solution. Over 80 percent of Americans polled agreed with the president's approach.[21]

The extent of public support of negotiations is also influenced by the implied meaning of this policy option. During the Iran crisis the term "negotiations" seemed fairly free of negative connotations. In contrast, during the TWA hijacking in 1985, "negotiations" seemed to mean bartering with perpetrators of violence and their backers. Thus, when President Reagan in a televised speech reaffirmed the American principle of never making concessions to terrorists and never asking other governments to do so, the media reported presidential assurances that Washington would not "negotiate" with terrorists.[22]

But even when the public understood that "negotiating" meant to make a deal with terrorists, the sentiment was for doing so in order to protect the lives of fellow citizens. During the 1985 TWA hostage crisis, when the hijackers had already killed one of their captives, the American target audience preferred a negotiated settlement even if that meant giving in to terrorists' demands. Polls conducted jointly by ABC News and the *Washington Post* showed that clear majorities (53 percent and 59 percent) wanted the government to negotiate rather than risk the lives of the hostages.[23] After the TWA hostages were freed, Americans were divided when asked whether or not the administration had in fact negotiated behind the scenes with the terrorists. Reminded by pollsters that President Reagan had opposed any deal during the crisis, 41 percent of the respondents said Reagan did negotiate, 43 percent believed he did not. Asked whether the President should have negotiated with the hostage-takers, more Americans (51 percent) rejected than supported (42 percent) this approach.[24]

Although a majority of the public wanted the Reagan administration to negotiate and in retrospect was just as soundly critical of possible secret bargains during the TWA incident, this is not a confirmation of an erratic mass public. Many Americans simply remembered Reagan's unequivocal and repeated promises not to negotiate with the Beirut captors; a majority disapproved of the President saying one thing publicly and secretly doing the opposite—regardless of what they themselves would have preferred during the crisis.

In the fall of 1986, before the arms-for-hostages scandal made headlines, 57 percent of respondents rejected negotiations with Lebanese terrorist groups to gain the release of several American hostages. About three years later, in early August 1989, many Americans seemed affected by the news that terrorists had killed William Higgins, when by 58 percent to 39 percent they expressed support for direct U.S. negotiations with terrorists in Lebanon. By May 1990 public sentiment had changed: 48 percent of respondents opposed negotiations with Middle Eastern terrorists holding Americans while 45 percent approved of negotiating.[25] When the hostages were no longer in acute danger of being executed by their captors, the public was more reluctant to support direct dealings between the U.S. government and terrorist hostage-holders.

People's attitudes are very volatile when it comes to the issue of whether or not to negotiate with terrorists. But significant opinion swings and reversals are based on rational calculation and deliberation on the part of a public "sensitive to the difficulties associated with terrorist hostage-taking incidents and the need to give the government some room to maneuver."[26] In general, a majority of Americans rejects negotiations with terrorists, but when U.S. hostages are threatened, a majority has valued the lives of fellow citizens over policy principles.

Military Actions to Save American Lives

Two daring rescue missions during the 1970s were widely reported and taken as evidence that terrorists can be fought and defeated. The first of these counterterrorist measures occurred on July 4, 1976, when Israeli special commandos stormed a hijacked Air France airliner at the airport of Entebbe, Uganda, and rescued over a hundred passengers and crew members. On October 19, 1977, in a similarly raid, West German commandos took control of a hijacked Lufthansa jet parked on the tarmac at Mogadishu airport in Somalia and freed 86 passengers and crew members. While in both instances rescuers could not prevent the loss of several lives, it was widely concluded that the Israeli as well as the German raid saved many more.

Immediately after learning of the Mogadishu rescue, President Carter asked top military officials about American counterterrorist capabilities. In November 1977, the Delta Force had been established under the command of Charles Beckwith, who for years had argued for a special counterterrorist force.[27] Beckwith expected at the time that it would take two years to build an effective counterterrorist commando unit. Exactly two years later, the Iran hostage crisis began. Soon thereafter public debate began about whether Delta Force offered a realistic option to resolve the Teheran crisis.

The logistical difficulties of sending commandos on a rescue mission into Teheran were reported and discussed in the press, and a solid majority of the public opposed attempting a rescue. Also under extremely difficult circumstances but with the advantage of a more accessible location (Beirut), opposition against a rescue mission was less pronounced in the early days of the TWA hostage crisis when 48 percent of the public opposed and 39 percent supported this option. The American public did not reverse its attitude with respect to rescue missions by the summer of 1989. When asked about an effort to rescue the American hostages in Lebanon, 40 percent of respondents favored, 50 percent opposed such an enterprise.[28] The last poll was conducted shortly after the press had reported that terrorists in Lebanon had killed one of their hostages (William Higgins) and threatened to murder other Americans as well. In this situation four of ten Americans backed a rescue attempt "even if some American lives might be lost." Public support for the use of military force or of military action in general terms was recorded when pollsters asked explicitly whether military measures would be favored if American hostages were killed or otherwise harmed. During the many months of the Iranian hostage ordeal about two thirds of the public consistently supported military action if Americans in Teheran were severely hurt or killed by their captors.[29]

In 1989, 62 percent of Americans questioned expressed support for using military force in Lebanon in an effort to free U.S. hostages. Even when asked in a follow-up question whether they would still approve of a military option if hostages were killed during such an action, 43 percent did not change their mind while 15 percent withdrew their support and 4 percent were no longer sure of their position.[30] While most Americans were still not ready to endorse military measures that might harm the hostages themselves, a substantial minority had simply lost hope that a peaceful solution would be found.

During the first several months of the Iranian hostage crisis, the American public was unwilling to back the use of force against Iran if innocent American hostages were endangered in the process. The option of military measures if some of the hostages were put on trial, otherwise harmed, or killed, was viewed quite differently from the resort to military force in the absence of such mistreatment, with the possibility of jeopardizing the lives of fellow Americans. But by March 1980 for the first time since the hostage-taking in early November 1979 more Americans supported than opposed military means to free the hostages.[31] In this case, public patience had its limits.

During the Iraqi annexation of Kuwait Saddam Hussein held hundreds of Americans civilians against their will as human shields against American attack. At the time, three of four Americans favored U.S. military action if any of the hostages were harmed.[32] In this respect, public opinion had not changed in the ten years since the Iranian hostage situation. In this instance, the predicament of the hostages was only one of the problems in the Persian Gulf, and the public took a tough stand right from the start. Asked a few days after the invasion of Kuwait and the developing hostage situation in August 1990 whether the United States should engage in combat even if Iraq continued to hold American civilians hostage, 61 percent of the respondents favored and 30 percent opposed combat. The support for combat regardless of the presence of U.S. hostages declined to 57 percent in October and to 55 percent in November while opposition increased to 32 percent and 34 percent respectively.[33] But as long as Hussein held the hostages, a solid majority of Americans did not want this sub-crisis to affect Washington's decision making within the overall Persian Gulf crisis.

Military Retaliation

Polls reveal that even when deeply troubled and frustrated during on-going hostage situations, most Americans oppose strictly retaliatory military strikes in order to punish terrorists and their supporters after hostages have been freed. During the Iran hostage crisis, for example, three of four Americans expressed opposition when asked about military retaliation against Iran once the hostages were freed.[34] This rejection of retaliation also prevailed during the TWA hijacking incident, when at different stages of the crisis 50 percent to 60 percent of Americans believed that military revenge would be a mistake once the crisis was resolved.[35]

The Use of Force Against State Sponsors

Whatever the original intentions of the so-called students who took control of the U.S. embassy in Teheran in November 1979, their move escalated very quickly into a durable hostage situation backed by the Ayatollah Khomeini and the revolutionary Iranian government. Yet there was little discussion of state sponsored terrorism during this particular crisis.

Several years and many terrorist spectaculars later, terrorism experts inside and outside the U.S. government began to identify several governments (e.g., Libya, Iran, Syria, and Cuba) as sponsors of anti-western and especially anti-American terrorism. Polls have revealed that Americans consider state sponsorship of terrorist groups and actions as utterly despicable. During the TWA hijacking between 50 and 54 percent of the American public favored military action against any Middle Eastern nation found to be supportive of anti-American terrorism.[36] A series of polls conducted over a sixteen month period in 1985 and 1986 found increasing American sentiment for the use of military force against governments that actively "created the conditions, the climate, and the frenzy that have led to attacks on Americans."[37]

In the days immediately following the release of the TWA hostages in early July 1985, 56 percent of respondents were opposed to U.S. military action against state sponsors. But after the bloody terrorist spectaculars during the rest of the year as well as in 1986, public opinion on this issue changed: throughout 1986, between 51 percent and 61 percent of the U.S. public endorsed military action against state sponsors of terrorism. Even before the Reagan administration made the final decision to bomb Libya in mid-April 1986, a majority of Americans (i.e., 55 percent in March) supported such an action. Indeed, one day before the air raids, 67 percent of the public was supportive of military actions specifically against Libya: 47 percent endorsed limited air strikes and an additional 20 percent approved a military invasion.[38]

In spite of the sound majority that favored military retaliation against Libya before and after the actual air strikes, a series of polls revealed that from July 1985 through March 1986 a majority of Americans consistently supported military retaliation against one country—Iran. In July 1985, for example, 52 percent of the public endorsed retaliatory moves against Iran while 49 percent supported military actions against Libya. However, by January 1986, after Libya's leader Moammar Qaddafi had been linked to terrorist attacks at the airports in Rome and Vienna, 60 percent of the public favored retaliation against Libya while nearly as many (59 percent) wanted military moves against Iran.[39] The Reagan administration's intensive anti-Libyan propaganda campaign and the President's very personal anti-Qaddafi rhetoric were probably strong influences on the public's views in this particular case.

A notable exception to Americans' willingness to retaliate against proven state sponsors of terrorism occurred in the aftermath of the bombing of Pan Am flight 103: about three weeks after the deadly incident those questioned rejected military retaliation by 51 percent to 41 percent even if the bombing could be traced to a particular country. The bombing of Flight 103 was widely seen as a retaliatory act for the accidental downing by U.S. forces of an Iranian civilian airliner over the Persian Gulf some six months earlier.[40]

Eight months later, Americans were evenly split when asked whether they supported the bombing of military and economic targets in Iran because of that country's links to the Lebanese captors of Americans.[41] In this instance, 45 percent of those polled may have feared that a military move against Iran might worsen the predicament of the American captives in Beirut, while the same percentage wished to end the ordeal, one way or the other.

During the Persian Gulf conflict of 1990–1991 terrorist groups that had enjoyed Iraqi support threatened violence against Americans anywhere if the U.S. and its allies attacked Iraq or attempted to liberate Kuwait. More than two thirds of the public supported a military response if terrorists loyal to Saddam Hussein killed Americans in the United States or abroad. At the same time, 48 percent of the public approved of going to war in response to anti-American violence by Saddam Hussein's terrorist friends, whereas 44 percent were against an all-out war to counter terrorism on behalf of Iraq.[42] At no time were Americans as poised as during the pre-war phase of the Persian Gulf conflict to retaliate militarily against a state sponsor of terrorism. Of course, in this case leading terrorists such as Abul Abbas and Abu Nidal made no secret of their close ties to Iraq and especially their sponsor Saddam Hussein. In a statement published days after the Kuwaiti invasion, Abbas warned, "We will strike at American and imperialist interests immediately any foreign soldier sets foot on Arab territory."[43]

American-Israeli Relations

Terrorism in the Middle East and by Middle Eastern groups elsewhere has almost always something to do with terrorists' and state sponsors' opposition to Israel and to the traditionally close ties between the United States and Israel. Adversaries of Israel in the region believe that the Jewish state could be dealt with on their terms were it not for Israel's strong American support. While much of the terrorism that originates in this region is committed to further the short-term goals of a specific group (i.e., the release of fellow terrorists from Israeli prisons), the desire to weaken the close relationship between the United States and Israel ranks high on the list of the long-term objectives of such groups and their state sponsors.

Pollsters for ABC News and the *Washington Post* repeatedly asked a cross section of American adults during the TWA hijacking crisis:" Tell me if you agree, disagree, or if perhaps you have no opinion . . . : The U.S. should reduce its ties to Israel in order to lessen acts of violence against us in the Middle East." Three days after the hijacking 53 percent of the respondents rejected this proposition. Several days later, however, after the American and Israeli governments had disagreed about their respective responses to the terrorists' demands, only 41 percent of the respondents opposed the suggestion. This was a substantial change concerning a long established area of American foreign policy.

Once the crisis was resolved 48 percent of those polled objected to weakening the ties between the U.S. and Israel. This particular survey series demonstrated that terrorism has the potential to alter public opinion concerning longstanding foreign policy principles.[44] Whether such changes tend to be temporary or durable remains an open question.

The Public and Terrorism News

Terrorists reach and manipulate their target audience in the United States through the print and electronic media. Given the centrality of the mass media in terrorists' strategies and tactics, public perception and evaluation of important issues involved in the coverage of terrorism take on added significance. Polls during the 1980s revealed that most people were well aware of the relationship between the press and terrorism. Hinckley found evidence of a widespread public belief in the 1980s "that terrorist successes depend on the publicity they receive from the media and that the media often exaggerate terrorist incidents, playing into terrorists' hands by giving them the coverage they seek."[45]

But the public did not accept the argument that terrorist violence would not occur if media organizations simply stopped covering these sorts of incidents. Asked specifically about the coverage of the *Achille Lauro* hijacking, the TWA hijacking and the

91

Iran hostage crises, a total of 67 percent of the respondents in one in-depth survey believed it "very" (28 percent) or "fairly" (39 percent) likely that these terrorist incidents would have occurred "even if news organizations did not cover them."[46] Although three of four Americans in this survey thought that newspapers, news magazines, and television networks did an "excellent" or "good" job in reporting terrorist events, 51 percent also believed that news organizations had given "too much" coverage to such events. It seems that reservations about media coverage concerned the quantity, not the quality, of reporting.[47] Public satisfaction with the content of the news seemed confirmed by attitudes toward television interviews with hostages: following the controversial airing of interviews and press conferences with the TWA hostages in Beirut, 56 percent of those surveyed approved of these broadcasts—even though the captors controlled the format of the question-and-answer sessions.[48]

The Rational Public

While a large segment of the public is well aware that terrorists depend on the media for communication, this recognition does not mean the American audience is immune to terrorist demagoguery and other messages concerning terrorism in general and violent spectaculars in particular. By paying attention to terrorist spectaculars, the public learns something about the complexities of terrorism-related problems: consequently it may tend to form more dogmatic attitudes concerning abstract policy principles and more pragmatic attitudes concerning actual acts against innocent victims. Yes, terrorists can and do manipulate the public during times when they already hold hostages or threaten violence. But in those situations, terrorists influence the views and actions of policy makers as well (see chapter 6). The frequent opinion changes in the course of specific terrorist events are not caused by "raw" or "knee-jerk" views that are carelessly expressed by people "without real consideration of the consequences."[49] On the contrary, it is precisely because the public considers and distinguishes between different policy options in different stages of terrorist events that attitudinal swings and reversals occur frequently. This is by no means proof of a whimsical public but rather of an Americans populace that responds reasonably and rationally to news and information about terrorism. Certainly, terrorists stage the news and provide a great deal of information in this context and thereby force average citizens and political elites to reconsider their policy preferences. But opinion changes here are not necessarily the result of uninformed attitudes but of realistic assessments of most difficult situations.

If, indeed, Americans have a good grasp of the complexities of terrorism, how do they evaluate a president's management of terrorist incidents? How solidly does the public support the chief executive who must respond to this sort of political violence? The following chapter examines the tendency to "rally-round-the-president" during and after terrorist and counterterrorist incidents.

CHAPTER FIVE

TERRORIST SPECTACULARS AND PRESIDENTIAL RALLIES

There is a big difference between the short-term, when people are rallying around the flag, and what happens month after month.

—JAMES MCGREGOR BURNS

When the American embassy in Teheran was overrun on November 4, 1979, President Carter's prospects for reelection were very poor. Less than one third of the American public approved of his job performance. The President knew he would be challenged at the Democratic convention and, as he later recalled, "at the time Senator Edward Kennedy had been an overwhelming favorite" to win the nomination of the Democratic party.[1] But within less than a month after the embassy takeover Carter's approval ratings jumped to 51 percent; and in mid-December, when the Gallup poll found a 54 percent approval rating, George Gallup characterized the turnaround as "stunning" and "the largest increase in presidential popularity recorded in the four decades the Gallup poll and Gallup organization have made these measurements."[2] Americans were, as the media reported, rallying behind their president.

Patrick Caddell, the White House pollster, cautioned ecstatic Carter supporters not to be misled by such high public approval ratings, because they could change.[3] Sure enough, by early March 1980, with the hostage crisis still unresolved, more Americans disapproved than approved of the President's performance.

Why are presidents and their advisers, other politicians, journalists, and scholars interested in presidential approval ratings? Increased fragmentation of power in Congress, the decline of political parties, and reforms in the presidential selection process are major reasons why "postmodern" presidents, far more than their predecessors, must rely on popular support as an important source of influence in the Washington power game.[4] Even earlier presidents were more likely to persuade other political actors to support them and their agenda if the public was behind them, because, as Richard Neustadt recognized, political players in the capital "think about the public outside Washington. They have to gauge his [the president's] popular prestige. Because they think about it, public standing is a source of influence for him, another factor bearing on their willingness to give him what he wants."[5] Following the 20 point plunge in President Bush's approval rating between August and October 1990 that expressed public dissatisfaction with the President's role in his budget fight with Congress and perhaps growing doubts over his handling of the Persian Gulf crisis, Kevin Phillips observed that the President's "prestige on Capital Hill and within his own party, never matching his strong ratings, now trails even his current mediocre public approval."[6] Certainly, a president's public standing does not automatically translate into comparable levels of support or opposition among Washingtonian influentials or in ayes and nays in Congress. At the very least, popular support is, in the words of George Edwards, "an important background resource for leadership"[7] and at most, as Lyndon Johnson concluded, "a major source of strength in gaining cooperation from Congress."[8]

Strong public support for presidential policies does at times convince political elites to switch their positions. This happened, for example, in case of the Grenada invasion in the fall of 1983.

ame clear that President Reagan's military interven-
rongly supported by the public, House Speaker
p" O'Neill and other members of Congress aban-
_____ their initial opposition and joined the President's supporters. Hedrick Smith reported in the *New York Times* that "many
lawmakers seem to sense a public wave of patriotism over the
Grenada operation, and have responded to it."[9] The editorial position of the *Washington Post* switched from skeptical to supportive as well.[10]

In recalling that before the seizure of the U.S. Embassy in Iran
Senator Kennedy had been favored in the upcoming primary sea-
son, President Carter was keenly aware that an "incumbent president's standing with the public appears to be related to the ease
or difficulty with which he wins renomination for another term
in office."[11] Public approval or disapproval during a president's
second term is likely to influence his "place in history" and the
election prospects for his party's candidate.

Ultimately, in Richard Brody's words, "presidential poll ratings are important because they are thought to be important."[12]
While a significant power source in normal times, broad public
approval is crucial when a president is faced with a crisis, especially one involving actual or potential military actions. More
than two months into the Persian Gulf crisis, when George
Bush's public support was rapidly declining, Henry Graff, a leading presidential historian, advised the President in an op-ed article to "travel the nation to explain the purpose and goals of his
intervention." He recalled that the Korean War "stained Harry
Truman's Presidency and the Vietnam War destroyed Lyndon B.
Johnson's—in both instances because public support for the
respective wars, thin to begin with, faded fast."[13]

Conventional wisdom has it that Americans line up behind
their president in times of serious international events in a
surge of patriotism. John Mueller has characterized significant
increases in popular approval ratings associated with specific,
dramatic international events that involve the United States
and the President directly as "rally-round-the-flag" phenome-

na.[14] Writing soon after World War II, Nelson Polsby conclud that a boost to the president's popularity at such a moment almost certain to occur, "regardless of the wisdom of the policies he pursues."[15]

However, not all international events that fulfill Mueller's criteria result in sudden jumps in presidential approval ratings. Scholars who have identified and compiled lists of "rally events" meeting Mueller's requirements have shown that outbursts of popular presidential backing are far from automatic. George Edwards, for example, identified 85 rally events from 1953 to 1988, of which only 24 resulted in actual rallies that fulfilled the minimum threshold of a five percentage point gain established by Edwards.[16] Selecting potential rally events during the Truman, Eisenhower, Kennedy, Johnson, Nixon, Ford, Carter, and Reagan presidencies, Brody and Catherine Shapiro compiled a list of 65 cases from 1948 through 1986. Of these only 16 qualified as rallies displaying at least a five point jump in public support.[17] Lowering the threshold to a three point approval increase, Larry Hugick and Alec Gallup found 74 events that resulted in actual rallies between 1938 and 1991.[18]

One point that Mueller alludes to and others emphasize is that even specific, dramatic international events that involve a president result in rallies only if they are extensively and prominently covered by the mass media and thereby become highly salient to the public. Front page coverage or lead stories in TV network newscasts lasting only a day or two is not enough. For this reason Hugick and Gallup excluded from their list events that technically met Mueller's requirements but "did not attract a very high volume of news coverage."[19]

Rallies around the flag and around the crisis-managing president have been interpreted as public outbursts of patriotic sentiment. But why did similar events—the Pueblo incident in 1968 and the Mayaguez seizure in 1975—lead to vastly different public reactions: President Johnson's approval decreased by seven percent in 1968, whereas President Ford's improved by eleven percent in 1975. Given such vastly different public reactions and the recognition that news coverage plays a crucial role in the public's reactions to events, Brody and Shapiro offer a plausible explanation that connects rallies to the reactions of opinion leaders. They propose that public rallies occur when the debate in the mass media reflects opinion leaders (i.e., members of Congress, high administration officials, ex-officials, interest group leaders, policy experts) who either support the president or abstain from criticism. When the news reveals that opinion leaders are neither rallying behind nor hiding their disagreement with a president's handling of a crisis, the public "appears to look to the events themselves for information with which to update its judgment of how well the president is handling his job."[20]

Terrorist Spectaculars and Rallying Round the President

There is no doubt that the anti-American terrorist spectaculars during the Carter, Reagan, and Bush years that occurred abroad meet both the widely accepted conditions Mueller established as well as the requirements for saturation media coverage and public salience.

Research has established that "[b]y far the most important kind of event affecting public opinion has involved war or armed conflict."[21] According to David Broder "terrorism is a form of warfare" and "like all other forms of warfare intended for political and geopolitical ends."[22] But whether one accepts his characterization of these sorts of incidents or not, terrorist "spectaculars" qualify in either case as major crises which even in the absence of conventional warfare tend to have "substantial (and often abrupt) effects on public opinion."[23] If one applies the three percent threshold, as Hugick and Gallup do, all six of the most dramatic terrorist incidents in the period 1979–1990 (see Table 3.1) fit the rally category.[24] However, only four events caused presidential rallies, if one adopts the five point minimum approval jump that Edwards and others prefer as an admittedly somewhat arbitrary qualification marker.[25]

Table 5.1
Terrorist Events and Changes in Presidential Approval

	% Change from Last Pre-Event Poll	% Change from First to Second Post Incident Poll
Carter		
Iran hostage crisis		
November 1979–		
January 1980	+6%	+13%
Reagan		
TWA hijack crisis		
June 1985	+5%	+2%
Achille Lauro hijacking		
October 1985	+3%	-1%
U.S. bombing of Libya		
April 1986	+6%	-7%
Bombing Pan Am flight 103		
December 1988	+6%	N.A.
Bush		
Killing of William Higgins		
August 1989	+3%	+1%

Source: Gallup Organization; N.A. = not applicable.

By any measure, the president gained public support in all six incidents. Thus, compared to other events that fulfill the requirements established by Mueller, international terrorist spectaculars would seem to result in approval gains. However no trend is discernible with respect to the durability of these rallies. In three cases examined in table 5.1, the initial approval gains over the last pre-event polls were also followed by upswings; in two incidents, by losses in the second post-even surveys; in the sixth case—the bombing of Pan Am flight 103—the second post-event poll measured the public approval of President Reagan's successor.

Because party identification is a strong determinant of American political attitudes, "Democrats, Republicans, and Independents do not always react the same to the president and to the events and conditions by which they evaluate him."[26] While presidential partisans will tend to be more supportive all along and are perhaps more prone to rally during a crisis, one would expect that strong rallies occur when a segment of those Americans who identify with the opposition party or characterize themselves as independent voters decide to back the president in a particular foreign policy dilemma. These kinds of reactions occurred in the wake of terrorist spectaculars: Rallies resulted from non-partisan public reactions. For example, before the Iranian hostage taking, only 18 percent of those American respondents who identified themselves as Republicans and 31 percent of Independents approved of Jimmy Carter's job performance. Even Democrats were lukewarm in their support, at 40 percent. By early December, the President's approval among Republicans and independent voters had increased by 24 percent, and by 22 percent among Democrats.

Before the TWA hijacking incident in June 1985, President Reagan's approval among Republicans (87 percent) and independents (58 percent) was significantly higher than among Democrats (35 percent). But the first poll after the crisis recorded a 6 percent gain among independent and a 4 percent gain among Democratic approval of Reagan's job performance while Republicans remained at 87 percent. Obviously, as far as Republicans were concerned, the presidential approval level had reached ceiling territory. The first survey after the U.S. bombing of Libya in April 1986 showed that Reagan's approval had increased 8 percent among Democrats (from 43 percent to 51 percent), 6 percent among independents (from 63 percent to 69 percent), but just 2 percent among Republicans (from 86 percent to 88 percent). As in the case of the TWA hijacking, the "ceiling effect" explains the insignificant approval increase among Republicans.[27]

Surveys before and after the terrorist bombing of Pan Am flight

100

103 in December 1988 revealed a 9 point gain among Republicans (from 84 percent to 93 percent) and a 7 point gain among Democrats (from 31 to 38 percent), and a surprising 2 point decline among independents. While Republican support "went through the ceiling," perhaps as a sign of affection for Reagan just a few weeks before the end of his term in office, there is no explanation for the reaction of independents.

During the Iran crisis, independent voters were the first to leave the rally in significant numbers: the very first strong decline in Jimmy Carter's approval ratings occurred in a two-week period at the end of January and the beginning of February 1980, when the President's approval among independents declined by 8 points from 56 percent to 48 percent. At the same time, approval declined merely 2 points among Democrats and Republicans. A month later, Republicans (with an 18 point decline from 43 percent to 25 percent) and Democrats (with an 11 point decline from 65 percent to 54 percent) followed the trend, while among independents approval dropped an additional 9 points to 39 percent. With a few notable exceptions, foreign policy in the United States has been nonpartisan since World War II. By and large partisan cleavages had little influence on the way the three groups evaluated the President's overall job performance during the first five months of the Iran situation.

During the TWA hijacking the non-partisan pro-Reagan rally was in fact followed up by slight additional approval gains among Republicans (3 percent) and independents (4 percent) while Democrats remained at the same approval level. The decline in approval following the initial nonpartisan rally triggered by the Libyan bombing occurred more along party lines: President Reagan's approval among his own partisans fell negligibly (a loss of 2 percent) while the declines were larger among Democrats (a loss of 11 percent) and independents (a loss of 5 percent). It is probably no coincidence that those who identified with Democrats and Independents parted ways with Republicans in a case that concerned not terrorist aggression but military counterterrorist action initiated by the President.

Research has revealed that the opinions of men and women and of whites and nonwhites move in parallel patterns.[28] By and large, these findings were confirmed by polls measuring presidential approval after terrorist or counterterrorist incidents but there have been exceptions as well.

About a month after the hostage taking in Teheran, Jimmy Carter's approval had increased 19 percent among men (from 30 percent to 49 percent) and 20 points among women (from 34 percent to 54 percent). There were no significant gender differences throughout the crisis in the president's approval. The reactions of men and women were similar in the case of the TWA hijacking and the bombing of Pan Am flight 103, when President Reagan's approval increased 7 and 8 points among women and 3 and 5 points among men, respectively. While presidential approval gains were slightly higher among women than men in those incidents in which terrorists struck at Americans, in the case of the Libyan bombing the President's approval gains were higher among men (8 percent) than among women (5 percent).

While gender variations in the examined cases were not significant, they seem to confirm that "the largest and most important [gender] differences concern violence and the use of force. In practically all realms of foreign and domestic policy, women are less belligerent than men."[29] It seems that women are somewhat more inclined than men to rally behind a president who tries to find a peaceful solution to a dramatic terrorist event and somewhat more reluctant to support a chief executive who resorts to military retaliation.

Nonwhites tend to rally more quickly than whites. The initially modest presidential rally (+6 percent) in the earliest phase of the Iranian hostage crisis consisted of a strong 12 point approval jump among nonwhite Americans (from 36 percent to 48 percent) and a 4 percent increase among whites (from 32 percent to 36 percent). This approval gain among nonwhites was particularly impressive because President Carter had a higher level of support among nonwhites than among whites before the crisis began. Similarly, the 5 point rally after the TWA hijacking included a 10 point jump in approval among nonwhites (from 26 percent to 36 percent) and a 4 point gain among whites (from 62 percent to 66 percent). In this case, however, the pre-incident support for President Reagan was very low among nonwhites and quite high among whites. Following the American bombing of Libya, the reactions of whites and nonwhites were very similar; presidential approval increased 6 points among whites (from 66 percent to 72 percent) and 8 percent among nonwhites (from 30 percent to 38 percent). Finally, after the bombing of Pan Am flight 103, President Reagan's approval among nonwhites increased 9 points (from 25 percent to 34 percent) and 6 points among whites (from 61 percent to 67 percent).

If one subscribes to the thesis that presidential rallies in the face of international crises are, at least initially, caused by patriotic reflexes, the major terrorist and counterterrorist incidents in the past offer evidence that nonwhites are more patriotic and rally more readily around the flag. But while the president is likely to achieve larger approval gains among nonwhites immediately after a terrorist incident, the differences tend to disappear by the time the second post-event surveys are conducted.

President Carter and the Iranian Hostage Crisis

The Teheran hostage crisis produced a quantity of rich opinion data that offer a unique opportunity to test several important propositions concerning the rally phenomenon as it relates to terrorism.

Not all dramatic international events that involve the United States and its president result in rallies. Therefore, the proposition that the reactions of opinion leaders provide answers to the rally puzzle is an attractive one. Indeed, Brody and Shapiro have produced evidence that the public lines up supportedly behind a crisis-managing president, if the media debate is dominated by elites supporting the administration, and that public rallies do not occur if opinion leaders are reported by the media to be openly critical of the president's crisis management.[30] The Iranian hostage crisis is one of the cases studied by Brody and Shapiro, and I have further examined the thesis of opinion leadership by comparing approval ratings with elite messages drawn from systematic qualitative and quantitative analyses of relevant news reports.

I classified the Iran coverage of the CBS Evening News and the *New York Times* during the first five-and-a-half months of the crisis according to positive and negative statements and attitudes concerning President Carter's crisis policies that were attributed to domestic elites. I also tallied statements attributed to Iranian sources that were critical of Carter's position, since negative "foe messages" might also influence public opinion. The focus was on major policy issues (for example, whether the United States should return the Shah to Iran, or whether military force should be used to resolve the crisis) and on the President's handling of the incident (e.g., support or criticism of Carter's crisis management and his decision not to participate in primary debates and other campaign activities). The results are listed in table 5.2.

Studies of the rally phenomenon have made use solely of surveys that reveal the public attitude about overall presidential job performance (Gallup and other survey organizations frequently ask the standard question: "Do you approve or disapprove of the way President X is handling his job as president?") Intuitively, one would expect that surveys revealing the level of public support for the way in which a president handles a specific event are even better indicators of the depth or shallowness of presidential support than are overall performance ratings. Instead of solely focusing on general approval as the measure of magnitude and durability of rallies, responses to incident-specific survey questions (for example, "Do you approve or disapprove of the way President Carter is handling the Iranian hostage crisis?") should also be considered to understand fully the complexities of this phenomenon.

The buildup to the Persian Gulf war supports this proposition: during October 1990, while President Bush's overall public

Table 5.2
Domestic Elite and Iranian Citations

	positive domestic	negative domestic	negative Iranian
November 4–15, 1979	55	9	25
November 16–30, 1979	52	5	21
December 1–15, 1979	49	2	11
December 16–31, 1979	17	13	2
January 1–15, 1980	13	13	10
January 16–31, 1980	8	7	7
February 1–15, 1980	11	14	10
February 16–29, 1980	12	7	7
March 1–15, 1980	13	7	5
March 16–31, 1980	3	13	6
April 1–15, 1980	11	13	0

Sources: CBS Evening News and *New York Times*

approval was on a steep downhill slide reflective of growing public frustration over his bitter budget fight with congressional Democrats, Americans were far more supportive of his management of the Persian Gulf crisis.[31]

The chief executive is ideally situated to communicate with the public through presidential addresses to the nation and White House news conferences. The ability to use the mass media to appeal to millions of Americans is a powerful tool to shape and manipulate the public perception of how a president is handling a given crisis. The modern president's imperative to "go public" becomes especially urgent in times of critical international events such as terrorist spectaculars.[32] Eytan Gilboa found that President Reagan's efforts during and after two terrorist incidents improved his public approval ratings.[33] But not all efforts to persuade the public are successful. "By virtue of going public," Kernell suggests, "a president may actually contribute to unfavorable swings of opinion in the country."[34]

The full range of variables necessary for a comprehensive explanation of the rally phenomenon include general and incident-specific approval ratings, the blend of media citations of domestic opinion leaders and foreign foes, and presidential attempts to lead public opinion.

Referring to his efforts to enlist public support to convince Congress to vote for his energy initiatives, Jimmy Carter recalled that his "repeated calls for action on energy had become aggravating, and were increasingly falling on deaf ears among American citizens. In spite of the subject's crucial importance, the public lacked interest in energy except when long gas lines formed or sudden price increases made people angry."[35] Several presidential addresses could not persuade the public to pressure Congress into supporting Carter's energy policy. Instead, with gasoline lines getting longer, the President's standing in the polls "dropped to a new low."[36]

The experience was fresh in Carter's mind when the Iran crisis began. Perhaps this was why the White House waited 24 days before scheduling a nationally televised news conference on November 28, 1979. By then a modest increase in general approval (6 percent) had already occurred and the President's management of the Iran situation had the support of 67 percent of the public. Following the news conference, which was dedicated exclusively to the situation in Teheran, Carter's overall approval jumped 13 points to 51 percent and his rating for handling the crisis jumped another 10 points to 77 percent (see figure 5.1 for the effect of Carter's public appeals on his general and incident-specific approval ratings).

However, the solid gains in presidential approval nearly four weeks after the hostage-taking also reflected the reactions of domestic opinion leaders (administration officials, members of Congress, and former government officials) and of foes in Iran (the hostage-holders, the Ayatollah Khomeini, and other government officials). During the earliest stage of the incident, when most Americans expected that the hostage situation would be shortlived like a similar incident in the U.S. embassy in Teheran in February 1979, Carter was criticized repeatedly—especially by his rivals for the upcoming election year. Immediately after the hostages were taken, CBS correspondent Marvin Kalb report-

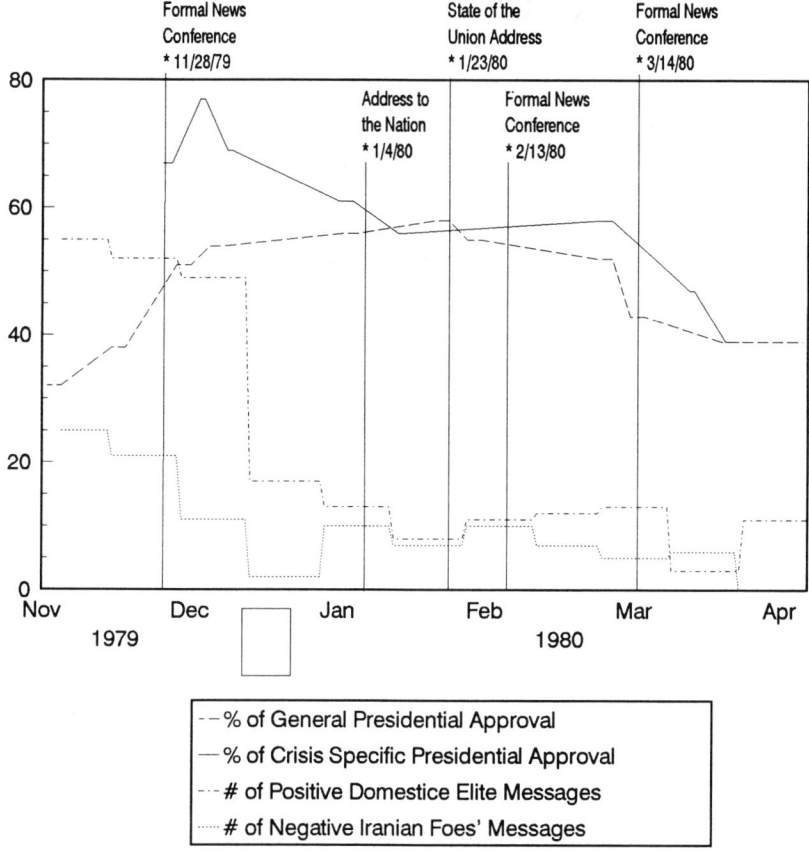

Figure 5.1
Presidential Support and the Iranian Hostage Crisis

ed that Republican John Connally had charged that the President
was guilty of "appeasement" because of his Iran policy.[37] Four
days later, Democratic Senator Edward Kennedy and Republican
Senator Robert Dole both made critical remarks. Dole com-
plained that "it becomes increasingly clear that pleading with
the Ayatollah is producing no tangible results."[38] The President's modest gains in general approval about two weeks into
the crisis may well have been affected by these and other critical
comments.

There was less domestic criticism in the second half of November and supportive messages from domestic elites remained at a very high level. Thus, the general and specific approval jumps were probably the combined results of Carter's news conference and of domestic opinion leaders affecting public opinion. Former President Richard Nixon called on the public to rally around their president when he said that "the American hostages will be released if the nation stands firmly behind President Carter in his efforts to resolve the situation."[39] Brody and Shapiro suggest that negative messages attributed to foreign sources are likely to enhance, not harm, presidential approval. Very negative statements by the Iranian captors and their supporters, especially the Ayatollah Khomeini, were plentiful in the media coverage all through November.

Domestic critics were practically silent during the first half of December but while the president's general approval rating rose, there was an 8 point drop in public support for his handling of the Iran situation. One possible explanation is that the crisis-specific approval level of 77 percent was a spontaneous reaction to President Carter's news conference in late November that declined just as quickly once the amount of negative Iran messages began to drop.

Carter's support declined sharply in the second half of December when the volume of negative statements from domestic elites increased dramatically. Political opponents attacked Carter's decision not to participate in primary debates or in other campaign activities as long as the American hostages were held in Iran. William Safire wrote, "The President is better off running against Khomeini and Ghotbzadeh than Kennedy and Brown, which is why—for the first time—Mr. Carter finds the White House a refuge instead of a trap." The columnist also criticized the President's crisis management directly, pointing out that, "The reason Mr. Carter's political exploitation of the crisis will fail is that after eight weeks, Americans are awakening to the fact that their president has been doing nothing."[40]

Domestic critics began to openly question the President's management of the crisis during a time when the news contained surprisingly few negative Iranian foe messages. Once the critics at home had entered the public debate in force, they did not retreat in the first part of January when news reports reflected a new outburst of verbal attacks by foes in Iran. On the contrary, the attacks on the President's handling of the Iran crisis became increasingly caustic. One of his rivals in the Democratic primaries, Governor Jerry Brown of California, said in early January: "I'll tell you one thing, I wouldn't let the Ayatollah Khomeini dictate the terms of my campaign."[41] He and others who criticized the "Rose Garden strategy" that kept the President in the White House argued that Carter's participation in primary debates would not hurt the hostages.

Notwithstanding the striking change in the Iran debate between the first part of December and late January, Carter's overall approval rating rose another 4 points to its peak of 58 percent. The problem with associating elite leadership and general approval, especially over longer time periods, is that other variables come into play. In this case, the Soviet invasion of Afghanistan in late December and the President's prime time address to the nation in response to the Soviet action helped maintain his respectable overall approval. The President's State of the Union Address on January 23, 1980, which dealt with both Afghanistan and Iran, also gave his public support a boost.

But during this same period, public support for Carter's handling of the hostage ordeal took a nosedive, declining 13 points to 56 percent by mid-January. During the weeks when another international rally event—the Soviet invasion of Afghanistan—was very much in the news, the Iran-specific approval polls showed that the public had increasingly lost confidence in Carter's management of the Iran crisis. By the middle of January his incident-specific approval rating had lost 21 percentage points from its highest level in the first half of December.

Even while the general approval rally was sustained in the wake of the Afghanistan situation, there were increasing signs of growing elite dissatisfaction with the President's overall job performance. The Iran problem was merely one of many areas of dissatisfaction. During a telecast of "Meet the Press" *Washington*

Post columnist David Broder posed a question to the President that summarized the many factors considered in an evaluation of Carter's effectiveness. Broder told the President: "With all due respect, we still have 5.8 percent unemployment. Inflation has risen from 4.8 percent to 13 percent. We still don't have a viable energy policy. Russian troops are in Cuba and Afghanistan. The dollar is falling. Gold is rising. And the hostages, after 78 days, are still in Teheran. Just what have you done, sir, to deserve renomination?" A few minutes later, Judy Woodruff spoke about the President's "misery index."[42] A week later, for the first time since the beginning of the hostage crisis, public approval of Carter's overall job handling decreased.

In the early part of February, for the first time since the hostage taking, the record of domestic sources in the Iran coverage contained more negative than positive messages. Neither a modest increase in negative messages attributed to sources in Iran nor a formal presidential press conference on the evening of February 13, 1980 halted the loss of approval. Page and Shapiro have presented evidence that popular presidents (whose approval ratings are 50 percent or more) have some impact on public opinion and that unpopular presidents (whose approval ratings are less than 50 percent) "definitely do not have much success at opinion leadership."[43] While Carter was technically still a "popular" president, his general approval was falling, losing 12 points between early February and early March. During these weeks, Carter simply lost his effectiveness to lead and shape public opinion. Moreover, threats, accusations, and demands by the Iranian captors and their supporters no longer boosted the President's public support at home. Americans had become inured to the reports of anti-American and anti-Carter outbursts by the Ayatollah Khomeini and others in Iran.

Brody and Shapiro suggest that when domestic leadership "does not rally or run for cover" and the media reflect this debate, the public takes its clues for evaluating presidential performances from event-related developments.[44] During a two week period ending in early March, several American diplomats who had been hiding in the Canadian embassy in Teheran, left Iran with false passports. Their homecoming, followed by a reception at the White House, and an outpouring of gratitude for the courage of Canadian diplomats in this quiet rescue of six Americans was the first good news about the Iran situation. In addition, the newly elected Iranian president, Abolhassan Bani-Sadr, and other officials in Teheran signaled their willingness to take control of the hostages in a first step to resolve the crisis. These developments explain the temporary halt in the slide of—and a 2 point gain in—the President's crisis-specific approval rating. Obviously, the public shifted to a wait-and-see, and perhaps even a slightly hopeful, attitude.

Both the general and the incident-specific approval of the President's performance took massive blows in the first part of March, when Ayatollah Khomeini announced his opposition to the transfer of the American hostages from the control of their captors at the U.S. Embassy to Iranian government officials. As hopes for the resolution of the crisis vanished, the public blamed the President for the continuing deadlock and his approval ratings dropped sharply by 9 points (general approval) and 11 points (Iran-related approval). For the first time since the beginning of the crisis, President Carter's crisis-specific approval fell below the 50 percent mark. The occasional surges of positive media messages attributed to domestic elites could not stop the declines: by this time the President and high officials in his administration were the sole sources of supportive messages, but they had lost their credibility and were unable to influence the public. For the same reason, formal and informal presidential news sessions did not work as they had in the earlier stage of the Iran crisis. By late March both approval ratings had slipped to 39 percent—a dismal level for a President faced with a major foreign policy crisis.

The Failed Rescue Mission and the Polls

Two weeks before the April 24, 1980 attempted rescue mission, 39 percent of the public approved and 50 percent disapproved of the way Jimmy Carter handled his job as President. The first poll after the ill-fated mission revealed a 4 point gain in overall approval. In the crisis-specific approval polls there was a more robust presidential rally: a 7 point increase from the last pre-mission to the first post-mission poll. But after this quick surge—a combination of patriotic reflex, momentary elite reluctance to criticize the President's decision, and President Carter's swiftly addressing the public—both approval measures dipped below their previous dismal levels before the rescue attempt.

The Iran case also demonstrates that the public is willing to completely reverse its evaluation if circumstances change drastically. Because the crisis ended minutes after President Reagan had been sworn into office, no approval questions concerning Jimmy Carter were conducted after the hostages' release. But another survey item is telling in this respect: Beginning in April 1980 and throughout the year, more than 60 percent of the public characterized President Carter's handling of the Iran incident (according to Louis Harris/ABC News polls) as a failure; but in January 1981, after the hostages had been freed, 61 percent of the American people called the then former President Carter's handling of the crisis a success.

For Jimmy Carter and his supporters this turnaround came about three months too late, and it strengthened the argument of those who had come to believe strongly that the hostage ordeal cost Carter a second term in the White House. It will never be known whether President Carter would have been reelected in spite of his poor approval ratings before the takeover of the American embassy. But given the tremendous surge in public support for the former President once the hostages were safe, voters probably would have rallied around the President had the Iran episode ended before the election.

President Reagan and the TWA Hijacking

A few days before Shiite terrorists hijacked TWA flight 847 en route from Athens to Rome in mid-June 1985, a Gallup poll found that 58 percent of the public approved of President Reagan's performance. About a month later and more than ten days after the resolution of the TWA incident, Reagan's approval stood at 63 percent. Moreover, the presidential approval rating rose another 2 points in a subsequent survey.

The TWA case, like the Iranian hostage crisis, confirms that incident-specific surveys are more accurate indicators of how the public evaluates a president during highly salient international events than overall approval ratings. Poll data presented in table 5.3 reveal a quick, initial rally round the president expressed in a 5 point general approval jump. But this surge was not accompanied by approval gains in crisis-related polls. In fact, approval of the President's foreign policy performance (in response to the question: "Do you approve or disapprove of the way Reagan is handling foreign affairs?") decreased slightly by 2 points to 46 percent. Three days after the hijacking, with Reagan's overall approval at 62 percent, only 48 percent of the public supported the way the President handled the hijacking crisis (in response to the question: "Do you approve or disapprove of Reagan's handling of the hostage situation?").

Table 5.3
The TWA Hijacking: Reagan's Public Approval Ratings

	general	foreign policy	incident specific
May 13, 1985	57%	48%	–
June 14—hijacking of TWA flight 847			
June 17, 1985	62%	46%	48%
June 18—nationally televised presidential news conference			
June 19, 1985	62%	55%	68%
June 22, 1985	62%	53%	69%
June 30—release of hostages			
July 1, 1985	65%	–	72%

Source: ABC News/*Washington Post*

Two days later, with Reagan's general approval rating unchanged, pollsters found the public rallying very strongly behind the president: the incident-specific approval rating surged 20 points to 68 percent, the favorable foreign affairs rating increased 9 points to 55 percent. After the crisis ended without further loss of life (Marine diver Robert Stethem had been murdered early in the hijacking) the overall and the crisis-related approval ratings made additional, modest gains.

What explains the modest rally in the general approval rating and the absence of strong public support for Reagan's handling of foreign affairs and the hijacking during the first days of the crisis? The media record of those first three days shows that President Reagan and other administration officials were virtually the only participants in the public debate. There was neither support nor criticism from the most likely elite quarters—members of Congress, experts, ex-government officials. It seems that the public, while perhaps instinctively rallying around the president in general terms, adopted the wait-and-see attitude of opinion leaders outside the administration with respect to Reagan's crisis-specific performance.

At the same time, the public reacted to the great amount of information the media provided with anger and demands to stand up to terrorism this time around. A report by Bernard Goldberg on the CBS Evening News on the third day of the crisis captured the general mood:

> Bernard Goldberg: From one end to the country to the other, Americans are speaking with a loud voice, a voice filled with frustration and anger. Dallas, Texas.
> Man: The ones—actual ones that did it, they ought to drag them off the plane and execute them right there.
> Man: I wish they put the Texas Rangers on them.
> Goldberg: Miami, Florida.
> Voice of Woman Radio Announcer: 6:10, WIOD, south Florida's information and sports authority.
> Woman Radio Caller: We're the strongest country in the world. We have more power, and this little band of maniacs can control us.
> Man: They should just move right in and say, look, you know, nobody gets out unless we get the hostages back.
> Goldberg: In the Midwest, there is a feeling of helplessness and outrage. Minneapolis, Minnesota.

Man: Helpless to the extent that we can't seem to do anything about terrorists and outraged that this happens to
Americans more and more often.

Goldberg: In the Rockies, the voices are voices of retaliation. Watkins, Colorado.

Man: Tell them they can have what they want and then
blow them up. [Laughs] That's what I'd do.

Goldberg: All over America, there is a feeling that it is time
to draw the line. Atlanta, Georgia.

Man: Eventually, you're going to have to take drastic measures, or you're going to find it knocking at your front
door.

Goldberg: A cab driver in San Francisco.

Cab driver: I think if we keep turning the other cheek, we're
going to be looked upon as a paper tiger.

Goldberg: And San Diego.

Man: We don't negotiate with them, that's for sure. We
retaliate and we teach them that you don't mess around
with Americans, in my opinion.

Goldberg: The voices are coming from all over America, the
message is plain and to the point, enough is enough.

In the absence of opinion leadership by political elites outside the administration, the public looked to the event itself and
formed its own attitudes about the President's handling of the
hostage situation. Finally, after several days, the public learned
how opinion leaders other than the President and his aides felt
about his crisis-management. Aware of growing public frustration with another hostage ordeal, Hamilton Jordan, who had
been White House chief of staff during the Iranian hostage crisis, publicly expressed his support of President Reagan. Recalling his experience in the Carter White House, Jordan pleaded
with the public to "give the benefit of the doubt to the President
and the people in the administration who are trying to resolve
this problem."[45]

Former National Security Adviser Zbigniew Brzezinski also
refused to criticize the President. Brzezinski said, "I believe at
this stage the President deserves our support. We would have
welcomed all the support we could have had during the difficult

115

Iranian hostage days. I'm going to support the President 100 percent and not second guess him."[46] Former President Carter urged Americans to "give President Reagan our full support and encouragement."[47] And Senator Alan Cranston, after a White House meeting with the President, remarked that the President had "the support of members of Congress."[48] Even editorial page editors, who were otherwise not reluctant to criticize President Reagan, came to his support. The *New York Times*, for example, did not remind Reagan of his hawkish attitude during the Iranian hostage crisis and instead concluded, "The question honed by the hijacking and cowardly murder is not whether the President is behaving consistently but whether he is behaving wisely, and so far the answer is yes."[49] Toward the end of the crisis, CBS News anchor Dan Rather summed up the position of domestic opinion leaders when he observed that "criticism, if any, about how the U.S. government has handled this hostage situation has been understandably muted."[50]

The little criticism that was voiced came from quarters generally supportive of Ronald Reagan. Unhappy with his non-military approach to resolving the crisis, the *Wall Street Journal* criticized the President in an editorial under the headline "Jimmy Reagan." And former National Security aide William Quandt commented negatively on the news that Reagan was considering closing the Beirut Airport or a blockade of Lebanon. Quandt called such measures "little tokens. They—they will be laughed at by the people in the Middle East. They . . . make the United States look, I think, like a helpless giant that it doesn't want to appear to be."[51]

The public followed opinion leaders: as long as elites and especially opponents of the President kept quiet, a modest general approval rally occurred—perhaps the result of patriotic reflexes. But when the mass media reflected positive domestic elite messages and continued negative messages from the Beirut terrorists and their supporters the public rallied around the flag and the President.

A 20 point crisis-specific approval jump occurred between the day before and the day after President Reagan's nationally televised news conference on the evening of June 17. No doubt, as Gilboa has suggested, "going public" had a strong influence on the positive evaluation of Reagan's crisis-management.[52] However, the strong rally was the result of several factors: presidential persuasion, the absence of domestic elite criticism, the preponderance of domestic elite support, and negative media messages from foes in Lebanon.

The Bombing of Libya

A solid majority of the American public (62 percent) was satisfied with President Reagan's job performance when he gave the green light for what he called retaliatory and preemptive bombing strikes against targets in Libya. In the preceding months, the administration had frequently blamed Libyan leader Moammar Qaddafi for sponsoring and masterminding deadly anti-American terrorism. The first full scale U.S. military counterterrorist action (other than attempts to rescue hostages or capture known terrorists) came at a time when such a move had been rumored, reported, and discussed in the mass media for several days.

Once the actual air raids had occurred, the reaction of domestic opinion leaders was swift: those who usually supported the President, as well as his traditional opponents, rallied behind him in what seemed like a spontaneous patriotic reflex. Contrary to their reactions in cases of terrorist-induced incidents such as the Iranian and TWA hijacking crises, most opinion leaders took an immediate stand.

Less than twenty-four hours after the air attacks, CBS anchor Dan Rather described the reaction in Congress: "In the great House of the people on Capitol Hill, the Capitol of the United States of America, as elsewhere in this country today, there was unusual solidarity and sentiment in support of the air strikes ordered by President Reagan against Libya." To illustrate this strong elite support, CBS showed a clip of House Speaker Thomas P. O'Neill, a Democrat, lining up behind the Republican President by stating that "all this has started because of the evil heart of a bad man. Every time he escalates we have to strike. He has to be brought to his knees on a thing like this. He has to learn a lesson."[53]

One day later, the *New York Times* reported that one leading Democrat had expressed reservations about the military action. Senator Robert C. Byrd (D-West Virginia) was quoted as saying, "I'm concerned about this approach we're taking. Are we going to do this again and again?"[54] In addition, a few lawmakers reserved judgment until they had more facts about the military mission.

The *Times* was among the first media organizations to lend strong editorial support to the President's decision to "punish" Qaddafi. In its April 15 edition, the *Times* editorialized that "even the most scrupulous citizen can only approve and applaud the American attack on Libya. It's emotionally satisfying to say that Colonel Qaddafi deserves whatever he gets; the Reagan Administration has now proved he richly deserves what he got."[55] Over the next five days, the *Times* published two additional and equally supportive editorials, one of them concluding that with the bombing raids "America sent a justifiable different message. The tiger bites."[56]

Table 5.4
Presidential Approval and the Bombing of Libya

	general	incident-specific
April 11–14, 1986	62%	–
April 14—nationally televised presidential address to the nation		
April 24–28, 1986	–	72%
May 15–19, 1986	–	70%
May 16–19, 1986	68%	–

Source:ABC News/*Washington Post* surveys

Given this strong support even among opinion makers normally inclined to oppose President Reagan, the 6 point gain in general approval in the aftermath of the attack on Libyan targets was not as strong as might be expected. This may have been due to the fact that the President's approval was already at a high level. But the event-specific public approval ratings in table 5.4 (in response to the question: "Do you approve or disapprove of the way Ronald Reagan is handling relations with Libya?")underline how substantial the rally was.

It seems that Americans rallied immediately to support the President's bombing decision: a CBS News/*New York Times* poll on April 15, the day after the U.S. attack on Libyan targets, revealed that 77 percent of the public approved of the military action. By the end of April, the level of public support was at 65 percent.[57]

One possible reason why neither the general nor the specific approval ratings went through the ceiling—as happened frequently in the wake of U.S. military interventions in, for example, Panama in 1989 and the Persian Gulf conflict in early 1991—was the widely held view that President Reagan's decision to fight terrorism militarily would trigger additional violence against American targets.This fear was justified: almost immediately after the bombing of Tripoli and Benghazi, terrorist attacks against U.S. targets were reported from different parts of the world. Hours after the American action against Qaddafi, an American working at the U.S. Embassy in Khartoum, Sudan, was shot and injured in what officials believed was a retaliatory attack. Two days later, Peter Kilburn, one of the American hostages held in Lebanon by terrorist groups, was killed in retaliation for the U.S. air attack. Also on April 17, the Marine guard compound at the U.S. Embassy in Tunis, Tunisia, was firebombed. A few hours later, four Libyans were caught by Turkish authorities as they were placing a bomb in an American officers' club in Ankara. Soon thereafter, an explosive device was defused at the American Express office in Istanbul.

The Bombing of the World Trade Center

The first terrorist spectacular inside the United States, in February 1993, was treated like a domestic emergency even though the international dimensions of the World Trade Center explosion were suspected and discussed by law enforcement officials, the media, and the public in the immediate aftermath. While the White House expressed concern and kept abreast of developments, President Clinton did not act as the crisis manager nor was he perceived to be, as were Presidents Carter, Reagan, and Bush during and after earlier terrorist actions abroad. President Clinton's stance did not change as evidence mounted that the terror in New York had its roots in the political turmoil of the Middle East.

With the President seemingly not directly involved in managing the "domestic" event, the bombing had no bearing on his public approval ratings. The rally phenomenon is, after all, closely tied to international events, especially crises, that directly involve the president.

In the future, however, the chief executive may have to assume the role of the crisis manager—even if the event occurs on American soil. Following the World Trade Center blast and the alleged multiple bombing plot that was to follow, future incidents of this kind may be viewed in the international, not the domestic, context.

What Drives Presidential Rallies?

Terrorist spectaculars during the Carter and Reagan years produced in their earliest phases more or less robust public rallies. Perhaps driven by patriotic reflexes in the initial stages of terrorist crises, presidential approval levels depended on the degree to which domestic elites and foreign terrorist foes participated in the mass-mediated debate. The public was especially sensitive to the support for or opposition to presidential action voiced by domestic opinion leaders. The cases in this chapter also established that a president with high approval ratings was in an excellent position to boost his public support by "going public" via televised addresses to the nation or news conferences.

Event-specific approval surveys were instrumental in detecting and explaining the underlying strength and weakness of each presidential rally examined in this chapter. The case studies suggest that the rally phenomenon cannot be understood fully by analyzing only general public approval ratings; overall presidential support can be and in many instances is affected by variables not related to rally or potential rally events. In the case of terrorist spectaculars abroad, the incident-specific approval was the most informative indicator. Based on this finding, there is reason to suspect that paying attention to crisis-specific presidential approval ratings in addition to the commonly consulted general job-performance measure also enhances our understanding of presidential rallies unrelated to international terrorism.

Because presidential rallies in response to international terrorist spectaculars are neither automatic nor irreversible, chief executives and their advisers are faced with tremendous difficulties in managing such crises. The following chapter deals with decision makers' dilemmas during major hostage situations.

CHAPTER SIX
_____

DECISION MAKERS AND
THEIR HARD CHOICES

The first principle in a terrorist situation in my view should be: what is in the best interest of the American people as a whole.

—ALEXANDER HAIG

Of all the methods of violence utilized by terrorists, hostage situations are the most stressful experiences for decision makers and, in the American setting, for the president. Hostage-taking has been called "smart" or "classic" terrorism because "the fundamental characteristic that distinguishes a hostage incident from other, more conventional, foreign policy problems is the constant and unyielding awareness that the lives and welfare of individual, identifiable human beings are at stake."[1] According to Gary Sick, the principal White House aide on Iran during the Iranian hostage crisis, such incidents are "generically different" from all other foreign policy problems.[2] Politically motivated hostage situations require the president and his advisers to make tough choices.

One day before the failed Iranian rescue attempt on April 24, 1980, President Carter insisted that the overall interests of the nation and the special interest of the hostages in Teheran had to be balanced, and that he had never had to face the problem of choosing between the two. Instead, Carter said, "I think every action that I've taken so far and every action that I would contemplate in the future would not be to abandon either one of those commitments of mine: our nation's prestige and interest on the one hand, the hostages' lives and safety and freedom on the other."[3] But regardless of how the President rationalized his then secret decision to launch a rescue mission, he was well aware that even his closest advisers had been unable to bridge the gap between the nation's interest as a superpower and the interests of the U.S. citizens held hostage in the Iranian capital.

The conflict between the desire to protect the life of each hostage and the need to act in the national interest was central to the considerations and deliberations of those involved in managing the Iran crisis. Secretary of State Cyrus Vance was a tireless advocate for the hostages (i.e., not doing anything that might endanger their lives), which in his view was compatible with the nation's geopolitical strategy, while National Security Adviser Zbigniew Brzezinski came down firmly on the side of the national interest. Unlike Carter and Vance, Brzezinski "was painfully aware that at some point perhaps a choice between the two might even have to be made."[4] In recommending the rescue mission and simultaneous retaliatory strikes Brzezinski argued that decision makers had "to think beyond the fate of the fifty Americans."[5] So strong was the disagreement between Vance and other top advisers on this issue that the Secretary of State decided to resign once Brzezinski's view prevailed and the President approved the rescue attempt.

Decision makers were confronted with the same dilemma during the long ordeal of several Americans held captive in Beirut by Shiite groups with close ties to Iran. Although insisting publicly that his administration would never make deals with terrorists, Ronald Reagan authorized secret arms-for-hostages exchanges with Iran. Like President Carter during the Iranian crisis, President Reagan rationalized his decision as serving both the national good (establishing ties to moderate factions in Iran) and the special cause of the hostages (winning their release).

In his memoirs, Reagan wrote, "To this day I still believe that the Iran initiative was *not* [in the first place] an effort to swap arms for hostages. . . . I still believe that the policy that led us to attempt to open up a channel to moderate Iranians wasn't wrong."[6] But at least two of his senior advisers saw it differently: Secretary of State George Shultz and Secretary of Defense Caspar Weinberger were vehemently opposed to the arms transactions because they were blatant violations of official U.S. policy which was formulated and actively promoted to serve the nation's goals.

President Bush, too, faced terrorist situations that brought him to the same hard choices as his predecessors. When Lebanese terrorists announced the murder of Lieut. Col. William Higgins in the summer of 1989 and threatened to kill other American hostages, George Bush agonized over a military response that would have furthered the overall national interest but endangered the lives of the remaining American captives in Lebanon. The administration strongly warned the Lebanese terrorists and their backers in Iran that the President was determined to put America's interest first should one more U.S. hostage be harmed. The captors and their sponsors backed down. Thus, we will never know whether or not Bush would have followed through with his threat. A year later, when Iraq's Saddam Hussein held hundreds of Americans captive in order to discourage American military action, families and friends of those held in Iraq wondered, "Is President Bush willing to impose a death sentence on Americans held hostage by Saddam Hussein?"[7] Bush's position was unequivocal: "Our hearts go out to the hostages and their families. But our policy cannot change. And it will not change," he told a joint session of Congress.[8] This stand was exactly what some administration officials had advocated for years and what ABC News anchor Peter Jennings had spoken of after the TWA hijacking: "As a citizen as well as a journalist, I would like the president to say at some point, 'Yes, I am concerned about the lives of 39 Americans, but I am responsible for 239 million Americans.' "[9]

Terrorism experts suspected nevertheless at the time that George Bush's resolve might weaken if hostages were harmed. Once again, the President's public decision was not tested because the Iraqi ruler released all hostages before the U.S.-led allied offensive commenced.

By targeting innocent individuals—especially by taking hostages—terrorists put a target government into a no-win situation: if decision makers decide that the national interest calls for a military response and the refusal to give in to terrorist demands, they jeopardize the lives of citizens; if they make a deal to spare hostages, they risk more violence and more demands. Either choice may undermine public trust in a government that is expected to protect both its citizens' lives and the national interest.

During hostage incidents like the Iranian crisis, the TWA hijacking, and the long captivity of Americans in Lebanon, international terrorists manage to cut even a superpower down to the size of a roaring mouse—mostly by creating this dilemma of the individual versus national interest. And there is little doubt that news coverage is the principal reason why governments in democratic states have such a hard time making choices that best serve the national interest. By emphasizing the human interest aspects of terrorist events, by focusing their reporting on the predicament of innocent victims and on the fears and tears of their mothers, fathers, wives, husbands, children, friends, and neighbors, the media tilt their coverage toward the more personal concerns of the victims and their loved ones while at the same time paying less attention to government officials and others who represent the broader interests of the nation as a whole.

Television highlights the plight of victims and the people close to them because dramatic and emotion-laden human interest shots of victims and their families satisfy the visual medium much more than pictures of "talking heads" typical of the coverage of the White House and other government beats. Prayer services, candlelight vigils, communities engrossed in putting yellow ribbons around trees, or letters-to-hostages campaigns make better stories for television than the speeches of administration officials. As a result, television transforms political problems and crises which call for rational responses into personal dramas and tragedies which demand compassionate reactions. Alexander Haig has suggested that "the emotional climate created by television in a hostage situation leads to national pronouncements in which the lives of the hostages take precedence over the broader interests of the American people as a whole."[10]

Henry Kissinger recognized the ability of TV coverage to frame the profound conflict between the special interests of the victims of terrorist acts and their families versus the broad interests of all Americans. The special interests persuade decision makers to satisfy the demands of hostage-holders and refrain from responding militarily; the broad interests reject concessions to terrorists and insist on protecting the vital interests of the nation—even by military means.[11] In spite of the solid arguments for the government to serve the national interest, the hostages and their families have other priorities. And a great deal of the news coverage during hostage situations favors those personal concerns.

George Will has characterized the way the news media report the suffering of the victims of terrorism and especially the concerns and anxieties of their relatives as the "pornography of grief."[12] But hostage families and the survivors of terrorist victims feel otherwise. Relatives of the victims of Pan Am flight 103 organized themselves into a lobbying group to pursue legal action against those responsible for the downing and they use the news media very effectively to apply pressure on reluctant decision makers in Washington.

Peggy Say, sister of Lebanon hostage Terry Anderson, did not agree with those who argued that media coverage prolonged the hostages' ordeals because publicity was among the foremost goals of terrorists and their sponsors.[13] While her brother and several other Americans were held by the Hizbollah, Say lobbied and pleaded relentlessly for substantial and frequent news coverage in order to force government officials to deal with the problem of "the forgotten seven" and make decisions in the hostages' best interests. When administration officials refused to rule out a military response to the TWA hijacking, she warned, "If they go in and bomb the terrorists, then Terry is a dead man; either the guards will kill him or we will."[14]

Say and other relatives of the longtime hostages in Lebanon were stunned by the attention the media paid to the TWA hijacking. Say described this as "the most traumatic time for the hostage families because all the attention that the passengers got could have been given to Terry and the others months and years before."[15] But during the TWA incident the press also reported about the other Americans held by Lebanese terrorists and thereby forced the Reagan administration to focus on the fate of these "forgotten" victims. As Peggy Say saw it, "The media had caused it. *Our* taking our cause to the media had caused it. We had won a commitment from the media and the government that these would never be the forgotten seven again."[16]

Terry Anderson's sister was not the only relative to recognize that media coverage was instrumental in putting the plight of the hostages permanently onto the administration's agenda. The family of Lebanon hostage Father Lawrence Martin Jenco, a Catholic priest from Illinois, was initially fairly unsophisticated in the ways of publicity and media exposure. But before long, they "stormed the country with a media plan so ambitious that a presidential candidate would have been proud of it. Thirteen Jenco relatives sat down and divided the entire nation among themselves like conquering generals."[17] They scheduled interviews with media organizations in 47 states and drew public attention to the situation of their brother and other hostages and the government's "do nothing" posture. "If it wasn't for the media," one of Father Jenco's brothers concluded, "the plight of the hostages would have been dormant."[18] Terrorists are delighted when relatives of hostages pressure and berate their governments. After Father Jenco was released by terrorists in Beirut, he told Peggy Say that his and Terry Anderson's captors had said to her brother, "Boy, your sister really sticks it to the government." Obviously pleased with Say, they asked Jenco to give her their condolences on the death of her father and brother.[19] The Shiite kid-nappers followed the American media and thus were well informed about her lobbying efforts on behalf of her brother.

While the media campaigns by Mrs. Say, the Jencos, and other relatives resulted in a great deal of news coverage, no act of international terrorism against American targets was more extensively reported than the 1985 TWA hijacking. The terrorists themselves and their Amal allies unleashed a publicity strategy unparalleled in the history of modern terrorism. They manipulated the U.S. media into highlighting sources who emphasized the hijacking victims and their relatives and friends. Robert Oakley, at the time the Director of the State Department Office for Combating Terrorism, described the circus-like atmosphere: film crews and correspondents rushed to Beirut where special events were arranged for them, including an exclusive television network interview with Amal leader Nabih Birri; another dramatic exclusive of TWA captain John Testrake in the cockpit with a hooded terrorist holding a pistol to his head; live briefings by terrorists, Amal representatives, and hostage spokesman Allyn Conwell; a press conference featuring many of the hostages; a surprise dinner hosted by the terrorists for the hostages at a beachfront hotel with TV coverage of the event. Family members were interviewed extensively and some were flown in to act as surrogate correspondents in obtaining information on their loved ones.[20]

But if hostage families were exploited by the media for the sake of human interest coverage, many of the relatives became members or leaders of a pressure group that used the press to lobby on behalf of the hostages. Gary Sick was impressed with the media skills of some members of this ad hoc lobby who "performed better than most assistant secretaries of state that I'd run into."[21]

These accounts are validated by systematic research. My quantitative analysis of CBS coverage of the TWA hostage crisis found that in its evening newscasts the network based nearly 2 1/2 times more of its reporting on news sources who clearly supported the special interests of the Americans held captive in

Beirut (i.e., the hostages, their families, friends, neighbors) than on sources perceived as protecting the national interest (the President and other administration officials). Next to media sources who provided descriptions, explanations, and background information, the hostages and the people closest to them were the most frequently covered news sources of the TWA drama, with President Reagan and other administration officials a distant third. The terrorists and their Amal allies got nearly as much network coverage as officials in the Reagan administration.Both the hostages families and America's foes in Lebanon insisted that only the fulfillment of the hijackers' demands—the release of hundreds of Shiites held in Israeli prisons—would free the hostages. Thus, a case can be made that the coverage of sources pushing for the special interest of a few over those associated with the national interest was in the ratio of 3 to –1. (See figure 6.1)

In the case of the TWA hijacking there was a striking difference in the source selection of CBS News and the *New York Times*. Both news organizations based the greatest part of their coverage on journalistic descriptions, background information, analyses, etc., but here the similarity ended. Unlike CBS, the *Times* devoted more attention to President Reagan and other administration sources (692 paragraphs) than to the hostages and their families, friends, and neighbors (560 paragraphs). Yet, if one categorizes the American foes in Lebanon (terrorists, their Amal allies, other sympathizers) as supporting the special interest views of the hijack victims and their loved ones, the source selection of the *Times*, too, turned out to be disadvantageous to the President and other administration officials who were perceived as protectors of the national interest (see figure 6.2). However, the ratio of special interest over national interest sources (773 versus 692) was not as extreme as in the CBS coverage.

During the first five-and-a-half months of the Iranian hostage crisis, the CBS Evening News coverage of the incident was tilted in favor of sources pushing for the U.S. government to act in the best interest of the hostages and their loved ones. My content

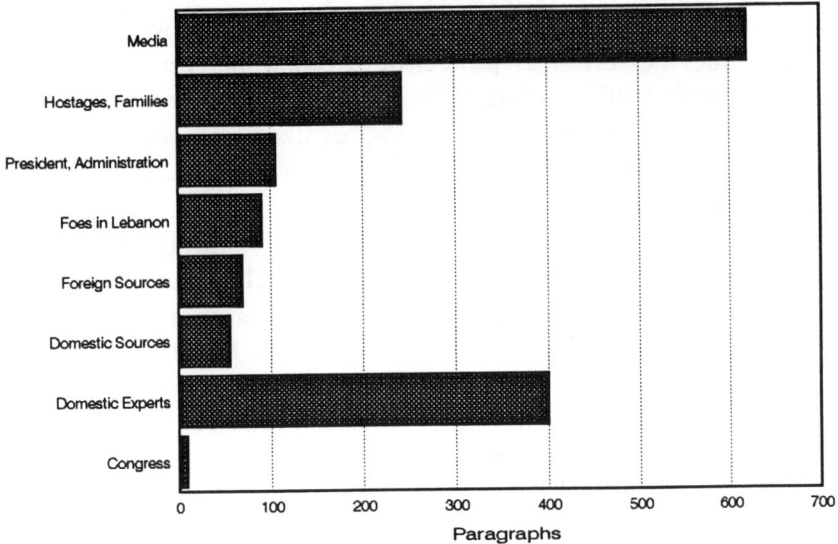

Figure 6.1
Coverage of TWA Hijacking Crisis on CBS News
from 6/14/85 to 6/30/85

analysis of relevant CBS transcripts revealed that 802 paragraphs were based on sources articulating the special interest and only 566 paragraphs on administration sources perceived as national interest advocates. In contrast, in the *New York Times* national sources (President Carter and other administration officials) had a slight advantage (2,877 paragraphs) over special interest sources, such as the hostages, their relatives and friends, and American foes in Iran (2,598 paragraphs).

The opposite occurred during the hijacking of the Italian cruise ship *Achille Lauro* in October 1985, when more incident-related coverage on the CBS Evening News focused on administration sources (69 paragraphs) than on ex-passengers, hostage families, and terrorists (57 paragraphs). In the *New York Times*, national interest sources had a slight advantage over special interest sources (662 paragraphs to 625 paragraphs).

These coverage patterns were not lost on the American public. As chapter 4 described, American attitudes toward terrorism are not static but responsive to incident-specific information that is

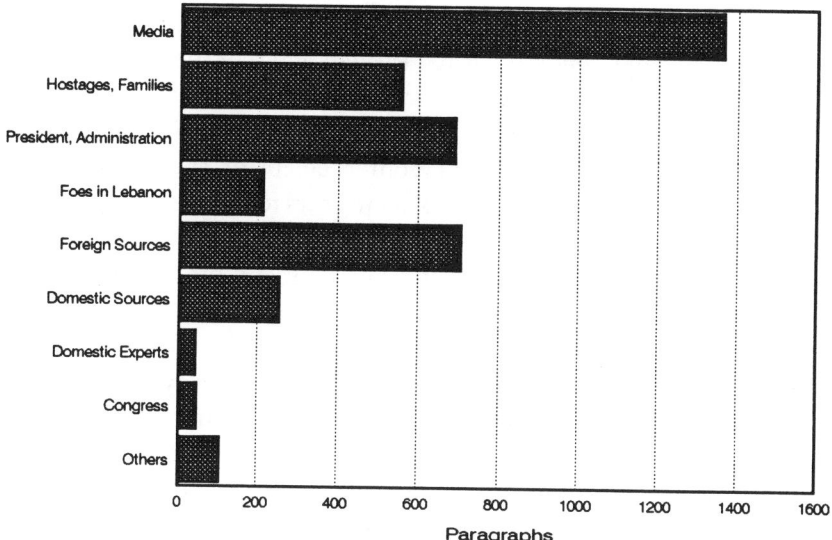

Figure 6.2
Coverage of TWA Hijacking Crisis in New York Times
from 6/15/85 to 7/1/85

mostly, if not exclusively, conveyed through the mass media. And since television typically favors sources promoting personal over national interest considerations, public sentiment is often swayed in favor of the victims: thus, during the TWA hostage situation, three public opinion polls found that 59 percent, 53 percent, and 57 percent, respectively, of respondents wanted the U.S. government to negotiate for the release of the hostages even if that meant giving in to terrorist demands.[22]

The Personalization of Terrorist Crises

Decision makers also get much of their information about terrorist incidents from the media. During the Iranian hostage crisis President Carter reportedly "spent more time watching the three television sets simultaneously beaming the latest news about the crisis into the Oval Office than he did reading CIA cables containing the latest evaluations of how to deal with it."[23] And when the TWA hijackers struck, President Reagan and others in his decision making team relied heavily on the media for information. Thus, when reporters asked Reagan whether the TWA crew was still aboard the hijacked airliner, the President answered, "Oh, yes, I saw it on television."[24]

Moreover, once the media confer celebrity status on the hostages and their families, decision makers feel more pressure to give in to relatives' demands for personal meetings. During the Iran crisis President Carter met repeatedly and his Secretary of State Cyrus Vance frequently with members of hostage families. Carter's National Security Adviser Brzezinski "deliberately decided to avoid such meetings in order not to be swayed by emotions."[25] He was convinced that the policy positions of Carter and Vance were affected by their emotional reactions to the personalization of the hostages. Media coverage and meetings between decision makers and hostage families gave the victims of terrorism a human face and transformed a foreign policy problem into a highly emotional human quandary with domestic implications.

During the earliest phase of the TWA hijacking, presidential advisers made great efforts to prevent Ronald Reagan from interrupting his normal schedule and thereby admitting that a handful of terrorists had forced him to deal with their actions. But before long the President did participate in the first of a number of White House crisis sessions and he reacted like most other Americans who followed the hostage drama on their TV sets—he valued the lives of the hostages more than his own declared policies. According to one account,

> Reagan was determined to end this outrage quickly. The public will demand satisfaction, he said, according to notes taken at the meeting. . . . The President turned to the prospects for a peaceful settlement. Release the hostages and we'll get the Israelis to release the Amal prisoners, the President suggested, according to the notes. Secretary of State Shultz had to argue strenuously to convince the President that the administration's policy of not making concessions to terrorists included not encouraging others to make concessions.[26]

While the TWA incident ended fairly quickly with the release of the hostages, the Americans already held by Lebanese terrorists before the U.S. airliner had been hijacked remained in captivity. And because the news media had repeatedly reported about the "forgotten Lebanon hostages" during the TWA ordeal, President Reagan became increasingly concerned, if not obsessed, with the remaining hostages and efforts to win their release. In his memoirs Reagan recalled his preoccupation with the fate of the Lebanon hostages:

> Our options were few, and I spent many hours late at night wondering how we could rescue the hostages, trying to sleep while images of those lonely Americans rolled past in my mind. . . . As president, as far as I was concerned, I had the duty to get those Americans home. Almost every morning at my national security briefings, I began by asking the same question: "Any progress on getting the hostages out of Lebanon?"[27]

Jimmy Carter described the long months of the Iranian hostage crisis in similar terms; it was the most difficult experience of his life. Recalling the agony of this period he wrote in his autobiography:

> The safety and well-being of the hostages became a constant concern for me, no matter what other duties I was performing as President. I would walk in the White House gardens early in the morning and lie awake at night, trying to think of additional steps I could take to gain their freedom without sacrificing the honor and security of our nation. I listened to every proposal, no matter how preposterous, all the way from delivering the Shah for trial as the revolutionaries demanded to dropping an atomic bomb on Teheran.[28]

President Bush also had to deal with the personal tragedies of hostages held by terrorist groups in Lebanon and their loved ones at home. The first crisis of his presidential term came when Lebanese terrorists released a videotape of hostage Lieut. Colonel William Higgins hanging from a scaffold and threatened to exe-

cute American hostage Joseph Cicippio next. Bush cut short a
trip through the western states and characterized the days following the murder of Higgins and the threats against other
hostages as "the most difficult time of my presidency."[29] One
week into the crisis observers noticed that "the strain in his face
was pronounced."[30]

Public Expectations and Governmental Options

As described above, the clash between policies dictated by the
national interest on the one hand and the personal priorities and
interests of the victims of terrorism on the other puts decision
makers in a bind. The challenge is to protect the lives of the victims without damaging the national interest. To make matters
more difficult, Americans have tremendous confidence in the
ability of their government to effectively counter terrorism.

More than four months after the takeover of the U.S. Embassy
in Iran, when the prospects of ending the stalemate were very
dim, pollsters asked, "Do you think there is anything the United
States government can do to free American hostages held in
Iran?"[31] Surprisingly, 49 percent of respondents said "yes." And
several weeks after the failed rescue attempt, 64 percent of those
questioned remained optimistic that "a president of the United
States" could make a real difference in getting the hostages out of
Iran alive.[32] At the time, however, most Americans no longer
believed that Jimmy Carter was the leader who could make this
kind of difference; President Carter's public approval had plum-
meted even before this survey was conducted.

In January 1986, after a year of increased violence against
Americans, a majority of the U.S. public was still convinced that
its government had the ability to do something "to significantly
reduce" terrorist attacks against its citizens.[33] An even larger
majority expressed doubts that the government was doing all it
could, and felt the government "should do more."[34]

In the aftermath of Lieut. Colonel Higgins' murder and
increased fears for the lives of the remaining hostages in Lebanon,

54 percent of the American public thought that the government had not made enough of an effort to get the hostages out. This poll followed an earlier survey which revealed that a majority of respondents believed President Bush's reaction to the hostage situation in Lebanon had not been tough enough.[35]

The deeply rooted confidence in the ability of the American superpower to deal with even the most difficult international problems is shared by political elites and decision makers. According to Margaret and Charles Hermann, "At the core of the problem for the public, for many policymakers, and probably for the president himself is the significant discrepancy between their image of the nation's capabilities and the harsh realities imposed by the terrorists' successful act of taking and holding hostages."[36] The result is a "sense of impotence that easily contributes to feelings of frustration and even anger."[37]

The rest of the world also watches as a hostage drama unfolds and comes to similar conclusions as the American public and elite. Recalling the Iranian hostage crisis, Sick observed "that the image of U.S. weakness generated by months of humiliating setbacks and frustrations was not healthy for relations with allies or adversaries."[38] All of this plays into the hands of terrorists and their sponsors who, after all, want to demonstrate the weakness of the government they fight.Some students of terrorism believe this quest for exposing the powerlessness of target governments ranks highest on the list of terrorist goals. Benjamin Netanyahu concluded, "whatever their specific motives or demands may be, the overriding consideration of all terrorist acts is to humiliate governments and expose their impotence. And this impotence is dramatized with special force and acuity when a handful of people are able to strike at anyone, anywhere, anytime."[39]

The President's Political Self-Interest

But no head of government, least of all a U.S. president, can survive for long without suffering irreparable political harm if a small group of terrorists manage to treat the leader like the tamer of a paper tiger. By appearing weak when challenged by terrorists, a leader risks his own political future and his place in history. Therefore, in addition to the need to protect the national interest and the lives of citizens, the political interest of the president enters into the decision making process as well.

All presidents want to be perceived as strong and effective leaders. The most important indicators of how a president is ultimately judged are (1) success in solving major problems, (2) successful reelection or helping a chosen successor to win the White House; and (3) public approval levels while in office. No chief executive and no White House adviser will ignore the president's political viability and effectiveness or the president's place in history.[40]

The ability of the media and especially television to "prime"— to focus on and thus draw attention to some among many events, problems, and issues—amounts to an ability to establish the context in which political evaluations and choices are made. Drawing on the results of their experiments, Iyengar and Kinder concluded that this priming function "suggests that television news does indeed shape the standards by which presidential performance is measured."[41]

When terrorists strike and take hostages, they force decision makers to consider the interests of all targets—the immediate victims, the nation as a whole, and the policy makers themselves, most of all the head of government. After a meeting with hostage families in the early days of the Iran crisis, President Carter told his chief of staff Hamilton Jordan: "You know, I've been worried all week about the hostages as a problem for the country and as a political problem for me. But it wasn't until I saw the grief and hope on the faces of their wives and mothers and fathers that I felt the personal responsibility for their lives."[42] Carter recognized clearly that the problem at hand had a strong bearing on three sets of interests (the national interest, the special interest of the hostages and their families, and the President's political interest) which were likely to call for different policy responses.

Conflicting Interests and Crucial Decisions

Personality traits and psychological predispositions are believed to affect decision makers—especially when they experience stress. It has been suggested that President Carter was "hypervigilant" in dealing with the stressful Iran situation, while President Reagan delegated responsibility in his efforts to free the hostages in Lebanon.[43] Clearly, Carter's very active approach and Reagan's detached crisis management affected the reactions and policies of their administrations during the hostage situations they faced.

Given the conflicting interests the President has to deal with in these kinds of crises, the $64,000 question is: what guides policy makers when they have to deal with hostage incidents? Which interest or interests did President Carter and his advisers hope to protect when the decision was made to approve a military attempt to rescue the hostages in Teheran? Which interest or interests motivated President Reagan and his advisers when they managed the TWA hijacking crisis or undertook the arms-for-hostages scheme? While both presidents have explained their decisions as being in the best interest of the nation and of the victims of terrorism as well, their choices were in reality more complex than they indicate.

The Iranian Rescue Mission

Soon after the takeover of the American Embassy in Teheran, the members of President Carter's cabinet and his closest advisers became identified with one of the conflicting interests. Secretary of State Cyrus Vance from the outset advocated a patient policy stance; he recommended diplomatic initiatives because he believed that peaceful approaches would protect the hostages. National Security Adviser Zbigniew Brzezinski was the strongest voice for a tough U.S. position; he recommended forceful responses and eventually military measures as the best means to protect America's "vital interests" and "national honor."[44] CIA Director Stansfield Turner noted that "Cy [Vance] was pushing in one direction and Zbig [Brzezinski] in another."[45] Chief of staff Hamilton Jordan, press secretary Jody Powell, and pollster Patrick Caddell were politically most astute and involved in the White House; they were concerned with the effect of the Iranian situation on the President's reelection chances in November 1980. A few weeks after the outbreak of the crisis, Jordan told Brzezinski "that Carter simply would not be reelected President if he did not act firmly."[46] When Carter's public approval skyrocketed during the first weeks of the crisis, Caddell warned that these ratings would not hold up for very long.

Aware of the concerns of these advisers Vance tried to find common ground, arguing that "in the long run the President will be judged by whether or not we get those Americans back safely and alive."[47] Jordan later recalled his own reaction: "That's it, I thought. He's worried that Jody and I are so preoccupied with Carter's reelection that we might encourage him to do something foolish because of political pressures. I assured him that I agreed with the present strategy and the ultimate objective of returning the hostages, but we also had to think about the posture of both the President and the nation."[48] Because the President is ultimately the person who must make the tough decisions, the various factions in the Carter White House competed for the president's ear. In the formal meetings of the National Security Council, participants spoke a great deal about the special interest of the hostages and the national interest. Brzezinski claims that "there was never any explicit discussion of the relationship between what we might have to do in Iran and domestic politics; neither the President nor his political advisers ever discussed with me the question of whether one or another of our Iranian options would have a better or a worse domestic political effect."[49]

Yet all the members of Carter's team were fully aware of the President's personal political stakes, his portrayal in the mass media, and how he fared with respect to public and elite opinion. Not only Carter's own memoirs but also the published recollections of his advisers are full of references to the domestic political environment the President was operating in during his last year in office.

For five-and-a-half months President Carter argued that a negotiated settlement was best for the hostages and the national interest, and he acted accordingly. In November and December 1979 he assured hostage families and the American people that he would not resort to military measures that would endanger the hostages. Why, then, did the President change his mind in late March, ultimately deciding in favor of a risky rescue mission?

Even though the President argued and probably had convinced himself that the rescue mission was for the benefit of the hostages and the American people telling his advisers that "it was time for us to bring our hostages home; their safety and our national honor were at stake."[50] The final decision was made at a National Security Council meeting on April 11, 1980, when Secretary Vance—whose objections to the mission were known—was out of town. Zbigniew Brzezinski recommended air strikes that he thought would be especially useful should the rescue fail. While Carter did not approve the retaliatory air strikes, he authorized the rescue operation.

In Carter's detailed account of this difficult period, there are no explicit references to the risks the rescue entailed for the hostages. However, CIA Director Turner recalled that a few days before approving the rescue attempt, Carter had refused to consider a mission "that, he thought, would almost certainly involve the loss of some hostages."[51] Brzezinski was aware that "casualties in the rescue mission would be unavoidable and we had to face the fact that the attempt might even fail."[52] Secretary of State Cyrus Vance, the only opponent of a rescue mission, was very clear about the stakes involved in a mission designed to free 50 hostages from a compound occupied by hostile guards in the center of a densely populated city more than six thousand miles from American shores. Vance was "convinced that the decision was wrong and that it carried great risks for the hostages and our national interests."[53] He resigned in protest after the decision was taken to proceed with the rescue attempt.The President and his top advisers—especially David Jones, the Chairman of the Joint Chiefs of Staff, and CIA Director Turner—knew or should have known the risks involved in the rescue mission. Had the attempt not been aborted because of the calamities en route to and at the desert staging area, the loss of human lives might have been far higher. According to Pierre Salinger, a CIA report issued more than a month before the attempted mission estimated that more than half of the American hostages might be killed during the actual rescue. Thus, Salinger concluded, "the American Government . . . had undertaken a rescue mission that its own intelligence service had predicted would result in the death of 60 percent of the people it was trying to liberate."[54] Admiral James L. Holloway, who headed a team investigating the failed rescue mission, concluded that the mission "had a 60 percent or 70 percent chance of success."[55] Lloyd Cutler, counselor to the President, learned from Defense Secretary Harold Brown that the military estimated a 65 percent success rate.[56]

Why did the President go with the high risk option? Negotiations with Teheran had broken down. But deadlocks of this type had been common in the first five months of the crisis. There were renewed threats against the hostages but these were less serious and alarming than in earlier stages of the ordeal. As Vance pointed out, there were no indications that "the danger to the hostages was so great that it outweighed the risk of a military operation."[57] Moreover, the Iranians would be able to seize other American hostages from among the journalists covering the crisis in Teheran, if the original captives were rescued.

If the rescue mission was not in the best interest of the hostages and their families, was the operation likely to serve the national interest and restore America's national honor and prestige in the world as the President and his National Security Council argued? Cyrus Vance feared that the initiative might push Iran to turn to Moscow for support, and such a development was hardly in America's interest. Moreover, the rescue was scheduled at a time when the State Department was pressuring American allies to join the U.S. trade embargo against Iran with the argument that Washington would otherwise resort to military actions—a step the allies tried to prevent.

In a memorandum to the President in early April, Brzezinski pointed out that "unless something is done to change the nature of the game, we must resign ourselves to the continued imprisonment of the hostages through the summer or even later."[58] The President was in a tough primary fight with Senator Ted Kennedy, who had won the important New York primary. Kennedy and other Democratic and Republican hopefuls openly criticized the President's handling of the crisis. Public opinion polls showed that the strong presidential rally had fizzled and that more Americans were critical than supportive of his crisis management. It was widely assumed that an on-going hostage situation would jeopardize the President's reelection chances. The politically attuned members of Carter's advisory team felt increasingly pressured to "do something" to counter the impression that Carter was a "do nothing" crisis manager. From his vantage point in the White House, Gary Sick observed, "The media contribute to the process of transforming an international issue into a domestic political crisis for the president. There is perhaps no other type of situation that subjects the president to such intense public scrutiny, and the president is aware that his image as a decisive and effective leader is constantly at risk."[59]

Stansfield Turner described the mood among Carter's closest foreign policy advisers:

> The impulse to "do something soon" was what brought most of us to favor the rescue mission; the hostages had been dominating American foreign policy for 156 days. Every evening we winced when Walter Cronkite signed off with a yet higher number of days. Although no one raised it in the NSC, a recent Gallup poll showed that approval of the President's handling of the crisis has fallen to 40 percent, down from 75 in November and 61 in January. The public expected something more than having its expectations alternatively raised and dashed.[60]

Did this pressure, closely tied to Carter's political survival, play a vital role in the decision to attempt a rescue? Years later, Turner addressed the question:

> What finally pushed him to the reluctant decision he had so long avoided? The Ayatollah had shut all the doors to a negotiated solution. We, the President's advisers, had boxed him in by voting against, or watering down, most other options—though there weren't all that many good ones. The only choice left was to wait it out, and the pressure of public opinion was making that difficult. It is easy to jump to conclusions that the President, with the Gallup Polls in mind, was looking ahead to the November election, and that this was a political decision. No President, of course, can ignore his electoral prospects. But it was clear that Jimmy Carter had agonized over this decision and had tried every way to postpone making it.[61]

When Hamilton Jordan first learned that Carter was seriously considering a rescue attempt, he thought that "here was a way to go in and snatch our people up and have the whole damn thing over! Not to mention what it would do for the President and the nation. It would prove to the columnists and our political opponents that Carter was not an indecisive Chief-Executive who was afraid to act."[62] Brzezinski "sensed increasing pressure from the public and from Congress for more direct action against Iran."[63] "In domestic politics," Sick recognized, "continued passivity not only condemned the president to self-immolation at the polls but it risked generating a public backlash in favor of forces who opposed everything Vance and Carter represented."[64] Brzezinski reports the President saying "that the American people were getting sick of the situation . . . and that he was sick of it as well."[65]

Recalling those times of difficult decision making, Lloyd Cutler, who had doubts about the rescue mission but did not participate in the decision, was quite sure that the President "certainly sensed that the public was getting angrier and angrier, and that something like this should be attempted." But Cutler also concluded, "I don't think Carter did it for political reasons."[66]

According to Cutler, there were a number of influential people in Washington who wondered why the United States did not bomb Teheran. In Cutler's judgment, the President could have easily gotten a declaration of war from the Congress. "And if he had asked for that and gotten it in the spring of 1980, the war would have been going on, in one way or another, through the election—and he would have probably won the election."[67]

Given that a military confrontation in the Gulf was firmly opposed even by traditional U.S. allies, Carter concluded that a rescue mission was the only prudent choice among the "do something" options. Cutler still believes that "in and of itself it [the rescue attempt] did not do any real harm; it helped us feel that at least we had tried something. It meant, however, that we could not try it again because they dispersed the hostages."[68]

Regardless how the President and others rationalized and justified the decision at the time, securing a successful presidency (with solid approval ratings and a victory in the November 1980 election) was an important consideration in making this decision—perhaps the most important one.

The Reagan Years and Terrorism

During the Iran crisis, Ronald Reagan criticized President Carter for not acting decisively. Several years later, President Reagan learned that decision making during international hostage incidents is a complex task and almost always a no-win situation. When militant Shiites hijacked TWA flight 847 in June 1985 with many Americans aboard, the Reagan White House was forced to deal with yet another terrorist act. At the time, the President's record with respect to international terrorism was dismal: 241 American service men had been killed when terrorists attacked the U.S. Marine headquarters at Beirut airport in October 1983, and dozens of U.S. citizens had died in other violent incidents. Seven Americans were being held hostage by Shiite groups in Lebanon—two of them for more than a year. In one of his first speeches as President, he had promised the American people toughness toward terrorists and "swift and effective retribution" if this kind of violence were committed against U.S. targets.

The TWA hostage situation once again involved the lives of hostages, their families, national interest considerations, and the political standing of the President. With media coverage and public opinion clearly favoring the hostages and their priorities, decision makers felt enormous pressure to act on behalf of the innocent victims and their loved ones. In their meetings top policy makers discussed what was best for the hostages and what was the best course of action with respect to the national interest.

In his memoirs, Reagan wrote, "After seventeen days, we had gotten them back without making any deals with terrorists."[69] He failed to mention that he had suggested a bargain with the hijackers but was dissuaded by Secretary of State Shultz who wanted to adhere to the President's official policy of "no concessions" to terrorist demands. But Israel was subtly pressured by Washington to agree to the release of more than 700 imprisoned Shiites and thereby satisfy the TWA terrorists' demands. With the President preferring a solution that above all protected the hostages' lives, national interest considerations—the official antiterrorism policy and the reactions of American allies constantly pressured to be tough on terrorism—were pushed aside.

Many expert observers believed that the press had limited the administration's options because "the media's focus on the plight of the victims precluded any balance between the short-term needs of the hostages and the long-term policy concerns."[70] This kind of reporting, one journalist concluded, "may not have helped the Administration in its efforts to attain their freedom, for the coverage tended to make the hostages' safety the major, if not the only consideration, and effectively forced the Administration, to the extent that it had ever thought seriously of doing so, to drop any idea of using force to free the captive Americans."[71]

The return of the freed Americans boosted the President's standing since "America had reason to rejoice when the hostages were freed."[72] Had the White House insisted on sticking to its declared national interest policy and had its hard line resulted in the killing of additional hostages, Ronald Reagan's political fortunes would have suffered. But the TWA situation also created a new headache for Reagan and his advisers: media coverage of "the forgotten seven" hostages in Lebanon had put their and their families' plight onto the public agenda. Sixty-seven percent of the American public was "highly disappointed" and 22 percent "somewhat disappointed" that the other hostages had not come home with the freed TWA passengers.[73] Moreover, a plurality of Americans (48 percent) felt that President Reagan had been "too weak" in efforts to win the return of the "forgotten seven."[74] Reminded by journalists during the TWA ordeal that Reagan had begun his presidency with the promise to deal effectively with terrorists, Americans expected better results. The Reagan administration was forced to put the hostage problem high on its policy agenda.

What motives and interests led to the secret arms-for-hostages transactions? During the TWA incident President Reagan became emotionally involved—in the judgment of some observers even obsessed—with the fate of the other Lebanon hostages. During a visit in Chicago he met with the family of Father Jenco and was chastised for not trying to do for the "forgotten seven" what he had been willing to do for the TWA hostages—make a deal for their freedom. A consistent demand of the terrorists who held the "other Lebanon hostages" was the release of fellow-terrorists from a Kuwaiti prison. If the Reagan administration could get Israel to free hundreds of Shiites to win the release of the TWA passengers, the Jencos reasoned, why not ask Kuwait to release 17 prisoners?

From this time on, the freedom of the hostages became Reagan's number one priority. According to one account,

> The seeds of the weapon sale were first sown just down the hall from the Oval Office in the emotionally charged days immediately following the TWA hijacking crisis. On July 3, the morning after Reagan had wept at Robert Stethem's

grave at Arlington Cemetery he spent more than an hour to direct a postmortem of the TWA incident at an NSPG meeting in the Situation room. . . . Reagan's concern made a big impression on his aides, most of whom were accustomed to his more usual passivity.[75]

In a meeting with George Shultz and Caspar Weinberger, his Secretaries of State and Defense, both adamantly opposed to the "initiative," the President tried to convince them that arms shipments to Iran were not the same as ransom payments to the terrorists. He hypothesized what he would do if one of his children were kidnapped and ransom was demanded:

> I don't believe in ransom because it leads to more kidnapping. But if I find out that there's somebody who has access to the kidnapper and can get my child back without doing anything for the kidnapper, I'd sure do that. And it would be perfectly fitting for me to reward that individual if he got me my child back. That's not paying ransom to the kidnappers.[76]

With this emotional logic, the President justified the arms transactions. While embracing the special interests of the hostages, Reagan and some of his advisers claimed from the beginning that American arms shipments to moderate factions in Iran would enhance the chances of reestablishing U.S.–Iranian relations so Iran would once again prevent Soviet expansionism in the region. In the eyes of those who supported the arms shipments, the hostages' priorities and the national interest coincided also in the person of hostage William Buckley, the CIA station chief in Beirut, whom the captors might have forced to reveal highly sensitive national security information.

But neither Shultz nor Weinberger accepted the national security rationale of arms-for-better-relations-with-Iran. When he first saw a draft proposal, Weinberger commented that it was "like asking Qaddafi over for a cozy lunch."[77] Shultz wrote that arms shipments to Iran were "contrary to our own interests."[78] Perhaps not even National Security Adviser John Poindexter and others who promoted the Iran initiative believed that arms shipments to Iran would enhance America's geopolitical interests. In his memoirs, Shultz described asking Poindexter point blank during a National Security Council meeting,

> "How can you say this is not an arms-for-hostages deal?"
> The President jumped in, asserting, "It's not linked!" Poindexter undercut him. "How else will we get the hostages out?" he asked me in accusing terms. In this flash of candor, Poindexter had ripped away whatever veil was left to the notion of a "changed Iran" as the rationale for our arms sales.[79]

While the dominant interest in the secret dealings with Iran was the President's preoccupation and concern with the hostages and his tendency to personalize this policy problem, nobody knew better than Ronald Reagan and his close political allies that the hostage situation could become a political liability like the Iran crisis had been for Jimmy Carter. In his memoirs Ronald Reagan revealed, "No problem was more frustrating when I was president than trying to get the American hostages home. It was a problem I shared with Jimmy Carter, a problem that confronted me when I entered the White House and that was with me when I left it."[80]

Had the arms-for-hostages scheme worked, it would have enhanced Reagan's political fortunes greatly, namely his popularity, his leadership in the last two years in office, and his place in history.

Abstract Principles and Actual Incidents

Since the early 1970s American policy toward international terrorists who hold Americans captive has not changed. No concessions, no ransom payments, and no pressure on foreign governments to do otherwise. These remain the cornerstones of the official U.S. position. But every president since Jimmy Carter has bent and violated these principles during actual terrorist incidents. Even when a president announces specific positions to deal with a specific hostage situation he does not necessarily follow his own pronouncements.

For more than five months, the determination to protect the lives of 52 Americans dictated President Carter's policy during the Iran hostage crisis. The rescue mission was ordered after media coverage, public opinion, and elite opinion had turned against the patient but unsuccessful White House approach. Stansfield Turner recognized the political reasons for a policy switch when he concluded that "Carter found it necessary to shift to a pro-active option because the pro-legal ones simply were not producing results; and he could not wait out Khomeini because the public, urged on by the drumbeat of the media, was impatient with what it perceived as our national impotence."[81]

Theodore Lowi recognized that a "peace-loving, religious man like Jimmy Carter did not take the risk of the Iranian rescue mission merely to give himself a convenient lever to move American public opinion. The leverage worked the other way: Public opinion had forced upon the president an act of sheerest adventurism."[82]

Neither in its handling of the TWA hijacking crisis nor in its decision to engage in an arms-for-hostages deal with Iran was the Reagan White House guided by its declared policies. The TWA deal was a result of the President's desire to save the lives of the hostages. The same motive was behind the arms shipments to Iran. In both instances, political considerations, too, affected the respective policy choices.

Since the late 1970s when international terrorists held and threatened hostages, the captors and their allies forced presidents to make hard choices between mostly incompatible interests. It seems that in those situations the special interest (of captives) and the political interest (of presidents) outweighed the national interest.

CHAPTER SEVEN

CONCLUSION:
MUST TERRORISTS SUCCEED?

American democracy rests on the belief, which the centuries have proved true, that people can and do make intelligent decisions about great issues if they have the facts.

—KATHARINE GRAHAM

In 1984, Secretary of State George Shultz called for a tough stand against terrorism, repeatedly affirming the official line of the Reagan administration: "We must not reward the terrorists by changing our policies or questioning our own principles."[1] About a year later, learning of the first transactions in the American-Iranian arms-for-hostages scheme, an indignant Shultz protested during a high level White House meeting convened by President Reagan that the exchange "was a betrayal of our policies."[2] Neither Shultz nor Secretary of Defense Caspar Weinberger were able to stop the repeated violations of the declared U.S. policy. Clearly, terrorism had succeeded: decision makers in Washington—with the knowledge and blessing of President Reagan—had violated their own policy principles.

This was neither the first nor the last time the U.S. government complied with the demands of terrorists or their sponsor states. In 1985, after the TWA hostages had been released by their captors, Sam Donaldson of ABC News asked a Washington insider, sarcastically, "The terrorists won, right?"[3] An ABC/*Washington Post* survey revealed that 43 percent of the American public also believed that the outcome of the TWA crisis was "more a victory for the terrorists" while 31 percent saw it as "more a victory for the United States."[4] Former CIA Director Stansfield Turner concluded,

> Whatever George Shultz and Ronald Reagan chose to call the swap, it amounted to their first accommodation with terrorists. They did not bomb, did not rescue, did not use political or economic pressure, and did not hold firm. Nor did the Jihad release the prisoners out of kindness of heart. It was a deal, and as deals go it must be judged only marginally successful. That is, the terrorists obtained a big piece of what they originally demanded, the release of their compatriots from jail, and that was bound to encourage them to strike again.[5]

Before the Hizbollah, which had close ties to Iran, freed the last of its Americans hostages in December 1991, the Bush administration had paid Iran $278 million for arms purchased by the Shah before his fall but never shipped to Iran. According to some reports, Iran transferred $86 million of the Washington payment to the Hizbollah. This led one critic of American softness on terrorists to conclude that "the hostage-takers made out like the bandits they are."[6]

Terrorists, especially by taking and holding American hostages, have had considerable success in achieving at least some of their shortterm or tactical objectives. The Iranians responsible for the long hostage crisis achieved one of their most important goals, i.e., to expose the Shah's oppressive regime and its ties to the United States government. The Carter administration agreed to the establishment of an international forum to investigate these grievances but the Iranians declined; they were looking for greater concessions.

While generally successful in terms of short-term objectives, "on the strategic front, however, the scoreboard of struggle between nation-states and terrorists is not so clear."[7] Some experts consider that international terrorism overall "is no success story."[8] But in several cases, terrorists were able to use violent acts to further and even achieve their ultimate goals. For example, the takeover of the U.S. embassy in Teheran and the long hostage ordeal were instrumental in removing American influence from Iran—one of the long-term goals of fundamentalist Shiite leaders in Iran and the region. By repeatedly attacking the U.S. embassy compound in Beirut, carbombing the U.S. Marine barracks at Beirut airport, and kidnapping Americans, the Hizbollah and similar groups advanced the same objective in Lebanon.

Shocking terrorist acts, beginning with the heavily covered assault of the "Black September" group on the Israeli team at the 1972 Munich Olympics, dramatized the cause of the Palestinians worldwide and marked the beginning of a long process toward the eventual recognition of Yassir Arafat and the PLO as legitimate political players by countries such as the United States, that had suffered terrorist violence from the PLO and other Palestinian groups. In the summer of 1993 Israel agreed to negotiate directly with representatives of the PLO at the Washington-sponsored peace talks. While Prime Minister Yitzhak Rabin emphasized that Israel's peace negotiators were meeting with individuals and not with an organization, there was no doubt, as the *New York Times* concluded, that "all parties recognize this as a significant change."[9] A few weeks later Rabin and Arafat shook hands on the South Lawn of the White House.

But terrorists are most victorious when they target the United States in their efforts to get attention, spread fear and anxiety, and expose the weakness and impotence of the American superpower in preventing these kinds of attacks and fighting these small groups and the governments which sponsor them. These successes, all preconditions to influencing the public and decision makers, could not be achieved to the degree they are without the American mass media news coverage described in this book.

Reviewing how the television networks had handled the videotape of the body of Lebanon hostage William Higgins hanging from a rope and the simultaneous threats to kill other hostages in Lebanon, media critic Walter Goodman observed that "television, by its nature, has helped to make the probable cost of action, the death of more hostages, seem too high to pay."[10] This is exactly what terrorists hope to accomplish: to stir public emotions and thereby influence what decision makers can and cannot do.

Nearly a decade before Higgins was killed, the Ayatollah Khomeini, too, had recognized the importance of the mass media and public opinion in America. While otherwise opposed to western progress and technology, during the Iranian hostage crisis he exploited the media for his own purposes by granting interviews to American and other western news organizations. During one television interview Khomeini mentioned public opinion polls in the United States which had revealed opposition to military actions against Iran. The Ayatollah took this as an indication that "Americans had come to their senses."[11] He was confident that decision makers in Washington would not act contrary to Americans' collective attitudes.

That was a shrewd observation. American decision makers are sensitive to public sentiments. In reaction to terrorist spectaculars and to a multitude of somewhat less dramatic incidents, presidents and legislators tend to propose and adopt new initiatives to prevent terrorism and to apprehend and punish its perpetrators. To be sure, politicians make genuine efforts to come up with effective antiterrorist policies. But most of these initiatives coincide with periods when terrorism ranks high on the public agenda. Commenting on the 99th Congress's extraordinary legislative output in the area of antiterrorism, two experts in the field wrote,

> Possibly at no time in the 20th century have so many questions been raised about the U.S. Government's ability to protect its citizens and property abroad. In the 1980s Americans came to feel increasingly at risk from terrorism. In 1983 and 1984, the bombings of the U.S. embassy in Kuwait

and the U.S. embassy and military barracks in Beirut dramatically exposed the vulnerability of diplomatic and military missions and personnel. American citizens traveling abroad no longer felt secure in the aftermath of the 1985 hijackings of TWA flight 847 and of the cruise ship *Achille Lauro*, as well as the murderous attacks at the Rome and Vienna airports. The scope and immediacy of the congressional response were linked to rising public alarm over this series of terrorist incidents. Congress answered mounting public frustration and fear by adopting legislation that reflected strong bipartisan support and close cooperation with the State Department and other executive agencies.[12]

In this instance, the result was the Omnibus Diplomatic Security and Antiterrorism Act of 1986 (PL 99–399). Still the centerpiece of U.S. antiterrorist policy, the act packaged a few new (i.e., maritime security) statutes and a multitude of existing, but significantly improved (i.e., diplomatic and aviation security) laws.

Most major terrorist and terrorism-related spectaculars have also been followed by the establishment of commissions or task forces. The failed attempt to rescue the American hostages in Teheran was investigated by the Holloway Commission; the attacks on U.S. embassies by the Inman Commission; the series of terrorist spectaculars in the mid-1980s by Vice President Bush's Task Force on Combating Terrorism; and the downing of Pan Am flight 103 in 1988 by the Presidential Commission on Aviation Security and Terrorism.

When the president and legislators appoint such bodies, conduct hearings, and propose new initiatives to combat terrorism, they hope most of all to erase the image of helplessness that they tend to project during and after terrorist incidents and replace it with the image of activism, of dealing with the problem, of "doing something." This was certainly the case when international terrorists struck within the United States. Following the World Trade Center bombing in early 1993 and revelations that the FBI had foiled similar terrorist conspiracies, Washington responded very quickly with congressional hearings and specific proposals for new laws and regulations concerning, for example, improved safety at nuclear power plants, tougher enforcement measures to prevent illegal immigrants from entering and staying in the country, and a mandatory death penalty for terrorists.

Because media coverage is the central link in the calculus of violence—international terrorism's heartbeat—some liberal democracies have adopted laws to restrict press coverage of terrorist activities and communications. In the early 1990s, for example, Greece enacted an antiterrorism law that gives state prosecutors the power to ban the publication of communications from terrorist groups following violent events. Editors who ignored this censorship were convicted under the new law and sentenced to jail terms.

The Federal Republic of Germany, too, adopted legislation that makes media glorification of terrorist violence a criminal offense. While it may be difficult to decide what constitutes "glorification," this law seems superfluous in a country with a degree of press-government cooperation during terrorist situations that amounts to self-censorship. Following a series of bloody attacks by the Red Army Faction (RAF) in the 1970s, the government and the media agreed to a policy of denying terrorists media access and working closely together in managing the news during such incidents. After industrialist Hans Martin Schleyer was kidnapped by the Red Army Faction in 1977, the news management model was tested. According to one account,

> Despite over a hundred RAF messages and communiques, almost no terrorist communications demanding the release of RAF prisoners were published. The media did agree to publish false reports of government efforts to arrange the release of terrorists whose freedom the RAF had demanded in exchange for Schleyer's life. For nearly two months the terrorists were denied a public platform, and the German people quietly accepted the news blackout. Schleyer died before he could be rescued, but the attempt to manage news coverage was a success.[13]

In the United Kingdom and in other European countries the public broadcasting corporations (television and radio) are prone to subtle government efforts to curb terrorism coverage. But this kind of censorship is quickly losing its effectiveness in the face of the rapid growth of private cable and satellite television in these countries.

Given the First Amendment protection that the American press enjoys, however, neither restrictive terrorism laws like the ones adopted in Greece and Germany nor joint government-press ventures like the German model are likely options in the United States. This does not mean, however, that media restrictions in one form or another are not discussed inside and outside the press. In fact, journalists are among the most outspoken advocates of restricting terrorism coverage. *Washington Post* columnist David Broder, for example, has stated that: "the essential ingredient of any effective antiterrorist policy must be the denial to the terrorist of access to mass media outlets. The way by which this denial is achieved—whether by voluntary means of those of us in press and television, self-restraint, or by government control—is a crucial question for journalists and for all other citizens who share our belief in civil liberties."[14]

While some of his colleagues share Broder's view, most journalists, editors, and producers reject any kind of government interference and point to the constitutional guarantee of press freedom and to the public's right to know. But, as one legal scholar has pointed out, the United States Supreme Court "has never adhered to an absolutist approach in its interpretations. The Court has deemed entire areas of expression outside the scope of protection."[15] Referring to the clear and present danger doctrine enunciated by Justice Holmes in 1919 and affirmed in several more recent Supreme Court rulings, Cherif Bassiouni has suggested that:

> the doctrine would appear to provide a basis for regulating media reporting of terrorist incidents in at least three instances: first, where the terrorist attacks are perceived as a "demonstrated risk of specific threats to the social order" and no opportunity or time exists to respond to the information disseminated; second, in those rare circumstances

where a media representative's remarks could be construed, in the context in which they are uttered, as an incitement to lawless action; and third, where media dissemination of specific information immediately jeopardized the lives of hostages. In each of these circumstances, a compelling state interest must outweigh countervailing first amendment values.[16]

Suppose that a reporter has learned that a hostage rescue mission is imminent. After a prior, failed attempt, the captors had killed several of their captives. The reporter's employers are determined to publicize the latest scoop about a second rescue effort. In such a case prior press restraint might be permissible. Referring to the Supreme Court's ruling in the Pentagon Papers case, one expert concluded, "It seems possible that a narrowly drawn criminal statute punishing media dissemination of information unnecessarily assisting the perpetrators or jeopardizing the lives of hostages may withstand constitutional scrutiny."[17]

Even in the United States the constitutional protection of the press is not unconditional; the constitution could be tested in this respect by an administration forced to deal with far greater terrorist threats than experienced so far. After the 1993 World Trade Center bombing terrorism experts warned that this was but the beginning of a new and more deadly wave of terrorist attacks inside and outside the United States. If these predictions are correct, increased demands to curb terrorism reporting may be expected.

But even if one considers international terrorism as a form of warfare and media coverage as the most effective terrorist ammunition, government imposed censorship is still the least desirable option to uncouple this central link in the calculus of terrorism. While debates about and critical reviews of terrorism coverage have been fashionable in the immediate aftermath of overcovered events such as the Iranian hostage crisis and the TWA hijacking incident, interest in establishing news guidelines wanes very quickly. Although most large media organizations have enacted their own rules for reporting hostage situations, the mere existence of such codes does not automatically translate into practice. Faced with an incident reporters, editors, anchors, and producers are tempted to present the most dramatic and sensational material.

While the research presented in this book demonstrates that the print press is not immune to terrorist manipulation, television—with its dependence on visual images and its live coverage—provides an attractive stage for shocking terrorist dramas. Nothing is more controversial than television's habit of broadcasting unedited live or taped material—even if it is provided or encouraged by terrorists. After the TWA hostage incident NBC anchor Tom Brokow recalled, "There was, in that hijacking coverage, too much of the kind of raw, unexpurgated television transmission coming from Beirut. The people were getting a kind of voyeurish experience. There was a real exploitation going on, which I don't think we should allow."[18] But when push comes to shove, most decisions are made in favor of presenting the most dramatic material for the longest possible time. Recalling the coverage of the Iranian hostage crisis Gary Sick observed,

> The crisis was the longest-running human interest story in the history of television, in living color from the other side of the world. Commercially it was a stunning success. Never had a news story so thoroughly captured the imagination of the U.S. public. . . . It may never be known how many pairs of pantyhose and how many tubes of toothpaste were sold to this captive audience as a direct result of the hostage crisis, but the numbers are substantial. Perhaps it was the true genius of America to transform a political disaster into a commercial bonanza.[19]

Media insiders deny that ratings and profit considerations enter into the decisions on how to cover terrorism news. Yet ABC anchor Peter Jennings was candid when asked about the reason for television's excessive terrorism coverage: "What accounts for the extraordinary intensity of media coverage of hijackings and hostage-takings? Ratings? The answer is yes. We work for commercial enterprises. We all want to be number one. Number one means dollars and cents to our corporations and so ratings are certainly important in our lives. Does it have to do with advertising revenue? Yes, I suppose it does, in that advertising revenue results from ratings."[20] While Jennings went on to say that these considerations are not conscious thoughts "in the news divisions which, by and large, operate independently from their parent corporations,"[21] the increasingly fierce competition between networks and cable television has magnified the importance of ratings—even among those who work in the news divisions. Because of these competitive realities, in-house critics or ombudspersons are just as unlikely as internal guidelines to affect either the quantity or the quality of terrorism coverage.

It has been suggested that one way to moderate the most objectionable features of terrorism coverage (e.g., live interviews with hostage holders and hostages, the excessive volume of reporting in the cases of spectacular events) would be increased peer review within the news industry. As a former president of the American Society of Newspaper Editors suggested, a media organization might be more willing to review critically and attack a competitor's coverage than to police its own.[22] There are some encouraging signs that news organizations may be shedding their traditional reluctance to scrutinize each other's coverage. After "Dateline NBC" aired faked film footage of General Motor trucks exploding in a crash in early 1993 without revealing that the test vehicles contained incendiary devices, other news organizations were openly critical of the manufacturing of the hoax. Similarly, after many television networks and local stations around the country repeatedly aired the videotapes of hanged hostage William Higgins and of Joseph Cicippio, whom his captors threatened to murder next, television critics and others in the media debated the appropriateness and the effect of presenting such shocking videotapes produced by terrorists. After ABC's "World News Tonight" refused to show the film of Higgins' body and of Cicippio's emotional farewell to his family, one critic concluded that "holding back on significant documents of a significant story out of concern for their impact on viewers, is a questionable practice for a news organization."[23]

I see nothing wrong with news producers deciding to exclude from stories the visual images provided by terrorists. Americans who hear and read about terrorists killing hostages without seeing images of their murdered compatriots are hardly deprived of their right to know. After all, producers and editors are constantly selecting which stories, which aspects of stories, and which visual images to include in their news presentations, and this process consists of excluding most of the available material.

Yet in covering terrorism, the media and especially television are damned if they do and damned if they do not exercise self-restraint. And peer review within the media—especially when it deals with the sensitive issues of whether, when, and how to restrict news coverage—is not likely to find a way out of this quandry. By and large news organizations have stuck to their coverage patterns and will continue to do so whenever terrorists strike. Katherine Graham spoke for many when she offered the following proposition: "Publicity may be the oxygen of terrorists. But I say this: News is the lifeblood of liberty. If the terrorists succeed in depriving us of freedom, their victory will be far greater than they ever hoped and far worse than we ever feared. Let it never come to pass."[24]

If terrorists commit violence simply to be heard and to get their grievances before a large audience, one way to solve the problem of terrorism would be for the mass media to grant these kinds of groups access before they resorted to hostage takings and other violent deeds. For example, when Croatian separatists hijacked a TWA airliner in 1976, they had but one demand and objective: an opportunity to publicize their grievances in the media.[25]

Perhaps this approach could also have some success in preventing domestic terrorism. But it is highly unlikely that international terrorists who target the United States would forego violence in exchange for media access. Yes, media coverage is central to their calculus of violence, but their media messages and demands would lose their bite without the frightening drama of a specific terrorist act behind them.

Terrorism is not a problem of the past. In the wake of the World Trade Center bombing, law enforcement officials revealed that dozens of similar groups operate within the United States. Some students of terrorism suspect that a loose international terrorist network has been established on American soil. There is evidence that the most notorious Middle Eastern terrorist groups such as Hizbollah, Hamas, Islamic Jihad, the Abu Nidal organization, and the Jordanian Muslim Brotherhood operate cells in various parts of the United States.[26]

But by arresting and indicting several suspects shortly after they had committed the first major act of terrorism in the United States and before others could execute a second plot, law enforcement agencies sent terrorists a powerful message: you can hit Americans at home but you are likely to be caught—either before or after you strike.

It is much safer and—as the previous chapters have described— much more advantageous in terms of media coverage to operate far away from American soil. Not surprisingly, following the New York arrest of the Egyptian cleric Sheik Omar Abdel Rahman, whose followers were linked to the World Trade Center bombing, several Shiite terrorist groups in Egypt and elsewhere in the region threatened to attack and capture Americans—in their region.

Must Americans simply accept their vulnerability to the calculus of violence as the price they pay for their democratic principles and values? Not necessarily. While media coverage is the most crucial element in the terrorist scheme, it is merely the means to the more important end of affecting the general public and decision makers. Therefore, different approaches to shortcircuiting terrorist objectives must come not only from the media but from decision makers and the public as well.

When faced with terrorism, recent presidents and other policy makers were directly and deeply affected by the way the news media reported such events. Not only the designated govern-

160

ment experts on terrorism but also other officials who are likely to respond to terrorist spectaculars, should be as familiar with the strategy of violence as they are with other important foreign and domestic policy problems. Awareness of this complex terrorist scheme would go a long way toward helping decision makers understand their own vulnerability to media-centered manipulation.

Such insight would equip leaders to enlighten the American public about the clever design behind anti-American violence. The standard plea of officials that terrorism's most effective weapon is fear and that Americans therefore must not succumb to fear, will not do. Decision makers and especially the president must level with the public and describe fully the hard choices before the nation when it is held hostage by terrorists.

When terrorists strike, the president should use the bully pulpit to explain the terrorist scheme and the pros and cons of various response options at hand. Of course, such an approach will only succeed if the public is convinced that the intention is to educate, not to manipulate or to lie, as has occurred in the past.

Katharine Graham is right: Americans "can and do make intelligent decisions about great issues if they have the facts."[27] This is a challenge to the mass media and to governmental policy makers, especially presidents. In the past, the American public reacted by and large rationally to information received through news coverage about terrorist events, threats, and demands. Better information, not simply less, may be the best available answer to the calculus of violence.

NOTES

Preface to the Paperback Edition

1. The FBI's code name **una**bom was chosen because persons associated with **un**iversities and **a**irlines were the first targets. Most media organizations referred to the mysterious killer as Unabomber.

2. The special task force was formed in 1993 after two mail bombs had exploded in Connecticut and California.

3. Peter Applebone, "Radical Right's Fury Boiling Over," *New York Times*, April 23, 1995.

4. Gustav Niebuhr, "Assault on Waco Sect Fuels Extremists' Rage," *New York Times*, April 26, 1995.

5. Tom Morganthau, "Janet Reno Confronts Waco's Bitter Legacy," *Newsweek*, May 15, 1995, p. 26.

6. James Bovard, "Waco Must Get a Hearing," *Wall Street Journal*, May 15, 1995.

7. Michael Harrison, editor and publisher of *Talkers Magazine*, was quoted in John Tierney, "How Talk Radio Gets at What's Real," *New York Times*, April 30, 1995.

8. Jares Sandberg, "Militia Groups Meet, Recruit in Cyberspace," *Wall Street Journal*, April 26, 1995.

9. According to a Gallup/CNN/*USA Today* poll of April 21–23, 79 percent of the respondents approved of the news coverage. A *Los Angeles Times* poll conducted April 26–27 found that 33 percent of the public felt that radio talk show hosts encouraged violence like the

Oklahoma City bombing, 53 percent did not feel that way, and 14 percent were not sure.

10. A Gallup poll conducted April 21–23, 1995, for example, found that 47 percent of the respondents considered it "very likely" and 42 percent "somewhat likely" that further terrorist acts would occur in the United States in the near future. In early May, an Associated Press poll revealed that 61 percent of the public expected violent acts like the Oklahoma City bombing within a year.

11. According to a poll conducted May 10–14, 1995, by ABC News and the *Washington Post.*

12. A *Time*/CNN/Yankelovic Partners Inc. poll on April 27, 1995, asked, "Based on what you've read, heard, or seen, do you think Clinton is trying to use this incident [the Oklahoma City bombing] for his own advantage, or don't you think so?" 31 percent of the respondents answered yes, 64 percent no, and 5 percent were not sure. For the mentioned approval ratings I relied on polls by Gallup, ABC News/*Washington Post,* and CBS News.

13. According to an NBC News/*Wall Street Journal*/Hart And Teeter Research Companies poll of June 2–6, 1995, 34 percent of the respondents believed that the Republican Party would be better in handling terrorism, 14 percent had more confidence in the Democratic Party, 28 percent in both, 15 percent in neither party.

14. According to CBS News (May 4–16), ABC News/*Washington Post* (May 10–14), and *Time,* CNN, Yankelovich Partners (July 19–20) polls.

15. "Chronicles," *Time,* August 7, 1995.

16. John Leo, "Give the Unabomber His 15 Minutes," *U.S. News & World Report,* Aug. 14, 1995.

17. Quoted in Leo, ibid.

18. Jonathan Adler, "Will It Be Publish—Or Perish?" *Newsweek,* July 10, 1995.

19. "An Open Letter to the Unabomber from Bob Guccione," *New York Times,* Aug. 3, 1995.

20. Ibid.

21. Reprinted in *The Economist,* Aug. 12, 1995.

22. Robert D. McFadden, "Times and the *Washington Post* Grant Mail Bomber's Demand," *New York Times,* Sept. 19, 1995.

Introduction: The Calculus of Violence

1. *Robert Kupperman and Jeff Kamen, Final Warning: Averting Disaster in the New Age of Terrorism* (New York: Doubleday, 1989), p. 14.

2. The nuisance argument is, for example, made by Walter Laqueur, *The Age of Terrorism* (Boston: Little, Brown, 1987).

3. Marius H. Livingston, *International Terrorism in the Contemporary World* (Westport: Greenwood Press, 1978), p. 20.

4. Anthony C. E. Quainton, "Terrorism: Policy, Action, and Reaction," in Lawrence Zelic Freedman and Yonah Alexander, eds., *Perspectives on Terrorism* (Wilmington: Scholarly Resources, 1983), p. 175.

5. Ronald H. Hinckley, *People, Polls, and Policy-Makers: American Public Opinion and National Security* (New York: Lexington Books, 1992), p. 91.

6. Hamilton Jordan, *Crisis: The Last Years of the Carter Presidency* (New York: G.P. Putnam Sons, 1982), p. 364.

7. Russell Watson et al., "The Hunt Begins," *Newsweek*, March 8, 1993, pp. 22–26; Bill Turque et al., "A Break in the Blast," *Newsweek*, March 15, 1993, pp. 28–31.

8. From President Clinton's address to the nation on June 26, 1993, according to transcript printed in the *Congressional Quarterly Weekly*, July 3, 1993, p. 1765.

9. Noel Koch, former director of special planning at the Pentagon, in a speech to the American Society for Industrial Security on March 12, 1987; cited in David C. Martin and John Walcott, *Best Laid Plans: The Inside Story of America's War Against Terrorism* (New York: Harper & Row, 1988), p. 365.

10. Martha Crenshaw, "Reflections on the Effects of Terrorism," in Crenshaw, ed. *Terrorism, Legitimacy, and Power* (Middletown: Wesleyan University Press, 1983), p. 6.

11. For more on terrorism as rational choice see Crenshaw, "The Logic of Terrorism: Terrorist Behavior as a Product of Strategic Choice," and Jerrold M. Post, "Terrorist Psycho-logic: Terrorist Behavior as a Product of Psychological Forces," in Walter Reich, ed., *Origins of Terrorism* (New York: Cambridge University Press, 1990).

12. Crenshaw, "The Logic of Terrorism," p. 18.

13. Quoted in Donna M. Schlagheck, *International Terrorism* (Lexington, Mass.: Lexington Books, 1988), p. 69.

14. Schlagheck, *International Terrorism*, p. 2.

15. Quoted by Brian Michael Jenkins, "Der internationale Terrorismus," *Aus Politik und Zeitgeschichte* B5/87: 25.

16. This slogan, once popular among the radical left and attributed to Huey Newton, is cited by Jenkins, "Der internationale Terrorismus," p. 25.

17. The letter was published in the *New York Times*, March 28, 1993, p. 35.

18. Albert Bandura, "Mechanism of Moral Disengagement," in Reich, ed. *Origins of Terrorism*, p. 172.

19. Schlagheck, *International Terrorism*, p. 67.

20. John O'Sullivan, "Media Publicity Causes Terrorism," in Bonnie Szumski, ed., *Terrorism: Opposing Viewpoints* (St. Paul: Greenhaven Press, 1986), p. 70.

21. For a report on the investigation following the Pan Am 103 downing see Steven Emerson and Brian Duffy, "The German Connection," *New York Times Magazine*, March 18, 1990.

22. Irving Louis Horowitz, "The Routinization of Terrorism and Its Unanticipated Consequences," in Crenshaw, ed., *Terrorism, Legitimacy, and Power*, p. 39. See also Crenshaw, "Reflections on the Effects of Terrorism," in Crenshaw, ed., *Terrorism, Legitimacy, and Power*.

23. See, for example, Robert Kupperman and Jeff Kamen, *Final Warning: Averting Disaster in the New Age of Terrorism* (New York: Doubleday, 1989), chap. 5; M. Cherif Bassiouni, "Terrorism, Law Enforcement, and the Mass Media: Perspectives, Problems, Proposals," in *The Journal of Criminal Law and Criminology*, vol. 72, no. 1 (1981); Abraham H. Miller, *Terrorism: The Media and the Law* (Dobbs Ferry, N.Y.: Transnational Publishers, 1982); Eric Morris and Alan Hoe, *Terrorism: Threat and Response* (London: Macmillan, 1987), chap. 12; L. John Martin, "The Media's Role in International Terrorism," in Charles W. Kegley, Jr., ed., *International Terrorism: Characteristics, Causes, Controls* (New York: St. Martin's, 1990).

24. The following books about terrorism and the media are among the best in the field: Alex P. Schmid and Janny de Graaf, *Violence as Communication: Insurgent Terrorism and the Western News Media* (London: Sage, 1982); Philip Schlesinger, Graham Murdock, and Philip Elliott, *Televising "Terrorism": Political Violence in Popular Culture* (London: Comedia Publishing, 1983); David L. Paletz and Alex P. Schmid, *Terrorism and the Media* (Newbury Park, Calif.: Sage, 1992).

25. Excellent incident studies are, for example, David Altheide, "Iran vs. U.S. TV News," in William C. Adams, ed., *Television Coverage of the Middle East.* (Norwood, N.J.: Ablex, 1981); Dan Nimmo and James Combs, *Nightly Horrors: Crisis Coverage by Television Network News* (Knoxville: University of Tennessee Press), chap. 5.

26. See, for example, Eytan Gilboa, "Terrorism and Trust: How We See the Middle East," in *Public Opinion*, Nov./Dec. 1986; Ronald Hinckley, "American Opinion Toward Terrorism: The Reagan Years," *Terrorism: An International Journal* 12(1989): 6.

27. Shanto Iyengar and Donald Kinder, *News That Matters: Television and American Opinion* (Chicago: Chicago University Press, 1987).

28. Iyengar and Kinder, *News That Matters*, chap. 11.

29. Shanto Iyengar, *Is Anyone Responsible? How Television Frames Political Issues* (Chicago: Chicago University Press, 1991), chap. 4.

30. Gabriel Weimann, " 'Redefinition of Image': the Impact of Mass-Mediated Terrorism," in *International Journal of Public Opinion Research*, 2(1):16–29. See also, Gabriel Weimann, "The Theater of Terror: Effects of Press Coverage," in *Journal of Communication* (Winter 1983), pp. 38–45.

31. Hinckley, *People, Polls, and Policy-Makers*, especially chap. 9.

2. Terrorism, the Media, and Foreign Policy

1. Roger Hilsman, *The Politics of Policy Making in Defense and Foreign Affairs* (Englewood Cliffs, N.J.: Prentice Hall, 1987), p. 222.

2. Molotch, H. and M. Lester, "Accidental news: the great oil spill as local occurrence and as national event," *American Journal of Sociology* 81: 235–260. See also Timothy E. Cook, "Domesticating a Crisis: Washington Newsbeats, Human Interest Stories, and International News in the Persian Gulf War." Paper prepared for the Social Science Research Council workshop on the Media and Foreign Policy, Seattle, Washington, September 1991; Patrick O'Hefferman, "What the Government Thinks: Post War Policy Makers' Perceptions of Media and Foreign Policy." Paper presented at the Social Science Research Council workshop on the Media and Foreign Policy, Seattle, Washington, September 1991.

3. Simon Serfaty, "The Media and Foreign Policy," in Serfaty, ed., *The Media and Foreign Policy* (New York: St. Martin's, 1991). See also other chapters.

4. O'Hefferman, "What the Government Thinks."

5. Martin Linsky, *Impact: How the Press Affects Federal Policymaking* (New York: W.W. Norton, 1986). This study of press influence covered both domestic and foreign affairs decision making.

6. O'Hefferman, "What the Government Thinks."

7. David R. Gergen, "Diplomacy in a Television Age: The Dangers of Teledemocracy," in Serfaty, ed. *The Media and Foreign Policy*, p. 52.

8. Lloyd N. Cutler, "Foreign Policy on Deadline," *Foreign Policy* 56, fall 1984, pp. 113–128.

9. Gergen, "Diplomacy in a Media Age."

10. W. Lance Bennett, "The Media and the Foreign Policy Process." Paper delivered at the fifth Thomas P. O'Neill Symposium in American Politics, Boston College, April 3–4, 1992.

11. Cook, "Domesticating a Crisis."

12. Bernard C. Cohen, *The Press and Foreign Policy* (Princeton, N.J.: Princeton University Press, 1963). The traditional and enduring press-

government relationship as well as the dominance of presidents and other administration officials in foreign news reporting, especially (but not exclusively) during crises, has been documented by a growing number of authors. See, for example, Montague Kern, P. W. and R. B. Levering, *The Kennedy Crises: The Press, the Presidency, and Foreign Policy* (Chapel Hill: University of North Carolina, 1983); Brigitte Lebens Nacos, *The Press, Presidents, and Crises* (New York: Columbia University Press, 1990); Daniel C. Hallin, *The "Uncensored War":The Media and Vietnam* (New York: Oxford University Press, 1986).

13. Robert M. Entman, *Democracy Without Citizens: Media and the Decay of American Politics* (New York: Oxford University Press, 1989), p. 19.

14. Mort Rosenblum, "Special Correspondent Quixote," *Gannett Center Journal*, Fall 1989.

15. Rosenblum, "Special Correspondent Quixote," p. 7.

16. Bennett, "The Media and the Foreign Policy Process."

17. Robert M. Entman and Benjamin I. Page, "The News Before the Storm: The Limits to Media Autonomy in Covering Foreign Policy." Preliminary discussion draft prepared for the SSRC workshop on Media and Foreign Policy, University of Washington, Sept. 1991. The preconditions and the need for a strong, participatory democratic polity are examined in Benjamin Barber, *Strong Democracy: Participatory Politics for a New Age* (Berkeley, CA: University of California Press, 1984).

18. W. Lance Bennett, "Marginalizing the majority: conditioning public opinion to accept managerial democracy," in M. Margolis and G.A. Mauser, eds., *Manipulating Public Opinion: Essays on Public Opinion as a Dependent Variable* (Pacific Grove, CA: Brooks Cole, 1989). Bennett, "The Media and the Foreign Policy Process;" Kern et al., *The Kennedy Crises*; Cook, "Domesticating a Crisis."

19. Bennett, "The Media and the Foreign Policy Process."

20. Nacos, *The Press, Presidents, and Crises.*

21. Entman and Page, "The News Before the Storm." For similar findings see Nacos, *The Press, Presidents, and Crises*, chapters 1, 2, and 6.

22. Hamilton Jordan, *Crisis: The Last Year of the Carter Presidency* (New York: G.P. Putnam Sons, 1982), p. 379.

23. For details about a useful Debate-Accountability Theory of the Media and Foreign Policy see Bennett, "The Media and the Foreign Policy Process."

24. Robert B. Oakley, "Terrorism, Media Coverage, and Government Response," in Serfaty, ed., *The Media and Foreign Policy.*

25. Stephen Hess, "The Golden Triangle: The Press at the White

House, State, and Defense," *The Brookings Review*, vol. 1 (Summer 1983), pp. 14–19.

26. Shanto Iyengar and Donald R. Kinder, *News That Matters* (Chicago: University of Chicago Press, 1987), p.45.

27. Entman and Page, "The News Before the Storm," p. 7. For more on newspaper readers and their special attention to front page stories see Leo Bogart, "The Public's Use and Perception of Newspapers," *Public Opinion Quarterly* (Winter 1984), pp. 716–17.

28. Entman and Page, "The News Before the Storm," p. 27.

29. Entman found congruence between the photographic images and the text in the printed press. See, Entman, *Democracy Without Citizens*, chap. 3.

30. CBS Evening News, Dec. 4, 1979.

31. Tony Atwater, "Coverage of the TWA Hostage Crisis." In A. Odasuo Alali and Kenoye Kelvin Eke, *Media Coverage of Terrorism: Methods of Diffusion* (Newbury Park: Sage Publication, 1991), pp. 69, 70.

32. While Atwater coded each story in the complete TWA coverage of all three over-the-air television networks, Nacos coded each paragraph of the CBS News transcript. Nevertheless, the results were very similar.

33. David A. Shimkin, "Differences in the Coverage of the U.S. Bombing of Libya in the *New York Post* and *The New York Times*." Unpublished paper, Columbia College, May 1992.

34. Bennett, "The Media and the Foreign Policy Process," p. 31.

35. Peggy Say and Peter Knobler, *Forgotten: A Sister's Struggle to Save Terry Anderson, America's Longest-Held Hostage* (New York: Simon & Schuster, 1991), p. 36.

36. Quoted by David C. Martin and John Walcott, *Best Laid Plans: The Inside Story of America's War Against Terrorism* (New York: Harper & Row, 1988), p. 43.

37. CBS Evening News June 17, 1985.

38. Philip Schlesinger, Graham Murdock, and Philip Elliott, *Televising "Terrorism": political violence in political culture* (London: Comedia Publishing, 1983), p. 166. For similar conclusions see also Alex P. Schmid and Janny de Graaf, *Violence as Communication: Insurgent Terrorism and the Western News Media* (London: Sage, 1982); David L. Paletz, John Z. Ayanian, and Peter A. Fozzard, "Terrorism on TV News: The IRA, the FALN, and the Red Brigades," in William C. Adams, *Television Coverage of International Affairs* (Norwood, N.J.: Ablex Publishing), 1982.

39. Schmid and de Graaf, pp. 96, 98.

40. Douglas Jehl, "The Slow Awakening to Terrorism Here." *The New York Times*, July 4, 1993, sect. 4, p. 1.

41. Paletz, Ayanian and Fozzard, "Terrorism on TV News," p.158.

42. Doris A. Graber, *Mass Media and American Politics* (Washington, D.C.: Congressional Quarterly Press, 1980), p. 239.

3. Terrorists and Their Goals

1. *Walter Laqueur, The Age of Terrorism* (Boston: Little, Brown and Company, 1987), p. 123.

2. John O'Sullivan, "Media Publicity Causes Terrorism," p. 70.

3. David C. Rapoport, "Fear and Trembling: Terrorism in Three Religious Traditions," *The American Political Science Review*, Vol. 48, No. 3 (Sept. 1984), pp. 668–69.

4. Rapoport, "Fear and Trembling," p. 665.

5. Rapoport, "Fear and Tembling," p. 660.

6. Marc A. Celmer, *Terrorism: U.S. Strategy and Reagan Policies* (New York: Greenwood Press, 1987), p. 6.

7. Tom Fenton reported his observations on the CBS Evening News on December 6, 1976. Similar references to the students' media skills were repeatedly made by CBS News and by other media organizations.

8. Laqueur, *The Age of Terrorism*, p. 125.

9. Seminar on "The Media and Terrorism," organized by the Center for Communications, Inc., October 23, 1985.

10. Edwin Diamond, "The Coverage itself—Why it turned into 'Terrorvision'," *TV Guide*, Sept. 21, 1985.

11. J.B. Bell, "Terrorist scripts and live-action spectaculars," *Columbia Journalism Review* 17, May/June 1978, p. 50.

12. CBS Evening News, December 6, 1979.

13. For an excellent essay on the issue of contagion see Robert G. Picard, "News Coverage as the Contagion," in A. Odasuo Alali and Kenoye Kelvin Eke, eds., *Media Coverage of Terrorism: Methods of Diffusion* (Newbury Park: Sage, 1991).

14. Paul Wilkinson, "Terrorism versus Liberal Democracy," in William Gutteridge, ed., *Contemporary Terrorism* (New York: Facts on File, 1986), p. 7.

15. Alex P. Schmid and Janny de Graaf, *Violence as Communication: Insurgent Terrorism and the Western News Media* (London: Sage, 1982), p. 215.

16. Michael X. Delli Carpini and Bruce A. Williams, "Television and Terrorism: Patterns of Presentation and Occurrence, 1969 To 1980," *Western Political Quarterly* 40:1 (1987), pp. 45–64.

17. For more on the goals of terrorism to get attention, recognition, and a degree of legitimacy see, for example: Yonah Alexander, "Terrorism, the Media, and the Police," in Robert Kupperman and Darrel Trent,

eds., *Terrorism: Threat, Reality, Response* (Stanford, CA: Hoover Institution Press, 1979); and O'Sullivan, "Media Publicity Causes Terrorism."

18. Elizabeth Kolbert, "New Coverage Plays Central Role in Story," *The New York Times*, February 27, 1993, p. 23.

19. Doris A. Graber, *Mass Media and American Politics* (Washington, D.C.: Congressional Quarterly Press, 1980), p. 228.

20. David L. Paletz, John Z. Ayanian, and Peter A. Fozzard, "Terrorism on TV News: The IRA, the FALN, and the Red Brigades," in William C. Adams, ed., *Television Coverage of International Affairs* (Norwood, N.J.: Ablex Publishing, 1982), p. 161.

21. These percentages were reported by William C. Adams, "The Beirut Hostages: ABC and CBS Seize an Opportunity," *Public Opinion* 8, August/September 1985.

22. Bagdikian's testimony is mentioned in "Closer Look at Network Coverage of TWA flight 847," *Broadcasting*, August 5, 1985.

23. Alexander Jones, *New York Times* media reporter, made this observation during the seminar "The Media and Terrorism," sponsored by the Center for Communications on Oct. 23, 1985.

24. Seminar "The Media and Terrorism."

25. Michael J. O'Neill, *Terrorist Spectaculars: Should TV Couverage Be Curbed?* (New York: Priority Press, 1986), p. 9.

26. O'Neill, *Terrorist Spectaculars*, p. 9.

27. Some of the research results presented in this chapter were previously discussed in the following articles: Brigitte Nacos, David P. Fan, and John T. Young, "Terrorism and the Print Media: The 1985 TWA Hostage Crisis," *Terrorism: An International Journal* 12:2, 1989; Brigitte L. Nacos, "International Terrorism and the Media," *Current World Leaders* 35–2, 1992.

28. Mentioned by Austin Ramney, *Channels of Power* (New York: Basic Books, 1983), p. 46.

29. Shanto Iyengar, *Is Anyone Responsible? How Television Frames Political Issues* (Chicago: University of Chicago Press, 1991), p.27.

30. Celmer, *Terrorism: U.S. Strategy and Reagan Policies*, p. 10.

31. Quoted in Cynthia L. Irvin, "Terrorists' Perspectives: Interviews," in David L. Paletz and Alex P. Schmid, eds., *Terrorism and the Media* (Newbury Park: Sage Publications, 1992), p. 75.

32. Quoted in George J. Church, "The Teror Within," *TIME*, July 5, 1993, p. 22.

33. CBS Evening News, November 20, 1979.

34. CBS Evening News, November 21, 1979.

35. From news conference excerpts published in *The New York Times*, June 21, 1985, p. A6.

36. CBS Evening News, June 20, 1985.

37. David C. Martin and John Walcott, *Best Laid Plans: The Inside Story of America's War Against Terrorism* (New York: Harper & Row, 1988), p. 353.

38. Quoted in Peggy Say and Peter Knobler, *Forgotten: A Sister's Struggle to Save Terry Anderson* (New York: Simon & Schuster, 1991), p. 201.

39. In an interview with the German news magazine *Der Spiegel* cited in Bonnie Szumski, ed., *Opposing Viewpoints: Terrorism* (St. Paul: Greenhaven Press, 1986), p. 114.

40. Edward Walsh, "Crisis Reflects Shiite Rivalries," *Washington Post*, June 26, 1985, pp. 1, A16.

41. Seminar on "The Media and Terrorism."

42. Neil Hickey, "The Impact on Negotiations—What the Experts Say," *TV Guide*, Sept. 21, 1985.

43. Michael J. Kelly and Thomas H. Mitchell, "Transnational Terrorism and the Western Elite Press," in Doris A. Graber, ed., *Media Power in Politics* (Washington D.C.: Congressional Quarterly, 1984), p. 287.

44. Iyengar, *Is Anyone Responsible?*, chap. 4.

45. Letter was published in *The New York Times*, March 28, 1993, p.35.

46. O'Sullivan, "Media Publicity Causes Terrorism," p. 73.

47. *Ibid.*

48. Hickey, "The Impact of Negotiations," p. 22.

49. For similarities in tv networks' terrorism coverage see, for example, David L. Altheide, "Three-in-one news: Network coverage of Iran," *Journalism Quarterly* 59, 1982, pp. 482–86.

50. Kelly and Mitchell, "Transnational Terrorism," p. 287.

51. According to surveys by CBS News/*The New York Times* (January 19–23, 1986) and by Gallup/Newsweek (March 26–27, and April 17–18, 1986).

52. According to ABC News (January 7, January 24–26, April 24–28, 1986) and NBC News/*Wall Street Journal* (April 28–29, 1986) polls.

53. Bernard C. Cohen, *The Press and Foreign Policy* (Princeton, N.J.: Princeton University Press, 1963), p. 13.

54. For more on the salience of terrorism see Ronald H. Hinckley, *People, Polls, and Policy-Makers: American Public Opinion and National Security* (New York: Lexington Books, 1992), ch. 9.

55. Roy L. Behr and Shanto Iyengar, "Television News, Real World Clues, and Changes in the Public Agenda," *Public Opinion Quarterly* 49(1), Spring 1985.

56. Iyengar, *Is Anyone Responsible?*, p. 39.
57. Iyengar, *Is Anyone Responsible?*, p. 29.
58. Picard, "News Coverage as the Contagion," p. 59.
59. Seminar on "The Media and Terrorism."

4. The Polls and the Theater of Terror

1. For an excellent account on the framers' view on the public's vulnerability to be misguided by demagoguery see Jeffrey K. Tulis, The Rhetorical Presidency (Princeton: Princeton University Press, 1987), especially chap. 2.

2. James W. Ceaser, Presidential Selection: Theory and Development (Princeton: Princeton University Press, 1979).

3. Tulis, The Rhetorical Presidency, p. 29.

4. Benjamin I. Page and Robert Y. Shapiro, *The Rational Public: Fifty Years of Trends in Americans' Policy Preferences* (Chicago: University of Chicago, 1992), p. 1. The two opposing views are described and contrasted in chapters 1 and 2. See also Robert Weissburg, *Public Opinion and Popular Government* (Englewood Cliffs, N.J.: Prentice-Hall, 1976), especially chap. 3.

5. Ronald H. Hinckley, *People, Polls, and Policy-Makers: American Public Opinion and National Security* (New York: Lexington Books, 1992), p. 6.

6. Robert Weissberg, *Public Opinion and Popular Government* (Englewood Cliffs, N.J.: Prentice-Hall, 1976), p. 33.

7. Hinckley, *People, Polls, and Policy-Making*, p. 92.

8. *Ibid.*

9. John Mueller, "American Public Opinion and the Gulf War: Trends and Historical Comparisons." Paper presented at the meeting of the Midwest Political Science Association, Chicago, Illinois, April 9, 1992, p. 2.

10. For more on "raw" opinion and "public judgment" opinion see Daniel Yankelovich, *Coming to Public Judgment* (Syracuse, N.Y.: Syracuse University Press, 1991). In his article "Foreign Policy after the Election," in *Foreign Affairs* 71-4 (Fall 1992), Yankelovich wrote, "If one looks at the full panoply of issues facing the nation, American opinion varies widely, ranging from 'raw opinion' on one extreme to responsible 'public judgement' on the other." In this context, Yankelovich equates raw opinion to "the knee-jerk view that people carelessly express without real consideration of the consequences." The author concludes that public opinion on many contemporary issues is of the "raw" variety.

11. NBC News/Associated Press polls of November 27 and December 11–12, 1979; Yankelovich, Skelly, and White polls of December 10–12, 1979, January 23–24, 1980, and March 19–20, 1980.

12. CBS News polls of June 18 and June 26, 1985.

13. Poll results were published in Barry Sussman, "Poll Finds Rising Sentiment for Distancing U.S. From Israel," *Washington Post*, June 26, 1985, p. A17. According to ABC News/*Washington Post* polls, the number of Americans who wanted Israel to release Shiite detainees without the United States making such a request rose from 61 percent on June 17, 1985 to 68 percent on June 22.

14. According to ABC News/*Washington Post* polls of August 2–3 and August 17–21, 1985.

15. According to a survey conducted by the Hart-Teeter Research Organizations, May 18–22, 1990.

16. Yankelovich, Clancy, Shulman poll of August 3, 1989; Associated Press/Media General poll of September 14–24, 1989.

17. The polls were conducted by NBC News/Associated Press on October 22–24, 1980, and by ABC News/Louis Harris and Associates on November 3 and December 3–6, 1980.

18. ABC News/*Washington Post* polls of November 13 and November 19, 1986, and January 13–19, 1987 revealed that 79 percent, 78 percent, and 79 percent of the respondents disapproved "of the United States government selling arms to Iran in order to get American hostages in Lebanon released."

19. Hinckley, *People, Polls, and Policy-Makers*, p. 95.

20. *Ibid.*

21. An ABC News/Louis Harris and Associates poll November 26–29, 1979 found that 72 percent of the public approved of efforts to negotiate a release of the hostages in Iran; a Harris survey on April 25, 1980, one day after the failed rescue attempt, revealed that 84 percent of the U.S. public approved of renewed efforts to negotiate a crisis settlement.

22. See, for example, "U.S. Says Its Policy Is Not To Give In." *New York Times*, June, 15, 1985, p. 4.

23. An ABC News/*Washington Post* poll on June 17, 1985 revealed 59 percent support for and 32 percent opposition to negotiations; on June 19, 1985 supporters led opponents 53 percent to 40 percent, and June 20–21, 1985, 57 percent to 36 percent.

24. According to ABC News/*Washington Post* polls conducted June 30–July 1, 1985.

25. According to polls conducted by NBC News/*Wall Street Journal*, October 6–7, 1986; Yankelovich Clancy Shulman, August 3, 1989; Hart-Teeter Research Companies, May 18–22, 1989.

26. Hinckley, *People, Polls, and Policy-Makers*, p. 103.

27. For more about Delta Force see Charlie Beckwith and Donald Knox, *Delta Force* (New York: Dell, 1983), and David C. Martin and John Walcott, *Best Laid Plans* (New York: Harper and Row, 1988).

28. For example, an ABC News/Louis Harris poll a few weeks into the Iran hostage crisis (November 26–29, 1979) found that 65 percent of the public was against and 26 percent for a rescue mission. NBC News conducted a poll during the TWA hostage crisis (June 18–19, 1985), Yankelovich Clancy Shulman its survey on August 3, 1989.

29. According to several surveys by NBC News/Associated Press, Yankelovich, Skelly, and White, and ABC News/Louis Harris.

30. According to an ABC News/*Wall Street Journal* poll conducted September 4–5, 1990, 72 percent of the respondents supported, 22 percent opposed, military action if any of the hostages were harmed.

31. Associated Press/Media General poll conducted September 14–24, 1989.

32. An NBC News/Associated Press survey conducted March 21–22, 1980 asked: "Do you think that it is time now to do whatever is necessary to try to free the hostages in Iran, even if it involves military action?" 45 percent of the respondents answered "yes," 44 percent "no." A *Washington Post* poll of April 9–13, 1980 found a 55 percent majority supporting military action if the hostages were not freed by a deadline set by the United States.

33. According to Gallup polls conducted August 9–10, October 18–19, and November 15–16, 1990 in which the question was: "Now that United States forces have been sent to Saudi Arabia and other areas of the Middle East, do you think they should engage in combat if Iraq continues to hold U.S. civilians hostage?"

34. Yankelovich, Skelly, and White polls of December 10–12, 1979, January 23–25, 1980, and March 19–20, 1980.

35. CBS News polls of June 18 and June 26, 1985.

36. ABC News/*Washington Post* polls of June 17, June 19, and June 20–22, 1985 found 54 percent, 50 percent, and 53 percent supporting versus 36 percent, 41 percent, and 36 percent opposing military measures against "any Middle Eastern nation that is found to be aiding terrorists against Americans."

37. Decision/Making/Information (now the Wirthlin Group) and National Strategic Information Center polls with the same question wordings were conducted January 11–12, March 6–11, June 7–11, July 1–3, September 6–9, and November 16–19, 1986. See also, Hinckley, *People, Polls, and Policy-Makers*, chap. 9.

38. NBC/*Wall Street Journal* poll of April 13, 1986.

39. Decision/Making/Information and National Strategic Information

Center polls of July 1–3, 1985, January 11–12, 1986, and March 6–11, 1986.

40. Yankelovich Clancy Shulman poll, January 9–19, 1989.

41. Yankelovich Clancy Shulman poll of August 3, 1989.

42. Surveys conducted for NBC News and the *Wall Street Journal* on August 18–19, September 4–5, and December 8–11, 1990, contained the following question: "Please tell me whether the U.S. should or should not take military action [Dec. 8–10: should or should not go to war] if terrorists loyal to Iraq kill Americans anywhere?" In the first two surveys respondents backed military action by 67 percent to 21 percent, and by 68 percent to 26 percent; in the last poll a 48 percent plurality supported going to war.

43. Quoted in Andrew Gowers, "Abu Nidal may launch attacks on US targets," *Financial Times*, August 11–12, 1990, p. 2.

44. The ABC News/*Washington Post* surveys were conducted on June 17, June 19, June 20–22, and June 30–July 1, 1985.

45. Hinckley, *People, Polls, and Policy-Makers*, p. 101.

46. Gallup/*Times Mirror* poll, July 10–24, 1986.

47. Gallup/*Times Mirror* poll, July 10–24, 1986.

48. ABC News/*Washington Post* survey on June 30–July 1, 1985.

49. Yankelovich, "Foreign Policy after the Election," *Foreign Affairs* 71–4 (Fall 1992), p. 6.

5. *Terrorist Spectaculars and Presidential Rallies*

1. Jimmy Carter, *Keeping Faith* (New York: Bantam, 1982), p. 482.

2. Gallup was quoted in Edward Walsh, "Rivals Doubt Carter will Retain Poll Gains after Iran Crisis," *Washington Post*, Dec. 17, 1979.

3. Caddell's comment was reported on the CBS Evening News, December 17, 1979.

4. For more on the presidential imperative to "go public" and to win public support as a source of effective leadership, see Samuel Kernell. *Going Public: New Strategies of Presidential Leadership* (Washington: Congressional Quarterly Press, 1986); George C. Edwards III, *The Public Presidency* (New York: St. Martin's Press, 1983); Barbara Kellerman, *The Political Presidency: Practice of Leadership* (New York: Oxford University Press, 1984); Richard Rose, *The Postmodern President* (Chatham, N.J.: Chatham House, 1991).

5. Richard E. Neustadt, *Presidential Power: The Politics of Leadership from FDR to Carter*(New York: Macmillan, 1980), p. 64.

6. Kevin Phillips, "The Bush Blueprint Bombs," *Newsweek*, Nov. 19, 1990, p. 40. It should be pointed out, however, that what Phillips characterized as "mediocre public approval" was an over 50 percent approval rating at the time.

176

7. George C. Edwards III, *At the Margins: Presidential Leader Congress* (New Haven: Yale University Press, 1989), p. 125.

8. Lyndon B. Johnson, *The Vantage Point: Perspectives of the Presidency, 1963–1969* (New York: Popular Library, 1971), p. 443.

9. Hedrick Smith, "Capitol Hill Outcry Softens as Public's Support Swells," *The New York Times*, Nov. 4, 1983, p. A18. See also, Brigitte L. Nacos, *The Press, Presidents, and Crises* (New York: Columbia University Press, 1990), pp. 177–80.

10. Nacos, *The Press, Presidents, and Crises*, p. 178.

11. Richard A. Brody, *Assessing the President: The Media, Elite Opinion, and Public Support* (Stanford: Stanford University Press, 1991), p. 19.

12. *Ibid.*, p. 22.

13. Henry F. Graff, "The Woolly Pulpit," *The New York Times*, Nov. 15, 1990, p. A27.

14. John E. Mueller, *War, Presidents, and Public Opinion* (Lanham: University Press of America, 1985), p. 208.

15. Nelson W. Polsby, *Congress and the Presidency* (Englewood Cliffs: Prentice Hall, 1964), p. 25.

16. George C. Edwards III, *Presidential Approval: A Sourcebook* (Baltimore: Johns Hopkins University Press, 1990), part II.

17. Richard A. Brody and Catherine R. Shapiro, "A Reconsideration of the Rally Phenomenon in Public Opinion," in Samuel Long, ed., *Political Behavior Annual* (Boulder: Westview Press, 1989).

18. Larry Hugick and Alec M. Gallup, " 'Rally Events' and Presidential Approval," *The Gallup Poll Monthly*, June 1991.

19. Hugic and Gallup, "Rally Events," p. 16.

20. Brody and Shapiro, "A Reconsideration of the Rally Phenomenon," p. 92.

21. Benjamin I. Page and Robert Y. Shapiro, "Educating and Manipulating the Public," in Michael Margolis and Gary A. Hauser, ed., *Manipulating Public Opinion* (Pacific Cove: Brooks/Cole Publishing, 1989), p. 289.

22. Quote taken from transcript of a seminar on "The Media and Terrorism," sponsored by the "Center for Communication, Inc." on Oct. 23, 1985, in New York.

23. Page and Shapiro, "Educating and Manipulating the Public," p. 300.

24. The approval data used in Table 3.1 and in this chapter are from Edwards, *Presidential Approval: A Sourcebook*. The crisis-specific survey results used in this chapter stem from several survey organizations. A complete list of the poll sources is published in the appendix.

25. Hugick and Gallup, after studying approval data, determined that

the more common "5-percentage point threshold was too stringent" to identify presidential rallies. Nevertheless, a 3 percent threshold increases the likelihood that sampling errors account for the approval change. Therefore, most researchers require an increase of at least 5 percent in presidential approval from the last pre-event to the first post-event poll for incidents to qualify as rally events.

26. Edwards, *Presidential Approval: A Soucebook*, p. 121. See also Benjamin I. Page and Robert Y. Shapiro, *The Rational Public: Fifty Years of Trends in Americans' Policy Preferences* (Chicago: Chicago University Press, 1992), chap. 5; and John Zaller, *The Nature and Origins of Public Opinion* (New York: Cambridge University Press, 1992).

27. For more on the "ceiling effect," see Zaller, *The Nature and Origins of Public Opinion*.

28. For more on similarities and differences along gender and race lines see Page and Shapiro, *The Rational Public*, chap. 7.

29. Page and Shapiro, *The Rational Public*, p. 295.

30. Brody and Shapiro, "A Reconsideration of the Rally Phenomenon." See also W. Lance Bennett, "The Media and the Foreign Policy Process," paper delivered at the fifth Thomas P. O'Neill Symposium in American Politics, Boston College, April 3–4, 1992.

31. According to polls conducted by Gallup and other polling organizations.

32. See especially Kernell, *Going Public*, and Rose, *The Postmodern President*.

33. Eytan Gilboa, "Effects of Televised Presidential Addresses on Public Opinion: President Reagan and Terrorism in the Middle East," in *Presidential Studies Quarterly* 20–1 (Winter 1990).

34. Kernell, *Going Public*, p. 178.

35. Jimmy Carter, *Keeping Faith*, pp. 108–9.

36. *Ibid.*, p. 114.

37. CBS Evening News, November 5, 1979.

38. "Candidates Cautious in Comments," *The New York Times*, November 9, 1979.

39. "Nixon Says U.S. Unity is Key to Fate of Hostages," *The New York Times*, Nov. 28, 1979, p. A12.

40. William Saffire, "Rejected Counsel's Return," *The New York Times*, Dec. 31, 1979, p. A15.

41. CBS Evening News, Jan. 7, 1980.

42. CBS "Meet the Press" broadcast of Jan. 20, 1980.

43. Page and Shapiro, *The Rational Public*, p. 349.

44. Brody and Shapiro, "A Reconsideration of the Rally Phenomenon," p. 92.

45. CBS Evening News, June 17, 1985.

46. Bernard Gwertzman, "Iran's Hostages: Worrisome Parallels," *The New York Times*, June 18, 1985, p.8.

47. Ronald Smothers, "Carter Calls on Americans to Give Reagan 'Our Full Support'," *The New York Times*, June 22, 1985, p. 6.

48. CBS Evening News, June 25, 1985.

49. "Twisting Reagan's Tail," *The New York Times*, June 20, 1985, p. A26.

50. CBS Evening News, June 28, 1985.

51. CBS Evening News, June 25, 1985.

52. Gilboa, "Effects of Televised Presidential Addresses."

53. CBS Evening News, April 15, 1986.

54. Steven V. Roberts, "From Capitol Hill, Words of Support Are Mixed with Some Reservations," *The New York Times*, April 16, 1986, p.A17.

55. "The Terrorist and His Sentence," *The New York Times*, April 15, 1986, p. A30.

56. "The Bombs of April," *The New York Times*, April 16, 1986, p. A26.

57. CBS News/*New York Times* surveys on April 15, and April 29 through May 1, 1986 asked respondents: "Do you approve or disapprove of United States jets bombing Libya?"

6. Decisionmakers and Their Hard Choices

1. Gary Sick, "*Taking vows: The domestication of policy-making in hostage incidents,*" in *Origins of Terrorism: Psychologies, Ideologies, Theologies, States of Mind* (New York: Cambridge University Press, 1990), p. 235.

2. *Ibid.*, p. 243.

3. Quoted in Zbigniew Brzezinski, *Power and Principle: Memoirs of the National Security Adviser 1977–1981* (New York: Farrar, Straus, Giroux, 1983), p. 470.

4. *Ibid.*, p. 484.

5. *Ibid.*, p. 484.

6. Ronald Reagan, *Ronald Reagan: An American Life* (New York: Pocket Books, 1990), p. 540.

7. This question was the lead paragraph in Robert S. Greenberger and Michel McQueen, "Americans Support Bush's Tough Hostage Strance, Backing Military Action Despite Their Presence," *The Wall Street Journal*, September 21, 1990, p. A16.

8. *Ibid.*

9. Seminar on "The Media and Terrorism," organized by the Center for Communication, New York, October 23, 1985.

10. Haig is quoted in Neil Hickey, "The Impact on Negotiations—What the Experts Say," *TV Guide*, September 21, 1985, p. 22.

11. Quoted in Neil Hickey, "The Impact of Negotiations."

12. Seminar on "The Media and Terrorism." Will was quoted by Gary Sick.

13. Peggy Say, "Free at Last," *The New York Times*, December 5, 1991.

14. Say and Peter Knobler, *Forgotten: A Sister's Struggle to Save Terry Anderson, America's Longest Held Hostage* (New York: Simon & Schuster, 1991, p. 60.

15. *Ibid.*, p. 61.

16. *Ibid.*, p. 62.

17. The Jencos media strategy is described in Jane Mayer and Doyle McManus, *Landslide: The Unmaking of the President* (Boston: Houghton Mifflin, 1988), chap. 5.

18. Mayer and McManus, *Landslide*, p. 107.

19. Say and Knobler, *Forgotten*, p. 149.

20. Robert B. Oakley, "Terrorism, Media and Government," in Simon Serfaty, ed., *The Media and Foreign Policy* (New York: St. Martin's, 1991), p. 97.

21. Seminar on "The Media and Terrorism."

22. The three polls were conducted by ABC News and the *Washington Post*.

23. This observation is attributed to President Carter's chief legal counsel Lloyd Cutler by John P. Wallach, "Leakers, Terrorists, Policy Makers, and the Press," in Simon Serfaty, ed., *The Media and Foreign Policy* (New York: St. Martin's, 1991), p. 88.

24. Seminar on "The Media and Terrorism." President Reagan was quoted by Gary Sick.

25. Brzezinski, *Power and Principle*, p. 481.

26. This account of a White House meeting is given by David C. Martin and John Walcott, *Best Laid Plans: The Inside Story of America's War Against Terrorism* (New York: Harper & Row, 1988), p. 186.

27. Reagan, *Ronald Reagan*, p. 492.

28. Jimmy Carter, *Keeping Faith: Memoirs of a President* (New York: Bantam, 1982), p. 459.

29. Dan Goodgame et al., "Not again," *Time*, August 14, 1989, pp. 14–25.

30. *Ibid.*

31. Poll was conducted by ABC News and the Associated Press on

March 20/21, 1980. 49 percent of the respondents anwered yes, 35 percent no, and 16 percent were not sure.

32. The ABC News/Louis Harris and Associates poll was conducted June 5–7, 1980 and asked, "Do you think that it is possible that a president of the United States can make a difference on getting the hostages out of Iran alive—or not?"

33. The CBS/*New York Times* poll January 19–23, 1986 asked, "Do you think there is anything the United States government can do to significantly reduce terrorist attacks that affect American citizens, or is this something the United States can't do much about?" 51 percent of the respondents said the U.S. could do something, 41 percent believed nothing could be done, 8 percent were not sure.

34. The CBS News/*New York Times* poll conducted January 19–23, 1986 asked the following question: "Is the United States government doing all it can to protect American citizens, or should it be doing more?" 55 percent answered that the government "should do more," 38 percent thought the government was doing all it could, 7 percent had no opinion.

35. An ABC/*Washington Post* poll conducted August 19–21, 1989 asked, "Do you think Bush's reaction to the situation in Lebanon [killing of William Higgins and threats to murder other American hostages unless Israel returned a Moslem clergymen it had abducted] has been too tough, not tough enough, or just about right?" Three percent thought Bush's response had been "too tough," 53 percent "not tough enough," 42 percent "just about right," and 2 percent had no opinion. The second poll was conducted by the Associated Press and Media General on September 14–24, 1986, and asked, "Do you think the United States government has done enough to try to free the U.S. hostages in Lebanon, or not?" Twenty-five percent answered yes, 54 percent no, and 21 percent had no answer/opinion.

36. Margaret G. Hermann and Charles F. Hermann, "Hostage taking, the presidency, and stress," in Walter Reich, ed., *Origins of Terrorism* (New York: Cambridge University Press, 1990), p. 212.

37. *Ibid.*, p. 212.

38. Gary Sick, *All Fall Down: America's Tragic Encounter with Iran* (New York: Penguin Books, 1986), p. 347.

39. Benjamin Netanyahu, *Terrorism: How the West Can Win* (New York: Avon, 1986), p. 200.

40. An excellent examination of the factors that determine whether or not presidents succeed can be found in Dean Keith Simonton, *Why Presidents Succeed: A Political Psychology of Leadership* (New Haven: Yale University Press, 1987).

41. Shanto Iyengar and Donald R. Kinder, *News That Matters: Television and American Opinion.* (Chicago: University of Chicago Press, 1987), p. 115.

42. Hamilton Jordan, *Crisis: The Last Year of the Carter Presidency* (New York: G.P. Putnam's Sons, 1982), p. 54.

43. Hermann and Hermann, "Hostage taking, the presidency, and stress."

44. Brzezinski, *Principle and Power*, chap. 13.

45. Stansfield Turner, *Terrorism and Democracy* (Boston: Houghton Mifflin, 1991), p. 59.

46. Brzezinski, *Principle and Power*, p. 483.

47. Quoted in Jordan, *Crisis*, p. 52.

48. Jordan, *Crisis*, p. 52.

49. Brzezinski, *Principle and Power*, p. 490.

50. Jimmy Carter, *Keeping Faith*, p. 507.

51. Turner, *Terrorism and Democracy*, p. 106.

52. Brzezinski, *Principle and Power*, p. 488.

53. Cyrus Vance, *Hard Choices: Critical Years in America's Foreign Policy* (New York: Simon & Schuster, 1983), pp. 409–10.

54. Pierre Salinger, *America Held Hostage: The Secret Negotiations* (New York: Doubleday, 1981), pp. 237–38.

55. Holloway is quoted in Paul B. Ryan, *The Iranian Rescue Mission: Why It Failed* (Annapolis: Naval Institute Press, 1985), p. 111.

56. Interview with the author in January 1991.

57. Vance, *Hard Choices*, p. 410.

58. Brzezinski, *Principle and Power*, p. 492.

59. Sick, "Taking vows," p. 242.

60. Turner, *Terrorism and Democracy*, p. 107.

61. *Ibid.*, p. 107.

62. Jordan, *Crisis*, p. 229.

63. Brzezinski, *Power and Principle*, p. 489.

64. Sick, "All fall down," p. 347.

65. Brzezinski, *Power and Principle*, p. 486.

66. Interview with author in January 1991.

67. Interview with author.

68. Cutler in interview with author.

69. Reagan, *Ronald Reagan*, p. 498.

70. Ronald D. Crelinsten, "Victims' Perspectives," in David L. Paletz and Alex P. Schmid. *Terrorism and the Media* (Newbury Park, CA: Sage, 1992), p. 215.

71. Peter Stoler, *The War Against the Press: Politics, Pressure and Intimidation in the 80s* (New York: Dodd, Mead, 1986), pp. 110–11.

72. *Ibid.*, pp.110–11.

73. According to a Louis Harris and Associates poll conducted June 28–30, 1985.

74. The poll conducted by Louis Harris and Associates June 28–30, 1985 asked, "Do you feel President Reagan has been too strong, too weak, or about right in getting back the seven Americans who had been kidnapped by terrorists in Lebanon before the TWA hijacking?" Two percent answered too strong, 48 percent too weak, 43 percent about right, and 7 percent were not sure.

75. Mayer and McManus, *Landslide*, p. 115.

76. Reagan, *Ronald Reagan*, p. 512.

77. Martin and Walcott, *Best Laid Plans*, p. 228.

78. *Ibid.*

79. George P. Shultz, "Something is Terribly Wrong Here," *TIME*, February 8, 1993, p. 45.

80. Reagan, *Ronald Reagan*, p. 490.

81. Turner, *Terrorism and Democracy*, p. 226.

82. Theodore J. Lowi, *The Personal President* (Ithaca: Cornell University Press, 1985), p. 173.

7. Conclusion: Must Terrorists Succeed?

1. George P. Shultz, "The U.S. Must Retaliate Against Terrorist States," in Bonnie Szumski, ed., Terrorism: Opposing Viewpoints (St. Paul: Greenhaven Press, 1986), p. 203.

2. George Shultz, "Something is Terribly Wrong Here," *TIME*, February 8, 1993, p. 39.

3. Donaldson's quote appeared in Edwin Diamond, "TV and the Hostage Crisis in Perspective: The Coverage Itself—Why it turned into 'Terrorvision'," *TV Guide*, September 21, 1985.

4. The ABC/*Washington Post* survey was conducted June 30–July 1, 1985. The question asked: "Would you say the way things worked out was more a victory for the United States or more a victory for the terrorists who took the hostages aboard a TWA plane?"

5. Stansfield Turner, *Terrorism and Democracy* (Boston: Houghton Mifflin Company, 1991), p. 194.

6. David H. Halevy, "The Terrorists' Payoff in the Hostage Deal," *New York Times*, December 27, 1991, p. A33.

7. Robert Kupperman and Darrell Trent, *Terrorism: Threat, Reality, Response* (Stanford: Hoover Institution, 1979), p. 7.

8. This is Robert A. Fearey's conclusion. See Feary, "Introduction to International Terrorism," in Marius H. Livingston, *International Terrorism in the Contemporary World* (Westport: Greenwood Press, 1978) p. 32.

9. "Israel drops the veil," *New York Times*, August 30, 1993, p. A28.

10. Walter Goodman, "Of Television Images and Hostage Realities," *New York Times*, August 10, 1989, p. C18.

11. Khomeini's remarks were mentioned in Maureen Johnson, "Fighting Flares in East Iran: Khomeini Summons Council," Associated Press wire story, December 21, 1979.

12. Richard W. Boyd and Martha Crenshaw, "The 99th Congress and the Response to International Terrorism," Congressional Research Service, September 1987.

13. Donna M. Schlagheck, *International Terrorism* (Lexington, Mass.: Lexington Books, 1988), p. 76.

14. Seminar on "The Media and Terrorism," sponsored by the Center for Communication, October 23, 1985. New York.

15. M. Cherif Bassiouni, "Terrorism, Law Enforcement, and the Mass Media: Perspectives, Problems, Proposals," *Journal of Criminal Law and Criminology*, 272(1):1–51, pp. 33, 34.

16. Bassiouni, "Terrorism, Law Enforcement, and the Mass Media," p. 39. The clear and present danger doctrine was enunciated in *Schenck v. United States*, 249 U.S. 47 (1919).

17. Bassiouni, "Terrorism, Law Enforcement, and the Mass Media," p. 41 The case referred to was *New York Times Co. v. United States*, 403 U.S. (1971).

18. Brokow is quoted by Kupperman and Kamen, *Final Warning* (New York: Doubleday, 1989), p. 161.

19. Gary Sick, *All Fall Down: America's Tragic Encounter with Iran* (New York: Penguin Books, 1986), pp. 258–9.

20. Seminar on "The Media and Terrorism."

21. Seminar on "The Media and Terrorism."

22. For more on possible measures to improve television's terrorism reporting see Michael J. O'Neill, *Terrorist Spectaculars: Should TV Coverage be Curbed?* (New York: Priority Press Publications, 1986).

23. Goodman, "Of Terrorism Images."

24. Graham, "The Media Must Report Terrorism," in Bonnie Szumski, ed., *Terrorism: Opposing Viewpoints*, p. 81.

25. For more on media access and terrorism see Abraham Miller, *Terrorism and Hostage Negotiations* (Boulder: Westview Press, 1980), chap. 5; Alex P. Schmid and Janny de Graaf, *Violence as Communication: Insurgent Terrorism and the Western Media* (London: Sage, 1982), chap. 5.

26. See, for example, Steven Emerson, "A Terrorist Network in America?", *The New York Times*, April 7, 1993, p. A23.

27. Graham, "The Media Must Report Terrorism," p. 81.

MEDIA COVERAGE OF THE EVENTS DESCRIBED IN THIS BOOK

Table 1
Iran Hostage Crisis—Frequency of Newsbeats, 11/4/1979-
4/20/1980
(CBS Evening News)

	Nov.	Dec.	Jan.	Feb.	Mar.	Apr.	TOTAL
White House	19	11	2	11	5	15	63
State Department	18	20	8	12	5	6	69
Pentagon	2	1	-	-	-	1	4
Capitol Hill	3	-	-	-	1	-	4
Heartland U.S.A.	8	1	1	1	-	2	13
Hostage Families/							
Ex-Hostages	12	6	4	4	3	10	39
Campaign	1	8	5	8	2	8	32
Other Domestic	14	8	1	2	-	3	29
Studio	10	4	2	1	3	3	23
All Domestic (n):	87	59	23	39	20	48	276
%	69.6	51.7	62.2	61.9	41.3	68.6	60.5
Teheran/Qom,							
etc.	31	45	10	15	20	17	138
UN	5	7	4	7	1	-	24
Other Foreign	2	3	-	2	6	5	18
All Foreign	38	55	14	24	27	22	180
%	30.4	48.3	37.8	38.1	58.7	31.4	39.5
Golden Triangle	39	32	10	23	10	22	136 29.8%
Other Domestic	48	27	13	16	9	26	140 30.7%
Teheran/Iran	31	45	10	15	20	17	138 30.2%
Other Foreign	7	10	4	9	7	5	42 9.2%

Percentage of Domestic Sources:
 Golden Triangle 49.3%; Other Domestic 50.7%

Table 2

Iranian Hostage Crisis: Frequency of Lead Story Beats
(CBS Evening News)

	Nov.	Dec.	Jan.	Feb.	Mar.	Apr.	TOTAL
Golden Triangle	11	11	5	6	2	4	39
Teheran/Iran	11	9	5	7	5	13	50
Other Domestic	3	-	-	1	2	1	7

Table 3

Iran Hostage Crisis—Front Page Story Datelines (New York Times)

	Nov.	Dec.	Jan.	Feb.	Mar.	Apr.	TOTAL
Washington	24	19	9	6	13	12	83
Teheran/Iran	25	24	10	15	11	7	92
New York	6	1	4	1	-	-	12
Heartland	-	1	-	-	-	-	1
Hostage Families/							
Ex-Hostages	1	-	-	1	-	1	2
UN	3	7	3	7	1	-	21
Other	1	4	2	1	3	2	13

Washington:	37% datelines
Teheran/Iran:	41% datelines

187

Table 4
Iran Hostage Crisis: New York Times Front Page Photographs

	Nov.	Dec.	Jan.	Feb.	Mar.	Apr.	TOTAL
President	3	3	-	1	-	2	9
U.S. Administration	-	2	1	1	1	-	5
U.S. Public	-	1	1	-	-	-	2
Hostages	3	3	-	-	-	-	6
Captors/ Sympathizers	8	3	-	-	1	-	12
Ex-Hostages	3	-	1	1	-	-	5
Hostage Families/ Friends, etc.	1	-	1	-	-	1	3
U.S. Visitors to Iran	-	4	-	-	-	-	4
Iranian Officials	-	-	-	3	2	-	5
Held U.S. Embassy	-	-	2	-	-	-	2
UN Session	2	4	-	3	1	-	10
Others	1	4	1	-	2	2	10

Table 5
New York Times Coverage of the Iran Hostage Crisis
By Sources and Paragraphs

Sources	Number of paragraphs	Percent of total
Media-based (descriptions/ background/analysis, opinion)	5,000	34.7%
President/Administration	2,877	19.9%
Hostages/Families/Relatives, etc.	632	4.4%
Experts	294	2.0%
Congress	212	1.5%
Rivals for Office	104	0.6%
Other Domestic Sources	1,492	10.3%
Foes in Iran	1,966	13.6%
Other Foreign Sources	1,854	13.0%
President/Administration		19.9%
Other Domestic Sources (Media included)		53.5%
Other Domestic Sources (Media excluded)		18.9%
All Foreign Sources		26.6%

Table 6
CBS Evening News Coverage of the Iran Hostage Crisis
By Sources and Paragraphs

Sources	Number of paragraphs	Percent of total
Media-based (descriptions/ background/analysis/anchor-texts)	1,923	49.9%
President/Administration	566	14.7%
Hostages/Families/Relatives, etc.	262	6.8%
Rivals for Office	110	2.9%
Congress	66	1.7%
Experts	40	1.0%
Other Domestic Sources	223	5.8%
Foes in Iran	540	14.0%
Other Foreign Sources	125	3.2%
President/Administration		14.7%
Other Domestic Sources (Media included)		68.1%
Other Domestic Sources (Media excluded)		18.2%
All Foreign Sources		17.2%

Table 7
TWA Hostage Crisis: Frequency of Newsbeats
and Number of Lead Stories
CBS Evening News, June 14-30, 1985

	Frequency of News Beats	Number of Lead Stories
White House, with President	15	1
State Department	4	-
Pentagon	6	-
CBS Studio Interviews with Adminstration Officials	1	-
Beirut	17	10
London Studio on Beirut	4	2
CBS Studio Interviews with Berri, other Amal officials	10	-
Heartland U.S.A.	11	-
Other Domestic Studio interviews with ex-hostages, experts, etc.	14	-
Tel Avis/Jerusalem	10	1
Other Foreign	11	2
	103	16
Golden Triangle originated/facilitated	26 (25.2%)	1 (6.3%)
Beirut originated/facilitated	38 (30.1%)	12 (75.0%)
Other Domestic	25 (24.3%)	-
Other Foreign	21 (20.4%)	3 (18.7%)

Table 8
CBS Evening News Coverage of the TWA Hijacking Crisis
By Sources and Paragraphs

Sources	Number of Paragraphs	Percent of Total
Media (descriptions/ background/analysis, anchor-texts)	620	38.9%
President/Administration	106	6.6%
Hostages/Families/Relatives, etc.	243	15.3%
Experts	400	25.1%
Congress	9	0.6%
Other Domestic Sources	55	3.5%
Foes in Lebanon	90	5.7%
Other Foreign Sources	69	4.3%
President/Administration		6.6%
Other Domestic Sources (media included)		83.4%
Other Domestic Sources (media excluded)		44.5%
All Foreign Sources		10.0%

Table 9

New York Times Coverage of the TWA Hijacking Crisis
By Sources and Paragraphs

Sources	Number of Paragraphs	Percent of Total
Media (descriptions/ background/analysis, opinion)	1,365	34.2%
President/Administration	692	17.3%
Hostages/Families/Relatives, etc.	560	14.0%
Experts	44	1.1%
Congress	47	1.2%
Other Domestic Sources	363	9.1%
Foes in Lebanon	213	5.4%
Other Foreign Sources	707	17.7%
President/Administration		17.3%
Other Domestic Sources (Media included)		59.6%
Other Domestic Sources (Media excluded)		25.4%
All Foreign Sources		23.1%

Table 10
CBS Evening News Coverage of the Achille Lauro Case
By Sources and Paragraphs

Sources	Number of Paragraphs	Percent of Total
Media (descriptions/ background/analysis, anchor-texts)	204	44.3%
President/Administration	69	15.0%
Families/Friends of Hostages	14	3.0%
Ex-Hostages/Passenger Not Aboard During Hijacking	16	3.5%
Experts	7	1.5%
Congress	19	4.1%
Other Domestic Sources	24	5.2%
Terrorists/Sympathizers	27	5.8%
Other Foreign Sources	81	17.6%
President/Administration		15.0%
Other Domestic Sources (Media included)		61.6%
Other Domestic Sources (Media excluded)		17.3%
All Foreign Sources		23.4%

Table 11
New York Times Coverage of the Achille Lauro Case
By Sources and Paragraphs

Sources	Number of Paragraphs	Percent of Total
Media (descriptions, background/analysis, opinion)	779	26.3%
President/Administration	652	22.0%
Families/Friends of Hostages	168	5.7%
Ex-Hostages/Passengers Not Aboard Ship During Hijacking	283	9.5%
Experts	69	2.3%
Congress	55	1.9%
Other Domestic Sources	75	2.5%
Terrorists/Sympathizers	174	5.9%
Other Foreign Sources	708	23.9%
President/Administration		22.0%
Other Domestic Sources (Media Included)		48.2%
Other Domestic Sources (Media Excluded)		21.9%
All Foreign Sources		29.8%

Table 12
CBS Evening News Coverage of the Libyan Bombing
By Sources and Paragraphs

Sources	Number of Paragraphs	Percent of Total
Media (descriptions, background/analysis, anchor texts)	367	54.9%
President/Administration	112	16.7%
Congress	6	0.9%
Experts	32	4.8%
Other Domestic Sources	55	8.2%
Qaddafi, other Libyan officials	23	3.4%
Terrorists, Sympathizers	5	0.8%
Other Foreign Sources	69	10.3%
President/Administration		16.7%
Other Domestic Sources (media included)		68.8%
Other Domestic Sources (media excluded)		13.9%
All Foreign Sources		14.5%

Table 13
New York Times Coverage of the Bombing of Libya
By Sources and Paragraphs

Sources	Number of Paragraphs	Percent of Total
Media (descriptions, background, analysis, opinion)	781	31.0%
President/Administration	689	27.4%
Congress	75	3.0%
Experts	146	5.8%
Other Domestic Sources	104	4.1%
Qaddafi, other Libyan officials	127	5.0%
Terrorists/Sympathizers	31	1.2%
Other Foreign Sources	563	22.5%
President/Administration		27.4%
Other Domestic Sources (media included)		43.9%
Other Domestic Sources (media excluded)		12.9%
All Foreign Sources		28.7%

BIBLIOGRAPHY

Adams, James. 1986. *The Financing of Terror*. New York: Simon and Schuster.

Adams, William C., ed. 1981. *Television Coverage of the Middle East*. Norwood, N.J.: Ablex.

——. 1982. *Television Coverage of International Affairs*. Norwood: Ablex.

Adams, William C. 1985. "The Beirut Hostages: ABC and CBS Seize an Opportunity." *Public Opinion* 8:45–48.

Alali, A. Odasuo and Kenoye Kelvin Eke, eds. 1991. *Media Coverage of Terrorism*. Newbury Park, Calif.: Sage.

Almond, Gabriel. 1960. *The American People and Foreign Policy*. New York: Praeger.

Altheide, David L. 1982. "Three-in-one news: Network coverage of Iran." *Journalism Quarterly* 59:482–86.

——. 1981. "Iran vs. U.S. TV News." In *Television Coverage of the Middle East*. Ed. by William C. Adams. Norwood, N.J.: Ablex.

Assersohn, Roy. 1982. *The Biggest Deal*. London: Methuen.

Atwater, Tony. 1991. "Coverage of the TWA Hostage Crisis." In *Media Coverage of Terrorism*. Ed. by Odasuo Alali and Kenoye Kelvin Eke. Newbury Park, Calif.: Sage.

Bandura, Albert. 1990. "Mechanism of Moral Disengagement." In *Origins of Terrorism: Psychologies, Ideologies, Theologies, States of Mind*. Ed. by Walter Reich. New York: Cambridge University Press.

199

Bani-Sadr, Abol Hassan. 1991. *My Turn to Speak: Iran, the Revolution, and the Secret Deals with the U.S.* Washington: Brassey's.

Bassiouni, M. Cherif. 1981. "Terrorism, Law Enforcement, and the Mass Media: Perspectives, Problems, Proposals." In *The Journal of Criminal Law and Criminology* 72:1–51.

Beckwith, Charlie A. and Donald Knox. 1985. *Delta Force.* New York: Dell.

Behr, Roy L. and Shanto Iyengar. 1985. "Television News, Real World Cues, and Changes in the Public Agenda." In *Public Opinion Quarterly* 49:38–57.

Bennett, Lance W. 1992. "The Media and the Foreign Policy Process." Paper delivered at the fifth Thomas P. O'Neill Symposium in American Politics, Boston College, April 3–4.

———. 1989. "Marginalizing the Majority: Conditioning Public Opinion to Accept Managerial Democracy." In *Manipulating Public Opinion: Essays on Public Opinion as a Dependent Variable.* Ed. by M. Margolis and G. A. Hauser. Pacific Grove, Calif.: Brooks Cole.

Bogart, Leo. 1984. "The Public's Use and Perception of Newspapers." In *Public Opinion Quarterly* 48(4):716–17.

Braestrup, Peter. 1983. *Big Story.* New Haven: Yale University Press.

Brody, Richard A. and Benjamin I. Page. 1975. "The Impact of Events on Presidential Popularity." In *Perspectives on the Presidency*, ed. by Aaron Wildavsky. Boston: Little Brown.

Brody, Richard A. and Catherine R. Shapiro. 1989. "A Reconsideration of the Rally Phenomenon in Public Opinion." In *Political Behavior Annual. Volume 2.* Ed. by Samuel Long. Boulder: Westview.

Brody, Richard A. 1991. *Assessing the President: The Media, Elite Opinion, and Public Support.* Stanford: Stanford University Press.

Brzezinski, Zbigniew. 1983. *Power and Principle: Memoirs of the National Security Adviser 1977–1981.* New York: Farrar, Straus, Giroux.

Cassese, Antonio. 1989. *Terrorism, Politics, and the Law: The* Achille Lauro *Affair.* Princeton: Princeton University Press.

Catton, William R. Jr. 1978. "Militants and the Media: Partners in Terrorism?" *Indiana Law Journal* 53:703–715.

Carter, Jimmy. 1982. *Keeping Faith: Memoirs of a President.* New York: Bantam.

Ceaser, James. 1979. *Presidential Selection: Theory and Development.* Princeton: Princeton University Press.

Celmer, Marc. A. 1987. *Terrorism, U.S. Strategy, and Reagan Politics.* New York: Greenwood.

Chomsky, Noam. 1989. *The Culture of Terrorism.* Boston: South End.

Christopher, Warren et al. 1985. *American Hostage in Iran: The Conduct of a Crisis*. New Haven: Yale University Press.

Cohen, Bernard C. 1973. *The Public's Impact on Foreign Policy*. Boston: Little Brown.

———. 1963. *The Press and Foreign Policy*. Princeton: Princeton University Press.

Cook, Timothy A. 1991. "Domesticating a Crisis: Washington Newbeats, Human Interest Stories, and International News in the Persian Gulf War." Paper presented at the Social Science Research Council workshop on the Media and Foreign Policy, Seattle, Washington.

Cooley, John K. 1991. *Payback: America's Long War in the Middle East*. Washington: Brassey's.

Crelinsten, Ronald D. 1992. "Victims' Perspectives." In *Terrorism and the Media*. Ed. by David L. Paletz and Alex P. Schmid. Newbury Park, Calif.: Sage.

Crenshaw, Martha, ed. 1983. *Terrorism, Legitimacy, and Power*. Middletown, Conn.: Weslyan University Press.

———. 1990. "The Logic of Terrorism: Terrorist Behavior as a Product of Rational Choice." In *Origins of Terrorism: Psychologies, Ideologies, Theologies, States of Mind*. Ed. by Walter Reich. New York: Cambridge University Press.

Cutler, Lloyd N. 1984. "Foreign Policy on Deadline." *Foreign Policy* 56:113–28.

Delli Carpini, Michael X. and Bruce A. Williams. 1987. "Television and Terrorism: Patterns of Presentation and Occurrence, 1969 to 1980." *Western Political Quarterly* 40:45–64.

Diamond, Edwin. 1985. "TV and the Hostage Crisis in Perspective: The Coverage Itself—Why it Turned into 'Terrorvision'." *TV Guide*, September 21.

Edwards, George C., III. 1983. *The Public Presidency*. New York: St. Martin's.

———. 1990. *Presidential Approval: A Sourcebook*. Baltimore: Johns Hopkins University Press.

Emerson, Steven and Brian Duffy, 1990. "The German Connection." *New York Times Magazine*, March 18.

Entman, Robert M. 1989. *Democracy Without Citizens: Media and the Decay of American Politics*. New York: Oxford University Press.

Entman, Robert M. and Benjamin I. Page. 1991. "The News Before the Storm: The Limits of Media Autonomy in Covering Foreign Policy." Preliminary Discussion Draft for the Social Science Research Council Media and Foreign Policy Project.

Farnen, Russell F. 1990. "Terrorism and the Mass Media: A Systematic

Analysis of a Symbiotic Process." *Terrorism: An International Journal* 13:99–143.

Feary, Robert A. 1978. "Introduction to International Terrorism." In *International Terrorism in the Contemporary World.* Ed. by Marius H. Livingston. Westport: Greenwood.

Freedman, Lawrence. 1986. *Terrorism and the International Order.* New York: Routledge.

Freedman, Lawrence Zelic and Yonah Alexander, ed. 1983. *Perspectives on Terrorism.* Wilmington: Scholarly Resources.

Gergen, David. R. 1991. "Diplomacy in a Television Age: The Dangers of Teledemocracy." In *The Media and Foreign Policy.* Ed. by Simon Serfaty. New York: St. Martin's.

Gilboa, Eytan. 1986. "Terrorism and Trust: How We See the Middle East." *Public Opinion* 9(4):52–55.

——. 1990. "Effects of Televised Presidential Addresses on Public Opinion: President Reagan and Terrorism in the Middle East." *Presidential Studies Quarterly* 20:43–53.

Graber, Doris A. 1980. *Mass Media and American Politics.* Washington, D.C.: Congressional Quarterly Press.

——. 1984. *Media Power in Politics.* Washington, D.C.: Congressional Quarterly Press.

Graham, Katharine. 1986. "The Media Must Report Terrorism." In *Terrorism: Opposing Viewpoints.* Ed. by Bonnie Szumski. St. Paul: Greenhaven.

Grossman, Michael B. and Martha J. Kumar. 1981. *Portraying the President.* Baltimore: Johns Hopkins University Press.

Gutteridge, William, ed. 1986. *Contemporary Terrorism.* New York: Facts on File.

Hallin, Daniel L. 1986. *The 'Uncensored War': The Media and Vietnam.* New York: Oxford University Press.

Herman, Margaret G. and Charles F. Herman. 1990. "Hostage Taking, the Presidency, and Stress." In *Origins of Terrorism: Psychologies, Ideologies, Theologies, States of Mind.* Ed. by Walter Reich. New York: Cambridge University Press.

Hess, Stephen. 1983. "The Golden Triangle: The Press at the White House, State, and Defense." *The Brookings Review,* Summer.

Hickey, Neil. 1985. "TV and the Hostage Crisis in Perspective: The Impact on Negotiations—What the Experts Say." *TV Guide,* September 21.

Hilsman, Roger. 1987. *The Politics of Policy Making in Defense and Foreign Policy.* Englewood Cliffs, N.J.: Prentice Hall.

Hinckley, Ronald. 1989. "American Opinion Toward Terrorism: The Reagan Years." *Terrorism* 12(2):387–99.

202

——. 1992. *People, Polls, and Policy Makers: American Public Opinion and National Security.* New York: Lexington.

Horowitz, Irving Louis. 1983. "The Routinization of Terrorism and Its Unanticipated Consequences." In *Terrorism, Legitimacy, and Power.* Ed. by Martha Crenshaw. Middletown: Wesleyan University Press.

Hugick, Larry and Alec M. Gallup. 1991. " 'Rally Events' and Presidential Approval." *The Gallup Poll Monthly,* June.

Irvin, Cynthia L. 1992. "Terrorists' Perspectives: Interviews." In *Terrorism and the Media.* Ed. by David L. Paletz and Alex P. Schmid. Newbury Park, Calif.: Sage.

Iyengar, Shanto. 1991. *Is Anyone Responsible? How Television Frames Political Issues.* Chicago: University of Chicago Press.

Iyengar, Shanto and Donald R. Kinder. 1987. *News That Matters.* Chicago: University of Chicago Press.

Jaehnig, Walter B. 1978. "Journalists and Terrorism: Captives of the Libertarian Tradition." *Indiana Law Journal* 53:717–44.

Jenkins, Brian M. 1987. "Der internationale Terrorismus." In *Aus Politik und Zeitgeschichte* B 5/87:17–27.

——. 1990. "International Terrorism: The Other World War." In *International Terrorism: Characteristics, Causes, Controls.* Ed. by Charles W. Kegley, Jr. New York: Macmillan.

Johnson, Lyndon B. 1971. *The Vantage Point: Perspectives of the Presidency, 1963–1969.* New York: Popular Library.

Jordan, Hamilton. 1982. *Crisis: The Last Year of the Carter Presidency.* New York: Putnam.

Kegley, Charles Jr. 1990. *International Terrorism: Characteristics, Causes, Controls.* New York: St. Martin's.

Kellerman, Barbara. 1984. *The Political Presidency: Practice of Leadership.* New York: Oxford University Press.

Kelly, Michael J. and Thomas H. Mitchell. 1984. "Transnational Terrorism and the Western Elite Press." In *Media Power in Politics.* Ed. by Doris A. Graber. Washington, D.C.: Congressional Quarterly Press.

Kern, Montague and P. W. and R. B. Levering. 1983. *The Kennedy Crises: The Press, the Presidency, and Foreign Policy.* Chapel Hill: University of North Carolina Press.

Kernell, Samuel. 1986. *Going Public: New Strategies of Presidential Leadership.* Washington, D.C.: Congressional Quarterly Press.

Key. V. O. Jr. 1961. *Public Opinion and American Democracy.* New York: Knopf.

Kingdon, J. W. 1984. *Agendas, Alternatives, and Public Policies.* Boston: Little, Brown.

Kupperman, Robert H. and Darrell M. Trent. 1979. *Terrorism: Threat, Reality, Response*. Stanford, Calif.: Hoover Institution Press.

Kupperman, Robert and J. Kamen. 1989. *Final Warning: Averting Disaster in the New Age of Terrorism*. New York: Doubleday.

Lang, Gladys Engel and Kurt Lang. 1983. *The Battle For Public Opinion: The President, the Press, and the Polls During Watergate*. New York: Columbia University Press.

Laqueur, Walter. 1987. *The Age of Terrorism*. Boston: Little, Brown.

Laqueur, Walter and Yonah Alexander. 1987. *The Terrorism Reader*. New York: NAL Penguin.

Lazarsfeld, Paul F., Bernard Berelson, and Hazel Gaudet. 1948. *The People's Choice*. New York: Columbia University Press.

Linsky, Martin. 1986. *Impact: How the Press Affects Federal Policy Making*. New York: Norton.

Lippmann, Walter. 1949. *Public Opinion*. New York: Free Press.

Livingston, Marius H., ed. 1978. *International Terrorism in the Contemporary World*. Westport, Colo.: Greenwood.

Long, David. E. 1990. *The Anatomy of Terrorism*. New York: Free Press.

Marks, John and Igor Beliaev. 1991. *Common Ground on Terrorism: Soviet–American Cooperation Against the Politics of Terror*. New York: Norton.

Martin, David C. and John Walcott. 1988. *Best Laid Plans*. New York: Harper & Row.

Martin, John L. 1990. "The Media's Role in International Terrorism." In *International Terrorism: Characteristics, Causes, Controls*. Ed. by Charles W. Kegley, Jr. New York: St. Martins.

Mayer, Jane and Doyle McManus. 1988. *Landslide: The Unmaking of the President, 1984–1988*. Boston: Houghton Mifflin.

McCombs, M. E. and Donald Shaw. 1972. "The Agenda Setting Function of the Mass Media." *Public Opinion Quarterly* 36:176–87.

Miller, Abraham H. 1980. *Terrorism and Hostage Negotiations*. Boulder: Westview.

——. 1982. *Terrorism, the Media, and the Law*. Dobbs Ferry, N.Y.: Transnational.

Molotch, H. and M. Lester. 1974. "Accidental News: The Great Oil Spill as Local Occurance and as National Event." *American Journal of Sociology* 81:235–60.

Morris, Erich and Alan Hoe. 1987. *Terrorism: Threat and Response*. New York: Macmillan.

Moynihan, Daniel P. 1975. "The Presidency and the Press." In *Perspective on the Presidency*. Ed. by Aaron Wildavsky. Boston: Little, Brown.

Mueller, John E. 1985. *War, Presidents, and Public Opinion*. Lanham: University Press of America.

——. 1992. "American Public Opinion and the Gulf War: Trends and Historical Comparisons." Paper presented at the meeting of the Midwest Political Science Association, Chicago.

Nacos, Brigitte Lebens. 1992. "International Terrorism and the Media." *Current World Leaders*. 35(2):311–31.

——. 1990. *Press, Presidents, and Crises*. New York: Columbia University Press.

Nacos, Brigitte, David Fan and John Young. 1989. "Terrorism and the Media: The 1985 TWA Hostage Crisis." *Terrorism* 12(2):107–115.

Netanyahu, Benjamin. 1986. *How the West Can Win*. New York: Avon Books.

Neustadt, Richard E. 1980. *Presidential Power: The Politics of Leadership from FDR to Carter*. New York: Macmillan.

Nimmo, Dan. 1987. "Televised Coverage of International Crises." *National Forum* 7:7–14.

Nimmo, Dan and James E. Combs. 1985. *Nightly Horrors: Crisis Coverage in Television Network News*. Knoxville: University of Tennessee.

Oakley, Robert B. 1991. "Terrorism, Media Coverage, and Government Response." In Simon Serfaty, ed. *The Media and Foreign Policy*. New York: St. Martin's.

O'Hefferman, Patrick. 1991. "What the Government Thinks: Post War Policy Makers' Perceptions of Media and Foreign Policy." Paper presented at the Social Science Research Council workshop on the Media and Foreign Policy, Seattle, Washington.

O'Neill, Michael J. 1986. *Terrorist Spectaculars: Should TV Coverage Be Curbed?* New York: Priority Press. A Twentieth Century Fund Paper.

O'Sullivan, John. 1986. "Media Publicity Causes Terrorism." In *Terrorism: Opposing Viewpoints*. Ed. by Bonnie Szumski. St. Paul: Greenhaven.

Page, Benjamin I. and Robert Y. Shapiro. 1992. *The Rational Public*. Chicago: Chicago University Press.

——. 1983. "Effects of Public Opinion on Policy." *American Political Science Review* 77:175–90.

——. 1989. "Educating and Manipulating the Public." In *Manipulating Public Opinion*. Ed. by Michael Margolis and Gary A. Mauser. Pacific Grove, Calif.: Brooks/Cole.

Paletz, David L. and Alex P. Schmid, eds. 1992. *Terrorism and the Media*. Newbury Park, Calif.: Sage.

Paletz, David L., John Z. Ayanian, and Peter A. Fozzard. 1982. "Terrorism on TV News: The IRA, the FALN, and the Red Brigades." In *Tele-*

vision *Coverage of International Affairs.* Ed. by William C. Adams. Norwood, N.J.: Ablex.

Picard, Robert G. 1991. "News Coverage as the Contagion." In *Media Coverage of Terrorism.* Ed. by A. Odasuo Alali and Kenoye Kelvin Eke. Newbury Park: Sage.

Polsby, Nelson W. 1964. *Congress and the Presidency.* Englewood Cliffs: Prentice Hall.

Post, Jerrold M. 1990. "Terrorist Psycho-Logic: Terrorist Behavior as a Product of Psychological Forces." In *Origins of Terrorism: Psychologies, Ideologies, Theologies, States of Mind.* Ed. by Walter Reich. New York: Cambridge University Press.

Public Opinion. 1981. "A Conversation with the President's Pollsters— Patrick Caddell and Richard Wirthlin." *Public Opinion* 3: 2–12, 63–64.

Quainton, Anthony D. E. 1983. "Terrorism: Policy, Action, and Reaction." In *Perspectives on Terrorism.* Ed. by Lawrence Zelic Freedman and Yonah Alexander. Wilmington: Scholarly Resources.

Ramney, Austin. 1983. *Channels of Power.* New York: Basic Books.

Rapoport, David C. 1984. "Fear and Trembling: Terrorism in Three Religious Traditions." *American Political Science Review* 48(3):668–77.

Reagan, Ronald. 1990. *Ronald Reagan: An American Life.* New York: Pocket Books.

Reich, Walter, ed. 1990. *Origins of Terrorism: Psychologies, Ideologies, Theologies, States of Mind.* New York: Cambridge University Press.

Romanov, Valentin. 1990. "The United Nations and the Problem of Combating Terrorism." *Terrorism and Political Violence* 2:289–304.

Rose, Richard. 1991. *The Postmodern President: George Bush Meets the World.* Chatham, N.J.: Chatham House.

Rosen, Jay. 1991. "TV as Alibi: A Response to Michael Schudson." *Tikkun* 6:52–54, 87.

Rosenau, James N. 1961. *Public Opinion and Foreign Policy.* New York: Random House.

Rosenblum, Mort. 1989. "Special Correspondent Quixote." *Gannett Center Journal,* Fall.

Rozell, Mark J. "President Carter and the Press: Perspectives from White House Communications Advisers." *Political Science Quarterly* (Fall 1990) 105(3):419–34.

Rubinstein, Richard E. 1987. *Alchemists of Revolution: Terrorism in the Modern World.* New York: Basic Books.

Ryan, Paul B. 1985. *The Iranian Rescue Mission: Why It Failed.* Annapolis, Md.: Naval Institute Press.

Said, Edward W. 1981. *Covering Islam: How the Media and the Experts Determine How We See the Rest of the World*. New York: Pantheon.

Salinger, Pierre. 1981. *America Held Hostage: The Secret Negotiations*. New York: Doubleday.

Say, Peggy and Peter Knobler. 1991. *Forgotten: A Sister's Struggle to Save Terry Anderson, America's Longest-Held Hostage*. New York: Simon and Schuster.

Schlagheck, Donna M. 1988. *International Terrorism: An Introduction to the Concepts and Actors*. Lexington, Mass.: Lexington Books.

Schlesinger, Philip, Graham Murdock, and Philip Elliott. 1983. *Televising 'Terrorism': Political Violence in Popular Culture*. London: Comedia.

Schmid, Alex P. and Janny de Graaf. 1982. *Violence as Communication: Insurgent Terrorism and the Western News Media*. Beverly Hills: Sage.

Schudson, Michael. 1991. "Trout or Hamburger: Politics and Tele-mythology." *Tikkun* 6:47–51, 86.

Schultz, Richard H. Jr. and Stephen Sloan, ed. 1980. *Responding to the Terrorist Threat: Security and Crisis Management*. New York: Pergament.

Serfaty, Simon, ed. 1991. *The Media and Foreign Policy*. New York: St. Martin's.

Shapiro, Robert Y. and Benjamin I. Page. 1988. "Foreign Policy and the Rational Public." *Journal of Conflict Resolution* 32:211–47.

Shultz, George P. 1993. *From Turmoil and Triumph: My Years as Secretary of State*. New York: Scribner's.

Shultz, George P. 1993. "Something Is Terribly Wrong Here." *TIME*, February 8, pp. 38–48.

Sick, Gary. 1991. *October Surprise*. New York: Times Books/Random House.

——. 1990. "Taking Vows: The Domestication of Policy-making in Hostage Incidents." In *Origins of Terrorism: Psychologies, Ideologies, Theologies, States of Mind*. Ed. by Walter Reich. New York: Cambridge University Press.

——. 1986. *All Fall Down: America's Tragic Encounter with Iran*. New York: Penguin.

Simonton, Dean Keith. 1987. *Why Presidents Succeed: A Political Psychology of Leadership*. New Haven: Yale University Press.

Speakes, Larry. 1988. *Speaking Out: The Reagan Presidency from Inside the White House*. New York: Avon Books.

Stoler, Peter. 1986. *The War Against the Press: Politics, Pressure, and Intimidation in the 80s*. New York: Dodd, Mead.

Szumski, Bonnie, ed. 1986. *Terrorism: Opposing Viewpoints*. St. Paul: Greenhaven Press.

Terry, Herbert A. 1978. "Television and Terrorism: Professionalism Not Quite the Answer." *Indiana Law Journal* 53:746–77.

Tulis, Jeffrey K. 1987. *The Rhetorical Presidency*. Princeton: Princeton University Press.

Turner, Stansfield. 1991. *Terrorism and Democracy*. Boston: Houghton Mifflin.

Vance, Cyrus. 1983. *Hard Choices*. New York: Simon and Schuster.

Vetter, Harold V. and Gary R. Perlstein. 1991. *Perspectives on Terrorism*. Pacific Grove, Calif.: Brooks/Cole.

Vincent, Billy. 1990. "Aviation Security and Terrorism." In *Terrorism: An International Journal* 13:397–439.

Weimann, Gabriel. 1990. "Redefinition of Image: The Impact of Mass-Mediated Terrorism." *International Journal of Public Opinion Research* 2:16–29.

——. 1983. "The Theater of Terror: Effects of Press Coverage." *Journal of Communication*, Winter, pp. 38–45.

Weinberg, Leonard and Paul Davis. 1989. *Introduction To Political Terrorism*. New York: McGraw-Hill.

Weissberg, Robert. 1976. *Public Opinion and Popular Government*. Englewood Cliffs, N.J.: Prentice-Hall.

White, Jonathan R. 1991. *Terrorism: An Introduction*. Pacific Grove, Calif.: Brooks/Cole.

White, Theodore H. 1973. *The Making of the President 1972*. New York: Atheneum.

Wilkinson, Paul. 1986. "Terrorism versus Liberal Democracy." In William Gutteridge, ed. *Contemporary Terrorism*. New York: Facts on File.

Yankelovich, Daniel. 1991. *Coming To Public Judgment*. Syracuse: Syracuse University Press.

——. 1992. "Foreign Policy after the Election." *Foreign Affairs* 71(4):1–12.

Zaller, John R. 1992. *The Nature and Origins of Mass Opinion*. New York: Cambridge University Press.

INDEX